Experiencing the New World of Work

Exploring the different facets of the new world of work (including the hacker and maker movements, platform work, and digital nomadism), this edited volume sets out to investigate and theorise how these new work practices are experienced by various actors. It explores such changes at both the micro- and macro-levels and endeavours to link them back to wider social, managerial, and political issues. In doing so, it aims to reflect on the similarities and differences between new and 'old' work practices and problematise discourses surrounding the future of work. This volume is characterised by the diversity of methods mobilised, the plurality of concepts, lenses, and theories deployed, as well as the richness of the empirical accounts used by the authors. It will appeal to a broad readership of management and organisational scholars as well as sociologists interested in current changes to the world of work.

Jeremy Aroles is an assistant professor in Organisation Studies at Durham University, UK. His research currently focuses on new ways of working, the management of culture, and the relation between fiction and organisational worlds. His research has notably been published in *Organization Science, Management Learning, New Technology, Work and Employment*.

François-Xavier de Vaujany is Professor of Management & Organization Studies at PSL, University of Paris-Dauphine. His research deals with collaborative practices in open contexts (e.g. open sciences, maker movement, co-working, digital nomads, campus tours, learning expeditions). He has authored or edited eleven books and more than 130 articles, chapters, and communications.

Karen Dale is Professor of Organisation Studies at Lancaster University. She has researched and written on embodiment, including *Anatomising Embodiment and Organisation Theory* (2001) and about architecture, space, and sociomateriality, including *The Spaces of Organisation and the Organisation of Space: Power, Identity and Materiality at Work* (co-authored with Gibson Burrell, 2008).

Experiencing the New World of Work

Edited by

JEREMY AROLES
Durham University

FRANÇOIS-XAVIER DE VAUJANY
Paris-Dauphine University

KAREN DALE
Lancaster University

CAMBRIDGE
UNIVERSITY PRESS

CAMBRIDGE
UNIVERSITY PRESS

University Printing House, Cambridge CB2 8BS, United Kingdom

One Liberty Plaza, 20th Floor, New York, NY 10006, USA

477 Williamstown Road, Port Melbourne, VIC 3207, Australia

314–321, 3rd Floor, Plot 3, Splendor Forum, Jasola District Centre, New Delhi – 110025, India

79 Anson Road, #06–04/06, Singapore 079906

Cambridge University Press is part of the University of Cambridge.

It furthers the University's mission by disseminating knowledge in the pursuit of education, learning, and research at the highest international levels of excellence.

www.cambridge.org
Information on this title: www.cambridge.org/9781108496070
DOI: 10.1017/9781108865814

© Cambridge University Press 2021

First published 2021

A catalogue record for this publication is available from the British Library.

Library of Congress Cataloging-in-Publication Data
Names: Aroles, Jeremy, 1989– editor. | Vaujany, François-Xavier de, editor. | Dale, Karen, editor.
Title: Experiencing the new world of work / edited by Jeremy Aroles, Durham University, François-Xavier de Vaujany, Université Paris-Dauphine, Karen Dale, Lancaster University.
Description: Cambridge, United Kingdom ; New York, NY : Cambridge University Press, 2021. | Includes bibliographical references and index.
Identifiers: LCCN 2020041321 (print) | LCCN 2020041322 (ebook) | ISBN 9781108496070 (hardback) | ISBN 9781108791090 (paperback) | ISBN 9781108865814 (epub)
Subjects: LCSH: Employees–Effect of technological innovations on. | Organizational change. | Industrial sociology. | Labor.
Classification: LCC HD6331 .E97 2021 (print) | LCC HD6331 (ebook) | DDC 331.25/6–dc23
LC record available at https://lccn.loc.gov/2020041321
LC ebook record available at https://lccn.loc.gov/2020041322

ISBN 978-1-108-49607-0 Hardback
ISBN 978-1-108-79109-0 Paperback

Contents

Tables

Contributors

Jeremy Aroles is an assistant professor in Organisation Studies at Durham University, UK. His research currently focuses on new ways of working, the management of culture, and the relation between fiction and organisational worlds. His research has notably been published in *Organization Science, Management Learning* and *New Technology, Work and Employment*.

Birgitta Bergvall-Kåreborn is Professor in Information Systems at Luleå University of Technology. She was a driving force in the development of Living Lab and among the first to study crowdsourcing as a new path to source labour, as well as identifying labour sourcing as a component missing from existing business models.

Claudine Bonneau is an associate professor at ESG UQAM (Montreal) and a co-director of the Laboratory for Communication and the Digital. Her work focuses on new work practices and has been published in the *Handbook of Social Media Research Methods* as well as in *Communication, Research & Practice* and *International Journal of Project Management*.

Fiza Brakel-Ahmed is an urban anthropologist with a background in Business with Modern Languages (BA), Communication Science (MSc) and Organizational Anthropology (MSc). She uses ethnographic methods to research and explore urban space and how users interact with such spaces. She is affiliated with the VU University Amsterdam as a lecturer and researcher.

Gibson Burrell is currently Professor of Organization Theory at both the Universities of Manchester and Leicester, each on a fractional basis. He was a founding editor of the journal *Organization*, became a Fellow of the Academy of Social Sciences in 2015 and was awarded a Research Fellowship by the Leverhulme Trust from 2014 to 2016. In 2014 he was awarded a 'Trailblazer' prize from the American Academy of Management Organization Theory Division for his contribution to the field. He has written or co-authored a number of books as well as writing several journal articles that are still cited.

Stewart Clegg is Distinguished Professor at the University of Technology, Sydney and a visiting professor at Nova School of Business and Economics and EM-Lyon. His research is driven by a fascination with power and theorising. Stewart is a prolific writer and the author or editor of a great number of books as well as articles in many leading journals. He is an EGOS Honorary Member, EURAM Distinguished Fellow, Fellow of the Australian Academy of the Social Sciences, among other honours.

Karen Dale is Professor of Organisation Studies at Lancaster University. She has researched and written on embodiment, including *Anatomising Embodiment and Organisation Theory* and about architecture, space and sociomateriality, including *The Spaces of Organisation and the Organisation of Space: Power, Identity and Materiality at Work* with Gibson Burrell (2008).

Edward Granter is a senior lecturer in Organizational Behaviour at Birmingham Business School, University of Birmingham. His research and teaching interests range from the sociology of work, to Frankfurt School Critical Theory, to organised crime. He is the author and editor of various books about work and organisation, including *Critical Social Theory and the End of Work* and the textbook *The Sociology of Work* (2019) with Steve Edgell.

John Hassard is Professor of Organizational Analysis at Alliance Manchester Business School. Previously he taught at London Business School and Cardiff and Keele universities. He researches Organization Theory and Management History, and has published in journals such as *Academy of Management Review*, *Journal of Management Studies* and *Organization Studies*.

Debra Howcroft is Professor of Technology and Organisation at Alliance Manchester Business School, the University of Manchester.

She is Deputy Director of the Work and Equalities Institute and Editor of *New Technology, Work and Employment.*

Wendelin Küpers is Professor of Leadership and Organization Studies at Karlshochschule International University in Karlsruhe and Affiliated Professor at ICN-ARTEM, Nancy. Combining a phenomenological and cross-disciplinary orientation, his research focuses on embodied, emplaced, emotional, creative and aesthetic dimensions of organising and managing.

Aurélie Leclercq-Vandelannoitte is a researcher at CNRS/IESEG School of Management. She holds a PhD in Management, which received three national awards. She is interested in new work practices and organisational forms enabled by the use of information technology. She relies particularly on Michel Foucault's thought. Her research has been published in leading journals in Organisation Studies and MIS.

Jonathan Morris is Professor of Organisational Sociology and Associate Dean for Research, Cardiff University Business School. His interests are in the sociology of work and organisation, managerial work and East Asian capitalism. He has published in journals such as the *British Journal of Industrial Relations, Human Relations* and *Organization Studies.*

Clare Mumford worked as a research associate at the University of Manchester between 2016–2020. She is now based at Manchester Metropolitan University. She specialises in qualitative research methods. Her research interests include the (changing) experience of work and working relationships.

Mickael Peiro is a PhD graduate at the University of Montpellier. His work is based on an embodied and committed ethnographic study of three forms of alternative initiatives (hackerspace, alternative currency, occupy movement) in order to observe within these organisations the tensions between founding values and organisational issues.

François-Xavier de Vaujany is Professor of Management & Organization Studies at PSL, Université Paris-Dauphine. His research deals with collaborative practices in open contexts (e.g. open sciences, maker movement, co-working, digital nomads, campus tours and learning expeditions). He has authored or edited 11 books and more than 130 articles, chapters and communications.

Jamie Woodcock is a senior lecturer at the Open University. He is the author of The Gig Economy (2019), Marx at the Arcade (2019) and Working the Phones (2017). His research is inspired by the workers' inquiry. It focuses on labour, work, platforms, resistance, organising and videogames.

Foreword

JOHN HASSARD AND JONATHAN MORRIS

In these incredibly turbulent and unpredictable times, the worlds of work, employment and organisation are facing a myriad of pressures to change, restructure and reform. This excellent book presents a critical social analysis of the types of transformations occurring in these 'new' worlds. Specifically, it focuses on three issues crucial to making sense of contemporary work, workplaces and their management: the *experience* of working; the effects of *digitalisation* on work; and the changing *politics* of work and the workplace. In the remarks that follow we lay personal (and hopefully provocative) ground for the many and varied discussions of 'new' work, ways of working and forms of organising presented in the chapters to come.

In contextual terms, work organisations, especially large ones, have in recent decades faced a range of pressures arising from international competition under neo-liberalism, a situation that many argue has placed 'shareholder value' central to the management of organisational affairs. In order to deal with these pressures, organisations have often responded by restructuring their operations in seemingly innovative ways. The espoused aim is often to make large organisations more 'agile' or 'flexible' – although minimising costs has arguably been the central theme of strategy-making during this era of 'investor capitalism'.

In such a context, workers, managers and other employees have generally come to experience increasing pressure when carrying out their activities, with commonly fewer personnel undertaking a far broader range of tasks. Several consequences have emerged from this work experience: not only of greater time and task pressures being placed upon individuals but also feelings of work insecurity allied to career uncertainty. Additionally, the escalating use of new forms of digital technology has often led to increased stress when working;

notably, through the obligation for workers and managers to work outside of the organisation and at times not traditionally rewarded in the employment contract. Those at the commanding heights of organisations, however, recurrently claim such technologies provide for greater work elasticity, notably in optimising the use of time and space, and with many employees now completing work wherever and whenever possible.

Nonetheless, such changes to the experience of work, and commonly those brought about in recent decades by digitalisation, can have perverse consequences, or paradoxes, in terms of working practices, particularly where employees are already under significant work (especially temporal) pressures. Digitalisation can serve to blur for example the locational boundaries of where work takes place, and when it starts and stops. This poses additional questions for workplace control in situations reflecting the confluence of new work practices and organisational systems. This is allied crucially to the emergence of technologies facilitating new ways of working, ways that can result in seemingly contradictory experiences for employees – making it easier for them to claim temporal control over when work is to be done, but also seeing their work extended into virtually any space where a smartphone, tablet or laptop can be operated.

We would argue that this propels the study of 'new' work and work experience into more nuanced areas. While formerly explorations of surveillance, for instance, have been influenced by Benthamite politics allied to Foucauldian histories – exemplified empirically in studies of new forms of shop-floor production – increasingly the context of 'new' means of organisational control reflects the spread of *self*-surveillance at work. Arguably, the economic context has been transformed too – principally to one where competition has internationalised and workers, managers and other employees are experiencing increased perceptions of job precarity.

Meanwhile work organisations often claim restructuring is directed at achieving 'leaner' forms of working. In such a scenario, employees must often deal with a significant increase in expected working hours, with this new 'normal working day' also being underpinned by recourse to innovative digital technologies. In realising the potential of using such devices, and in working, for example, from non-workplace locations, we see emergent work practices increasingly reflect qualities of 'distantiation' and 'dispersal', which can reflect moves to more diffuse and fragmented social relations. In such scenarios, organisational surveillance can be transformed into more subtle – self and peer – forms of control, as realised in situations offering workers ever more elastic opportunities for carrying out tasks.

However, digitalisation, which can often be welcomed by workers and managers, has often been singled out as responsible for generating adverse occupational outcomes, not least in terms of self-exploitation. In modern work organisations, there is often political pressure to shift the locus of control from employer to worker, as witnessed in demands for those working from home to 'prove themselves'. It has been argued that workers in such situations can be drawn increasingly into the all-embracing 'gaze' of such technologies. Moreover, the potential for greater autonomy and collaboration – which workers and managers have tended to assume in relation to the use of digital technology – is arguably reflective principally of occupational status and the ability to exercise control over the type of work such technology facilitates. Digital communication devices, for example, initially seemed to offer employees significant opportunities for redefining the temporal and spatial boundaries of their work, and notably to extend these boundaries at their personal discretion. There is, in fact, considerable evidence pointing to employees initially welcoming not only the flexibility such technologies presented but also the increased influence they appeared to be bestowing in terms of work routines and practices. It must be stressed, however, that increased autonomy at work can also be accompanied, politically, by increased control, notably as employees attempt to 'use' these technologies to demonstrate organisational commitment. Researchers point to workers, managers and other employees experiencing pressures to 'conform' temporally in organisations, and of digital technologies being used by workers politically to signal organisational loyalty in this regard. This can lead to workers and managers becoming caught in a collaborative spiral of escalating engagement – one that results in them working at all hours and in virtually any location. It has been argued that this reflects an autonomy paradox in relation to what elsewhere has been termed 'concertive' forms of control.

Digitalisation can therefore alter considerably the experience and politics of presence/absence in work and the workplace, and in turn the 'new' control of work. Political questions of organisational control are thus evident, and notably regarding so-called collaborative forms of working, which extend beyond direct visual observation and control. Autonomy can become a synonym for self-governance; one that can reflect major changes to the spatial packages of working life. Early studies of professionals using the BlackBerry, for example, found they viewed the technology positively, and that the device enhanced their sense of competence and influence. But conversely researchers also suggested its use could indicate expectations of increased responsiveness, as well as a degree of compulsion to be continuously accessible amid shifting norms of engagement. In their leisure time during the workweek, such professionals still checked their devices continuously, and up to once an hour on weekends. In other research, researchers reported professionals checking their email even on vacation.

Digital technologies have been viewed, therefore, as capable of escalating work engagement, raising work expectations and increasing work stress. Investigations have linked the use of digital technologies with work overload, expectations of worker availability and changes to the home–work boundary. The distorting of traditional work and non-work boundaries – in ways that appear (temporally, spatially and technologically) to be evermore 'permeable' – can certainly be viewed as reflecting important changes in the 'new' ways we define what it means to be 'working'. However, many of the descriptions and explanations of changes to contemporary working can arguably be considered as overly linear, deterministic and decontextualised. We would argue that much research in this area often underplays the amount of political choice and personal agency in the contemporary organisation and control of work. For us this represents a missing ingredient in the extant literature: identification of case examples that run counter to – or 'against the grain' of – linear and deterministic explanations.

This book seeks to remedy this situation by going deeper and more critically into the 'new' worlds of work, employment and organisation. It is a volume that very much fits the bill of presenting 'against-the-grain' arguments when analysing the experience of working, the effects of digitalisation on work and the changing politics of the workplace. Taking recourse to a range of methodological approaches, theoretical lenses and empirical cases, the book provides detailed and reflective analysis of new ways of working, new forms of employment and new modes of organising. In what is an extremely rich and varied set of contributions, the focus of work inquiry ranges from 'hackerspaces' to 'makerspaces', from 'peasantry' work to the 'post-work imaginary', from 'third-place' working to the lifeworld of 'digital nomads'. In sum, this is an important and thought-provoking book that offers nuanced and fine-grained explanations of the 'new' work experience.

Introduction
Experiencing the New World of Work

JEREMY AROLES, FRANÇOIS-XAVIER DE
VAUJANY AND KAREN DALE

The New World of Work

Over the past few years, much has been written on the changing world
of work, with discussions focusing, for instance, on the rise of
automation (Spencer 2018), changes in the nature of the employment
relationship (Sweet and Meiksins 2013), the (failed) promises of the gig
economy (Cant 2019; Wood, Graham, Lehdonvirta & Hjorth 2019)
or new ways of collaborating and co-producing (de Vaujany, Leclerq-
Vandelannoitte & Holt 2020). Importantly though, these discussions
are not novel, neither are the phenomena they seek to describe. The
history of work is full of *déjà vu*. Communities, participatory systems,
horizontality, democracy at work and nomadism are far from being
new topics per se. In the nineteenth century, the Arts and Crafts
Movement, socialist utopian communities, anarchy and Marxism had
already involved public debates around these topics (see Granter 2016;
Leone and Knauf 2015; Tilly 2019). Yet, there is clearly a renewed
interest for these themes in research attempting to grapple with the
multifaceted nature and the complex meaning of contemporary work
(see for instance Aroles, Mitev & de Vaujany 2019; Fayard 2019;
Simms 2019; Susskind 2020).

One of the guiding threads of many analyses of new ways of
working (and their matching forms of management) is certainly collaboration (Garrett, Spreitzer & Bacevice 2017; Spinuzzi 2012).
Collaborative techniques, practices, spaces and sensibilities lie at the
heart of this new world of work. This almost sounds counterintuitive,
in that the current world of work is often depicted as increasingly
fragmented, individualised, digitalised, entre/intrapreneurial, gig-
orientated and compartmentalised for the sake of flexibility, speed
and integration. Platforms, projects, complex matrix-based structures
and Artificial Intelligence allow the materialisation of the 'minimal'
form of socialisation and integration required to act together and most

1

of all to be constitutive of a society. In this world made of individuals 'alone together' (Spinuzzi 2012), in the neo-liberal and post-human context of our societies (Hayles 1999), collaboration is no longer a given maintained through structures, shared routines as well as public standards and institutions. Collaboration then requires new 'conditions of possibilities', continuously reinvented by those contributing to this new world of work. But strangely and paradoxically, collaboration, both in what is claimed about it and sometimes in its actuality, appears more as an individualistic form of collaboration (as opposed to what might have traditionally been thought of as collaboration). Communities are particularly evanescent and ephemeral. They become a strange utopia that is never really fulfilled, a cool, atmospheric, apolitical construct, far from the true public spaces and agora described and expected by Arendt (1998). Interindividual relationships prevail in a neo-liberal order that seems to be more than ever triumphant and calling indefinitely for novelty and rupture in ongoing work practices.

Focus of This Edited Volume

This volume revolves around two dimensions of the new world of work, namely (1) the *lived reality* (lived experiences) and (2) the claimed *novelty* of 'new' work practices. Experiences are varied, diverse and located within broader socio-economic conditions and relations; they also embody different interpretations of those relations. The lived reality of new work configurations is explored through many different perspectives in this edited volume. Some chapters, for instance, engage in an experiential, sensible or phenomenological exploration of the so-called new world of work. Such a stance provides deep insight into the embodied dimension of work practices (Dale 2000, 2005; Küpers 2014; de Vaujany & Aroles 2019) and allows accounting for the differential ways in which the aforementioned changes and transformations are experienced. In addition, it gives us a vocabulary to understand the fabric of obviousness and the taken-for-grantedness of our world, as it is produced by our moods, emotions, affects and activities. Other chapters provide more macro-level forms of theorisation around the manifestations of the new world of work and their implications for those involved in such work configurations. This helps to locate new work practices within broader socio-economic, historical and cultural conditions and relations.

The issue of novelty is equally crucial to our understanding of new work practices. This volume argues that work, management and organising processes are full of spatio-temporal continuities and dis-continuities that become manifested at different levels. The current world of work is necessarily different from, yet similar to, its predecessor: current collaborative practices and processes extend older ones, present forms of precarity reflect past ones, contemporary resistance to automation resonates with very old social movements such as the Luddites and so on. Chapters in this edited volume investigate and unpack these changes and repetitions in the ways in which work activities are both conceptualised and carried out in practice.

Connecting these two concerns (experiences and novelty), this volume explores the following question: How is the 'new' world of work, envisioned since the late 1980s, lived and experienced? To address this question, we sought to put together a collection of chapters that would offer a provocative, diverse and hopefully agenda-setting account of the new world of work. Through various methodological approaches, theoretical lenses and empirical cases, this volume aims to provide an in-depth, qualitative, reflective and fine-grained analysis of new ways of working and new modes of organising. We contend that a critical, experiential and reflective stance is needed in order to go beyond (technologically driven) utopias, glamorising discourses and immaterial-ised visions and expectations that, more often than not, are mobilised to depict new work practices and the future of work in general.

Following this introduction, the volume is divided into three parts and comprises ten chapters. The first part focuses on a key tenet of new ways of working: co-presence, shared spaces and collaboration. In particular, it explores, conceptually and empirically, the immediate, sensible, embedded and co-present experience of work practices. The second part explores another key aspect of new ways of working and their experience, which seems to be the opposite of co-presence: digi-talisation, although the two are intertwined and interrelated in con-temporary work in ways that call out for a detailed exploration. It is an opportunity to explore further key temporal and spatial transform-ations at stake in new ways of working, in particular those activities that are more and more mediated by digital tools and platforms.

Lastly, with the third and final part, this volume explores the imaginaries, politics and narratives of new ways of working. This is an opportunity to stress the paradoxes, geopolitical absurdities and historical drifts sometimes produced by new ways of working in our experience of the world (of work). The first two sections of the volume focus more on the specificities of experiences of new ways of working, while the final section brings a broader historical and political sweep to bear on these changes. In the conclusion, we reflect on the changes and continuities explored in this volume through three dimensions: (i) creativity and changing skills; (ii) the time and space of work; and (iii) the changing nature of the employment relationship and beyond. In addition, this edited volume contains a foreword and an afterword, both of which offer insightful reflections on the future of work.

Part I Experiencing at Work

The first part of this volume comprises four chapters. The first chapter, written by Wendelin Küpers, is entitled 'Embodied Inter-Practices in Resonance as New Forms of Working in Organisations'. This first chapter is a theoretical consideration of new ways of working and what they mean in a relational and embodied way. It explores how a phenomenological approach can help to develop a more integral and relational understanding of embodied and resonant practices of new work in organisations. In such relational practices, material, economic, political and socio-cultural dimensions come together. Based on a phenomenology of embodied practising that sees work as situationally and temporally placed, the processual concept of 'inter-practice' is presented and explored. Afterwards, the relational mode of 'resonance', as developed by Rosa, is presented and critically discussed, with the chapter concluding with some implications and perspectives.

The second chapter, written by Fiza Brakel-Ahmed, is entitled 'Wherever I Lay My Laptop, That's My Workplace: Experiencing the New World of Work in a Hotel Lobby'. This chapter focuses on self-employed workers who work in hotel lobbies that were not primarily designed as co-working spaces. The number of self-employed workers has been growing exponentially over the past twenty years. In parallel, digital technologies have made it possible for people to work from literally anywhere in the world, providing they have the right devices and access to a Wi-Fi system. Self-employed individuals typically do not have an office in a firm they can go to every day in order to work. Digital technologies open up an array of possibilities – working is possible anywhere and at any time. Self-employed individuals can choose to work from home, a rented hot desk in a co-working space, in coffeeshops, hotel lobbies and even on the beach in a sunny resort on a beautiful island. This chapter explores how *other* spaces, in this case a hotel lobby, can be turned into an 'unintended' co-working space through the agency of self-employed individuals.

The third chapter, written by Mickael Peiro, is entitled '"So Many Cool Things to Do!": Hacker Ethics and Work Practices'. This research is based on an ethnographic study conducted in a political hackerspace in France between 2016 and 2018. The fieldwork combines direct participation with a long-term presence in the community and years of archived exchanges and interviews with all the hackers involved in the initiative. This chapter explores the daily activities of a group of hackers, thus making it possible to experience new forms of organisation and social relations. The analysis of the relationships between the means and ends of the organisation studied suggests that, far from being confined to individual values and attitudes, the pleasure and power given to 'doing' represent organisational principles within hackerspace. It highlights the structuring of the alternative project and how the hackers organise themselves according to their ethics. The hacker ethic is reflected in the organisational tasks and the constitution of a legitimate order; it is not linked to rational, charismatic or traditional motives, but to a real power given to the 'doing': the do-it-ocracy.

The fourth chapter, written by François-Xavier de Vaujany and Jeremy Aroles, is entitled 'Experiencing Making: Silence, Atmosphere and Togetherness in Makerspaces'. This chapter describes the 'experience of making' in two makerspaces, one located in France and the other in the United States. In particular, this chapter focuses on three concepts – silence, atmosphere and togetherness – in order to flesh out, or make visible, the specificities of Do-It-Yourself (DIY) and Do-It-Together (DIT) processes in makerspaces. Craftsmanship, making and do-it-ocracy are prominent elements of the so-called new world of work. The authors mobilise Merleau-Ponty's work and an aesthetic perspective on time and place in order to delve into the experience of making. They propose the concept of New Collaborative Experiences (NCE), which is defined as new modes of feeling and expressing the self and the world in a context that requires collective production and coordination, as a way of illuminating the two ethnographic accounts presented in this chapter.

Part II Digital Platforms and the New World of Work

The second part of this volume consists of three chapters. The fifth chapter, written by Debra Howcroft, Clare Mumford and Birgitta Bergvall-Kåreborn, is entitled 'Exploring Inequalities in Platform-Based Legal Work'. The aim of this chapter is to examine the neglected area of platform work and inequalities. Drawing on Acker's theoretical frame of inequality regimes, this study investigates whether platform work reproduces and/or augments inequalities. Extant research on platforms has focused predominantly on lesser skilled work based on repetitive transactions; in contrast, the authors explore experiences of higher-skilled work, specifically the provision of legal services. A qualitative approach was adopted based on participants using the People Per Hour (PPH) platform, which offers high-skilled professional services targeted at the small-business market. The study is situated in the context of structural disadvantages in the legal profession. The authors show that persistent inequalities within the offline legal profession are not simply mirrored, but amplified in platform work, contesting any optimistic claims that platform work has the potential to act as a leveller.

The sixth chapter, written by Jamie Woodcock, is entitled 'Workers Inquiry and the Experience of Work: Using Ethnographic Accounts of the Gig Economy'. This chapter considers how research that puts the workers' perspective at the forefront can be placed within a critical dialogue with the researcher. While there have been accounts of resistance taking place across Europe in delivery platforms, these have tended to take a broader analytical lens, rather than focusing on the specific practices being experimented with. In this chapter, the author presents a reflection on the experiences of joint writing with workers in the gig economy. The chapter is intended as a corrective to much of the abstract academic research on the 'gig economy'. As such, it is both an empirical and methodological intervention – presenting an account of this work from the perspective of a worker themselves, while also arguing that it is from this perspective that the work can be not only critically analysed but also transformed.

The seventh chapter, written by Claudine Bonneau and Jeremy Aroles, is entitled 'Digital Nomads: A New Form of Leisure Class?'. This chapter draws from Veblen's *Theory of the Leisure Class* to explore whether digital nomads can be seen to constitute a new form of leisure class. Digital nomadism refers to a mobile lifestyle in which freelancers, digital entrepreneurs or remote workers combine work with continuous travel. In particular, this chapter problematises digital nomadism through four dimensions, namely differentiation, emulation, visibility and institutionalisation. Drawing from a qualitative analysis of the mainstream promotional discourse underlying digital nomadism, this chapter shows the existence of a whole set of economic activities based on selling a romanticised work/lifestyle to others. These commercial propositions, which rely on online storytelling and visibility, constitute efficient means of emulation that contribute to framing images of success. This 'Veblen-inspired' analysis generates a source of questions not only relevant to the study of digital nomadism, but also to miscellaneous aspects of the new world of work.

Part III Politics, Imaginaries and *Others* in the New World of Work

The third part of this volume comprises three chapters. The eighth chapter, written by Gibson Burrell, is entitled 'Bypassing the Stage of Copper Wire? New Work Practices amongst the Peasantry'. This chapter is concerned with changes in work practices amongst the 'peasantry' still working upon the land in twenty-first-century India. This population may sound very far from the conventional understandings of shifts in technology that regularly affect how work is done in the 'West' but the rise of ICT technologies, especially the smart phone, have at least the potential to shift practices upon the land that have remained unchanged for centuries. Before the twenty-first century, large infrastructural requirements saw the triumph of copper, so that in some senses a whole material civilisation developed around the electrical and conductive properties of this metal. However, this centralised mode of organising based upon copper has become threatened by a Digital Revolution. New forms of working are allowed by the post-copper technologies and materials of the twenty-first century, but this chapter asks: How widespread and how deep does this rematerialising of organisation actually go?

The ninth chapter, written by Edward Granter, is entitled 'Critical Theory and the Post-work Imaginary'. This chapter presents an analysis of the intellectual heritage underlying the new world of work and seeks to illustrate continuity and disjuncture in the dynamics of what could be termed 'post-work imaginaries'. Advances in production systems and technology, particularly around automation and robotics, have been accompanied in recent years by a resurgence of debate about the future of work. Many contemporary accounts inhabit a utopian space where radical change is desired and envisioned. They point to profound, possibly revolutionary, change in the nature of work – perhaps the end of work. They place work at the centre of social life as presently known, and in so doing tend to offer up a critique of capitalist society *in toto*. During the twentieth century, Western economies grappled with the issue of automation, at the same time finding themselves oscillating between consumer-fuelled expansion and economic crisis. This produced an intellectual engagement with automation and post-work that has much in common with that of today's 'post-industrial utopians'. Even stretching back into antiquity, utopian thinkers imagined a world without toil, and so the notion of 'post-work', or the 'end of work' exists in the context of a long and distinctive intellectual heritage.

The tenth chapter, written by François-Xavier de Vaujany and Aurélie Leclercq-Vandelannoitte, is entitled 'Exploring the New in Politics at Work: A Temporal Approach of Managerial Agencies'. This chapter argues that new ways of working imply a crisis both of communities and politics in our societies. The authors introduce the concept of 'co-politicisation' to make sense of the transformative political power of managerial agency in society. In the context of ongoing work transformations, managerial agency increasingly seems to become a political agency, through its potential to transform society and the sense of togetherness. However, in the meantime, politics has entered into crisis – individuals express their own voice, but without building, in turn, any meaningful or resonant collective and community. This chapter argues that a temporal approach is needed to understand such a crisis of community. Drawing from Paul Ricoeur's thought on a 'crisis of the present', the authors suggest that new ways of working may be missing practices likely to produce the extra-temporality that managerial agency needs to perform. Without this extra-temporality, the managerial agency of new ways of working just keeps weakening our sense of togetherness.

References

Arendt, H. 1998. *The Human Condition*. Chicago: University of Chicago Press.

Aroles, J., Mitev, N. & de Vaujany, F. X. 2019. Mapping themes in the study of new work practices. *New Technology, Work and Employment*, 34 (3): 285–299.

Cant, C. 2019. *Riding for Deliveroo: Resistance in the New Economy*. Cambridge: Polity Press.

Dale, K. 2000. *Anatomising Embodiment and Organisation Theory*. Basingstoke: Springer.

    2005. Building a social materiality: Spatial and embodied politics in organizational control. *Organization*, 12(5): 64–678.

de Vaujany, F. X. & Aroles, J. 2019. Nothing happened, something happened: Silence in a makerspace. *Management Learning*, 50(2): 208–225.

de Vaujany, F. X., Leclercq-Vandelannoitte, A. & Holt, R. 2020. Communities versus platforms: The paradox in the body of the collaborative economy. *Journal of Management Inquiry*, 29(4): 450–467.

Fayard, A. L. 2019. Notes on the Meaning of Work: Labor, Work, and Action in the 21st Century. *Journal of Management Inquiry*. DOI: 1056492619841705.

Garrett, L. E., Spreitzer, G. M. & Bacevice, P. A. 2017. Co-constructing a sense of community at work: The emergence of community in coworking spaces. *Organization Studies*, 38(6): 821–842.

Granter, E. 2016. *Critical Social Theory and the End of Work*. Abingdon: Routledge.

Hayles, N. K. 1999. *How We Became Posthuman: Virtual Bodies in Cybernetics, Literature, and Informatics*. Chicago: University of Chicago Press.

Küpers, W. 2014. *Phenomenology of the Embodied Organization: The Contribution of Merleau-Ponty for Organizational Studies and Practice*. New York: Springer.

Leone, M. P. & Knauf, J. E. 2015. *Historical Archaeologies of Capitalism*. Abingdon: Springer.

Simms, M. 2019. *What Do We Know and what Should We Do about the Future of Work?* London: SAGE Publications Limited.

Spencer, D. A. 2018. Fear and hope in an age of mass automation: Debating the future of work. *New Technology, Work and Employment*, 33(1): 1–12.

Spinuzzi, C. 2012. Working alone together: Coworking as emergent collaborative activity. *Journal of Business and Technical Communication*, 26(4): 399–441.

Susskind, D. 2020. *A World Without Work*. London: Allen Lane.
Sweet, S., & Meiksins, P. 2013. *Changing Contours of Work: Jobs and Opportunities in the New Economy*. Thousand Oaks, CA: Sage Publications.
Tilly, C. 2019. *Work Under Capitalism*. New York: Routledge.
Wood, A. J. Graham, M. Lehdonvirta, V. and Hjorth, I. 2019. Good gig, bad gig: Autonomy and algorithmic control in the global gig economy. *Work, Employment and Society*, 33(1): 56–75.

PART I

Experiencing at Work

1 Embodied Inter-Practices in Resonance as New Forms of Working in Organisations

WENDELIN KÜPERS

Introduction

Why Work? (Merry 2019) is a recent book, asking critically about the status of a more sustainable form of economics and more integral work for people and planet.

The worlds of work have always changed, but in our time we face unprecedented transformation. Conditions, contents, processes and the role of technology are radically altering what it means to work and the future of work. As an intensifying and ambiguous process of individualisation, often with pseudo-autonomy at work, the working self is situated between freedom and social pathology (Ebert 2016), while experiencing altering of conventional work identity (Petriglieri, Ashford & Wrzesniewski 2019). Increasing flexibilisation 'liquefies' spheres of work. *Hyper-flexibilised working practices* make workers appear as a kind of appendix to organisational demands and expectations, which may result in sacrifice of personal coherence and fulfilment of meaningful work for systemic priorities. Alternatively, new work forms may render creative possibilities for different ways of operating and acting.

On the one hand, the colonisation of the lifeworld by encroaching modernist imperatives, which has been studied for quite some time, is causing new forms of alienation. On the other, changes in contemporary society and workplaces may also contribute to redesigning and enacting different understandings of what it means to work, play (Küpers 2017a) and live. Currently, the debate about the future of work seems mainly to be focused on disruptive technologies, and the impact of robotisation and artificial intelligence, etc. all with their opportunities and dangers.

Increasingly, virtualising organisations bring about new spatio-temporal and cultural challenges (Kingma 2019), and are calling for new arrangements for working. Considering the ubiquity of digital technology in twenty-first-century work (Cascio & Montealegre 2016), research has demonstrated the potentially ambivalent role of digital technologies and socio-material negotiations, especially in constructions of meaningfulness of work (Symon & Whiting 2019). New work in the digital age allows more nomadic identities, practices, communities and cultures (Aroles, Granter & de Vaujany 2020; Chen & Nath 2005; Garrett, Spreitzer & Bacevice 2017; Müller 2016) that call for dancing on a limen of transitional moves (Küpers 2011).

For example, working in a collaborative virtual platform with a mode of coordination whereby information and communication are decentralised, with a collective working community, requires nomadic qualities, such as strong autonomy and flexibility. Although the scenario of an ultra-flexible 'super-interim world of work' – similar to a new age Taylorism – could lead to an 'Uberised' world of subcontracting platform employment workers, which may lead to a two-tier society with a well-integrated techno-elite and a techno-proletariat (Benhamou 2017). However, being increasingly professionalised and economised, digitally mediated nomadic work as an example of a new work form carries both emancipatory and constraining powers, partly continuing and evolutionary, partly discontinuing and revolutionary. Simultaneously, this work form is rendering a 'real-virtual' or 'analogue-digital' 're-evolution' that calls for rethinking the status of the body, bodily dimension and the role of embodiment, while mapping themes in the study of new work practices (Aroles, Mitev & de Vaujany 2019).

Thus, one important question will be about the roles the body and ways of embodiment play in these new forms of work-practice. The situated human body becomes an interactive interface of digital technology in form of a technognosis in action (Davis 2015). For Davis, the embodied human sensorium itself remains that 'weird media' of real time flux of perception, feeling and cognition, as well as the neural substrate that conditions, and arguably causes, the ongoing mediation of reality, and has become the ultimate object of technical manipulation, augmentation and control.

Correspondingly, working bodies, or workers' bodies, are now part of affective and effective computational systems, like telework, telematics or networked computing, coming 'closer to computers' (Kozel 2007). This approximation makes bodies become extensions of performing workers' ways of touching, feeling, moving, thinking and acting. Ambivalently, new forms of sharing the working body (and thus embodied workers' jobs), via digital devices, foster both a more 'really virtual' and 'virtually real' orientation. This orientation is both collaborative and competitive, while mediating different bodily and emotional states' levels of conscious (un-)awareness of lived experience. The enabling, transformative, but also constraining potentials of what is happening between bodies and technologies, call for critical investigation and careful responsive and responsible designs.

Practices of new work are thus connected to artful design of, and for, work as well as sustainable processes in and beyond organisations (Küpers 2013a, b, 2016). Concretised by the role of habits and improvisation (Küpers 2011) and serious play and embodied performance in organisational lifeworlds (Küpers 2017a, b), the emerging new experimental 'crea©tive' ways of work–play are promising, but need to be seen as integrated into embodied and inter-relational practices. To understand and develop as well as perform practices of new work creatively and integrally invites us to consider agentic capacities and embodied agencies. These are characterised by emergent, partly subversive, incomplete and ambiguous powers. The forces of these powers help to mediate responsive processes and transformative performances that are contributing to radical social change (Denzin 2016, p. 153) and the development of new embodied practices.

The proposition of this chapter is that advanced forms of phenomenological exploration are helpful for an extended and integral understanding of embodied practices of new work. Following Merleau-Ponty's philosophy (1995, 2003, 2012) and an interdisciplinary approach, the chapter will present phenomenological reflections on an embodied and inter-relational understanding of new resonant working practices in organisations. Building on seeing work as situationally and temporally placed, the concept of 'inter-practice' will be discussed. In such relational practices, material, economic, sociocultural and political dimensions come together. Placed at various levels, relational practices are interpreted as both enabling and constraining or constrained as well as part of an overall bodily (somatic) contexture. Rosa's concept of 'resonance' will be presented as a relational mode of inter-practices of new work. Facing an unsustainable

Anthropocene, the chapter concludes with some implications and perspectives.

Phenomenological Understanding of Embodied Practice of New Work

By following the call to return to phenomena and to things or events in their lifeworldly situated-ness, a phenomenological orientation offers a specific approach to, and understanding of, practices of work as embodied. New working practices need to be seen as always and already being part of an embedding horizon of 'all activities and possible prâxis' (Husserl 1970, p. 142). And these are bodied ones, integrating senses and sense-making. This embedding and embodied dimension also concerns the present reconceptualising and redesign of work and workers by multiplying digital platforms, AI, algorithms, learning machines, etc. To explore them critically, Merleau-Ponty's thinking (1995, 2012) and corresponding phenomenological, techno-scientific interrogations in relation to digital technologies, and new media (Hansen 2006, 2014; Hoel & Carusi 2018) are highly relevant.

Work practices in the digital age still need to be considered and interpreted as an embodied and a situated nexus of ways of experiencing, intending, responding and acting. These incorporeal practices, even while being increasingly mediated by technologies, still provide the source of, and medium for, meanings in organisations understood as situated lifeworlds (Sandberg & Dall'Alba 2010).

Whatever and how the incarnated technologically enframed, constrained or enabled actors sense, feel, think, intend or do, or cannot do and make (not) sense in these worlds of organising and organised, they are embodied. This implies that, even in 'real–virtual' activities (e.g. in computer use, see Lupton 1995), they are bodily exposed to, relate and process their practising within a syn- or dis-chronised field of senses and sensations (Merleau-Ponty 2012, p. 237).

Within the sphere of such an experienced practice, as a kind of 'matrixed ontology' (Kaushik 2019) a member of an organisation does not only sense 'I know', but also 'I relate to' or 'I do', or when constrained, 'I cannot relate to' or 'I cannot do'. Moreover, members also experience these capacities as collective actors operating in teams with 'we-mode-intentionalities' (Küpers 2015a). In other words, the atmosphere within which practices are situated is not only what people or social agencies conceive, but also primarily what they live through together with their 'operative intentionality' (Merleau-Ponty 2012, pp. xxxii, 165) or being affected to as bodily beings. Intending and being affected as bodies via their pre-reflexive emplaced motility, they can be constrained or enabled and augmented by technology, for example in relation to mobility (Küpers 2015b).

With this understanding of 'body-based' there is a close link between what is actually given or intended and situated responses. This responsiveness refers to a specific answering practice (Waldenfels 2008). With their living bodies, practitioners respond to questions, problems or claims as well as various demands imposed on them in their embedding or affording contexts.

To consider the entwinement of life and world of practice phenomenologically (Sandberg and Dall'Alba 2009) and to develop new forms of working require integrating these bodily and embodied processes. Turning to the body and to practices as embodied helps in reintegrating ignored, neglected or undervalued phenomena that are constitutive of understanding the practising in organisations (Dale 2001; Yakhlef 2010). Concretely, a revived, embodied approach can recollect, disclose, recognise and up-value how living human and even more-than-human beings in new work-practice 'touch, smell, taste, (and) have sentiments and senses; they argue, yell, get nervous and even die' (Nicolini, Gherardi & Yanow 2003, p. 22).

Facing the ongoing 'absent presence' of the body and embodiment (Leder 1990) or the disembodied, marginalised understanding in organisational and management theory and practice, a phenomenology of the body contributes to a 're-membering'. This remembering allows criticising of reductionist understandings and one-sided interpretations of working practices that prioritise regulative or instrumentally orientated action (Hancock 2009). Due to an outcome-fixation and utilitarian orientation, such instrumentalism can fall into a short-sighted 'practicalism' that collapses 'pragma' with 'practicality'. Such a practicalist reductionism implies the loss of a sense of emergent processes, un(pre)determinable qualities, socio-ethical- or aesthetic dimensions or 'proto-wise' qualifications of embodied practices (Küpers 2013a).

A revived emphasis on the body in relation to enabling possibilities and restricting constraints in organisations can help to understand how power or control is achieved and maintained, as well as what forms of practising are excluded or superimposed in new forms of work. In particular, such a critical stance can reveal how specific embodied experiences, aspects and meanings of new work practices are discriminated, marginalised, degraded, ignored, dominated or subordinated. Thus, a critical approach towards embodied practice can be used for studying excluding regimes, the ordering and normalising effects of disciplinary techniques and the encumbering processes of forced or imposed imperatives on working practices at individual and collective levels. At a collective level, this also implies critically exploring group-dynamics or governing functional and structural issues within the organisational system that enforce certain practices and exclude others.

Reconsidering the body in relation to new working practice reveals how interacting members of organisations are related, both in distanced or connected ways, through or constrained by their bodies also with regard to each other and to used technology or being used by enframing technologies described by Heidegger as Gestell (Heidegger 1993; Wendland, Merwin & Hadjioannou 2018). According to this technological enframement, embodied workers make themselves an available resource or standing reserve (*Bestand*) ready to be called on in the service of a technological system.

Based on a phenomenological understanding of embodied practice, *sensu* Merleau-Ponty, practising and thus acting in arrangement of new work can be interpreted as inter-relational processes that are manifested and constrained concretely in various forms of bodies at work. For this, a phenomenology of embodied agency of performing and performative bodies at work is helpful (Küpers 2017a). Such an approach can reveal the processing of working and worked bodies in new work arrangements. This may include concrete cases of affective and emotional labour, including care work as well as aesthetic and presentational labour (ibid). The powerful enabling of multisensory experiences and interplay of sensual audio-scapes, smell-scapes, touch-scapes, etc. (Degen 2008) in new work contexts can cause personal, interpersonal and socio-cultural as well as systemic tensions and conflicts.

Bodily practices constitute an important means by which the norms, values and beliefs associated with a particular organisational culture are enacted and the proficiency of a cultural member is demonstrated. The lived experience of bodies and their intersection with norms and power can be seen as potential media for resistance to power (Ball

2005). Ball (2005) showed how embodied forms of antagonistic resistance are responses to totalising biometric surveillance practices in relation to the interface of informatised bodies and the categorising technologies that try to fix them. Moreover, tactics and micropolitical processes in relation to everyday-living (de Certeau 1984) can be studied as the employment of creative intelligence and practice of governance or subversive tactics. Through these tactics, embodied occupants of work environments or resisting groups subvert all-pervasive pressures to reassert and reappropriate a sphere of autonomous action and self-determination.

Trying to survive and undermine constrained, repressive domination can lead to everyday resistance (Scott 1985). This form of resistance manifests not as dramatic and visible as rebellions, riots, revolutions, other collective or confrontational articulations, but can be quiet, dispersed, disguised or otherwise seemingly invisible. Such low profile, undisclosed infrapolitics refers to the behaviour of subaltern groups – for example, escape, sarcasm, passivity, laziness, misunderstandings, disloyalty, slander, avoidance or theft – that exploited people use in order to both survive and undermine repressive domination. Consequently, bodily performances have the potential to subvert particular constraining, hegemonic norms, which affect constructions and politics of the self, others and identity. In addition to resistance and subversion, constraints are also powerfully linked to non-purposive, non-rational and silence(d) practices in organisational life and affect what is or cannot be practised or expressed. This may include unnoticed actions and omissions or what is strategically unthinkable, tabooed or supposedly undoable (Carter, Clegg & Kornberger 2008, p. 94).

In accordance with a phenomenological approach, for Kemmis (2012, p. 150), the happening-ness of practices is the embodied action itself. In addition, it is an action in all its materiality and, as such, affects the specific dimensions and configurations of practices that are historically, discursively, socially and culturally formed. In their concept of practice architecture, Kemmis and Smith (2008) discuss various forms of relating, sayings and doings in practices and how these three dimensions of practice simultaneously shape and are shaped by one another. In particular, they discuss the connection between material–economic arrangements (resources that enable and constrain actions and the doings of the practice), social–ethical and political arrangements influencing the sayings relating to the practice and cultural–discursive arrangements (language and discourses that constitute the sayings). Kemmis et al. (2009) argued that these practice architectures hang together in 'teleo-affective structures' that give a sense of purpose (the 'teleo' element) and shape participants' commitment in embodied realisation (the 'affective' element) as they are all present in practices. In addition, Kemmis and his colleagues (Kemmis et al. 2009, pp. 2–3) emphasised that practices are not only embedded in practice architectures but also 'clustered together in relationship with other practices' defined as meta-practices, that is, practices that shape other practices As such, they are part of praxis as an overarching configuration at a holonic metalevel.

Furthermore, there exist ecologies of practices that can be defined as distinctive, interconnected webs of human social activities – characteristic arrangements of sayings, doings and relatings – that are mutually necessary to order and sustain a practice of new work as a practice of a particular kind and complexity (Kemmis, Edwards-Groves, Wilkinson & Hardy 2012). Practices are ecologically arranged in two ways as they 'arise in relation to one another in a particular site' and as they are 'interdependent and inter-related' (Kemmis et al. 2014). Also, new and innovative practices of work are shaped by and shape the practices, meta-practices in praxis. In turn, practices, meta-practices and praxes determine and allocate resources, infrastructure and policies that influence, enable or constrain the conditions for practices of new work by focusing on different participants' ways of doing or technologies of operating as well as on how all of these are shaped by, and do shape, concrete actions as holonic parts of practices.

The 'practice architectures' function as and disclose existing preconditions that influence practices of new work in praxis as they are simultaneously produced by the particular doings, sayings and relatings that constitute any given way of practising some-thing. The complex assemblages of this architecture, with their associated material–economic, social–political and cultural–discursive spaces and arrangements, constitute and mediate practices, and are effectuating actionable or non-actionable processes as all domains that facilitate or impact practices in praxis. While there is no clear route, it is only through careful research, examining the specific practices and concrete actions in various contexts, that it is possible to approach and judge whether and how specific acts and decisions are likely to be beneficial for both individuals and the broader society, and thus the common good. Moreover, this conceptualisation makes it possible to determine how more praxis-orientated practices can be cultivated and qualified as practically wise to challenge the more reductive conceptions and effects of managerialism and neoliberalism (Küpers 2019). In order to understand the relational dimensions of embodied new work practices, the following offers the concept of 'inter-practice'.

Inter-practices

Following Merleau-Ponty's phenomenology, practice can be interpreted as an *'inter-practice'* (Küpers 2013a, b). Based on a post-dual ontology of 'inter-being' (Merleau-Ponty 2003, p. 208), such radicalised relational orientation understands practice and practising in organisations as an emerging event. The concept of inter-practice helps to reveal and interpret the inter-relationship between being, feeling, knowing, doing, sharing, structuring and effectuating in and through wisdom-orientated or wise action, both individually and collectively, as implicated in organisation and in leader- and follower-ship. Correspondingly, the concept of phronetic inter-practices can be used for inquiries into the negotiating interplay of the inherently entwined materialities, subjectivities, intersubjectivities and objectivities as they occur and are processed in organisational lifeworlds. Embedded within the complexities of human and systemic pragmatics, embodied inter-practice covers both: the experiential and social interactions of actors; as well as institutionalised operations of organisation (incorporations) as agency.

The mediating inter-practices are not only a collection of purposeful activities of self-contained individual actors and material things. Rather, these relational practices are also prepersonal, personal and transindividual, social and systemic events of emergent be(com)ing and meaning-giving complexes. Such processual practice is a mode of engagement with the world of organising and it in-tensions and extensions in the ongoing reconfiguration. Metaphorically, this practising resembles more an iterative way-finding and dwelling, as justpositioned to a planned navigation and building.

Phenomenologically, not only is practising embodied, but being embodied is always already a way of mediating the inter-practising by living bodies and embodiments within a situated, shared, responsive and creative practice in organisations. Thus, organising practices can be seen as a mediating function and emergences of vivid bodies, embodied inter-subjects and a dynamic embodiment of realities in which practitioners are inter-relationally embedded. In this way, inter-practice considers more inclusively the corporeality of practice-based dimensions (Yakhlef 2010) and its situatedness. Further, embodied, a(i)esthetic performative and wisdom-orientated dimensions of emergent, responsive inter-practices in relation to organising and leading have been discussed (Küpers 2011, 2013a, b, 2017a) Also the role of embodied and artful design for creative and sustainable inter-practising in organisations has been explored (Küpers 2016). The outlined relationships and inter-practice can be further described and qualified in relation to the concept of resonance as developed by Hartmut Rosa, presented and critically discussed in the next section.

Resonance and New Work Practices

The following develops a materio-socio-cultural phenomenology of embodied resonance related to new forms of working practices. Based on observable phenomena of alienation and acceleration in today's society and economy as well as organisations in particular, the concept of resonance as developed by Rosa (2019) will be presented and critically discussed.

For many people, alienating working life lacks meaningful resonance as it appears as atmospherically bleak, bare, lacking colour or as intimidating, while experiencing themselves and their inner world as pale, numb, deaf or deadening. Their empty relationship to their work and themselves appears as not swaying or oscillating in a meaningful way. Alienation in private and working life manifests itself in 'silent, cold, rigid, and repelling or failing world-relations' (Rosa 2016, p. 35). Thus, these relationships are experienced as unsatisfying, resulting from resonance-hostile or non-responsive social and object-specific configurations. Furthermore, the dominant form of 'being-in-the-working-world' employee encounters in technologically advanced and progressively digitalised societies is associated with unprecedented levels of acceleration, as part of escalatory dynamics of modern life (Rosa, Dörre & Lessenich 2017) as we are immersed in a globally extended, digitalised world.

The ultimate *raison d'être* of late-modern life forms with their tendency to colonise working (and private) life with obligations and activities – for example, by elevating endless to-do lists or emails – is symptomatic of a widespread social pathology associated with 'task-fetishism' to be processed and the pressure over ever shorter and dense time regimes. The primacy of *instrumental rationality* present in accelerated ways manifests an obsession with *means* over a critical engagement with *ends* as part of a hegemonic doxa of managerialist productivism, and the compulsive pursuit of innumerable targets. The pace of life and in particular in working life has been increasing on an unprecedented scale at various levels: socially, culturally, economically, politically, professionally, demographically, geographically, technologically, etc. If *acceleration* seems to move us further away from the possibility of 'the good life' the resonance provides us with the chance of realising it.

An adequate response to the alienation and escalatory logics of capitalist modernity (Rosa et al. 2017) is not just slowing down, but rather rehabilitating and cultivating resonance appears as an appropriate response. People suffer from a discrepancy or missing and estranged correspondence between who they are and what they do, between an embodied being and being-in-the-world. Being exposed to 'relations of relationlessness', the lack meaning social configurations of work and life are experienced as silent, indifferent and/or hostile disempowerment while meaning-seeking beings longing for social constellations that mean something to them, a reality that is the source of genuine engagement with vital aspects of a valuable existence, thus being fruitful and/or responsive, i.e. being in resonance.

What follows uses Rosa's recent account and concept and dialectics of 'resonance' with a specific focus on its role for new work practices. Following Rosa, resonance can be defined as 'a form of world-relation, in which subject and world meet and transform each other' (Rosa 2016, p. 298). The emergence of resonance is possible only 'through af-fection and e-motion (*sic*), intrinsic interest and expectation of self-efficacy' (ibid). And this is entailing the construction of a *meaningful*, *dynamic*, and *transformative* rapport between actors and their environment.

Resonance constitutes an experiential relationship based on *response* rather than *echo*. Strictly speaking, the term 'resonance' describes an acoustic phenomenon; for the Latin word '*re-sonare*' means 'to echo', 'to resound', or 'to reverberate'. But unlike a merely mirroring echo, resonance is not simply the product of a sequence of mechanistic-linear reactions. Resonant relationships are not reducible to forms of causal or instrumental (linear) mechanical entanglement, with its predetermined – and, in principle, predictable – pattern. Rather, resonance-laden activities emerge not as a causal effect, but form an open and embodied multilayered oscillating process, emanating from agential entities, capable of expressing their *own voice and stakes* when relating to one another. Resonance presupposes that those who participate in its relationship express or speak *with their own voice*, implying that every party involved in this experience enjoys a certain degree of autonomy.

Furthermore, resonance hinges on *normative evaluations and value-based judgements* that are not merely transactional, but species-constitutive, permitting human beings to establish morally guided and mutually empowering relationships. Put differently, resonance is linked inextricably to motivational background horizons shaped by value, rather than instrumental, rationality. Finally, an essential characteristic of resonance is a moment of constitutive unavailability, indicating that its obtainability cannot be taken for granted. Its constitutive unavailability has two major implications: first, resonance cannot be brought about at will or in a purely instrumental fashion; and second, resonance is unpredictable in its results. Moreover, social relations that are sustained by resonance are an *ambivalent* affair:

(a) They are *robust* because they represent an immanent force of human life. But they are also *fragile* because they can be undermined by co-existential conditions that hinder their development.
(b) They are *structural* because they are embedded in grammars of social interaction. But they are also *agential* in that they depend on people's capacity to interact with the world by relating to, working upon, and attributing meaning to the objective, normative and subjective dimensions of their existence.
(c) They are *closed* because they have to be sufficiently consolidated to enable those immersed in them 'to speak with their own voice' (Rosa 2016, p. 298). But again, they also need to be *open* because they have to be sufficiently adaptable to permit those experiencing them to be affected and reached by them.

For Rosa (2016), resonance 'is not merely an emotional state, but a relational mode' (ibid) This *relationalist* understanding of the human condition stresses the socio-ontological significance of the *rapports* that we, as resonance-seeking entities, establish with different facets of existence. For Rosa (2016), resonance-seeking activities form a constitutive component of everyday existence, which is inconceivable without the need to find meaning in their quotidian interactions with the manifold dimensions of their lifeworlds. With this, resonance gains a socio-ontologically privileged status for co-creating and developing meaning. This includes the relation to meaning in and through work in particular that might be linked to recent research on mappings and on paradoxes of meaningful work (Bailey et al. 2019; Lips-Wiersma and Morris 2017; Yeoman, Bailey, Madden & Thompson 2019) and its fostering (Lysova, Allan, Dik, Duffy & Steger 2019) and links to ethics (Lips-Wiersma, Haar & Wright 2020).

Recent research on meaningful work confirmed links to organisational resonance, work resonance and spiritual resonance. Organisational resonance included relatedness, environmental support, self-identification with organisation, personal growth and organisational alignment. Work resonance included contribution, competence, autonomy, learning, creativity, values, self-identity with work and personal growth. Spiritual resonance included higher purpose, values and autonomy. Complementary, spiritual resonance, refers to the combination of higher purpose, values and autonomy (self-transcendence). In other words, the work we do resonates with us when it speaks to our values and autonomous spirit and serves something bigger than ourselves.

However, while Rosa is trying to avoid making unjustified essentialisations about the *true essence* of human nature, the same is implicitly presupposed as a resonance-seeking orientation that constitutes an anthropological invariant – thus a foundational ontological condition that is built into *all* human societies and *all* human beings.

Given its multilayered nature, the concept of resonance can serve as a potential impulse for exploring world-relations especially also in the field of new work practices and describing qualities of these relations. It can be used as a yardstick to make judgements about the normative value of social arrangements in relation to a fulfilling, empowering working life that are always already and remain embodied.

Importantly, and related to Merleau-Pontian phenomenology, also for Rosa, 'resonance comes into being only if and when, through the vibration of one body, the frequency of another body is stimulated' (Rosa 2016, p. 282) – and vice versa. Resonant relatively autonomous bodies not only affirm their relationality and interdependent reciprocity but also retain a substantial degree of independence. Accordingly, relations of resonance 'lead to mutual reinforcement, thereby magnifying the amplitudes of the vibrations' (ibid, p. 282) by means of which agential elements can enter into mutually fruitful modes of communication. Far from being tantamount to a merely factual process of physical reactions between interrelated bodies, the human search for resonance is inextricably linked to the pursuit of a *meaningful* life, situated in spatio-temporally contingent structures. These are not only produced and reproduced but also potentially transformed by resonance-seeking practices. In a fundamental sense, resonance is a mode of *being-in-the-world* that is a specific kind of 'inter-relationalization' (ibid, p. 285) of subjects and their environment. As a *relational* concept, resonance 'describes a relationship between two (or more) phenomena or bodies' (ibid, p. 285).

The 'coming-into-being' of resonance in social and working life presupposes not only *relationality* and *reciprocity* between two or more bodied phenomena. Rather, for Rosa this requires also a minimal degree of relative sovereign *autonomy* and agency. In Rosa's 'sociology of world-relations', experiences of resonance possess socio-ontological preponderance. Life seems pointless to humans unless its different facets 'speak to' – and, thus 'resonate with' – them in one way or another. The 'triad of converging movements of body, mind, and the experiential world' (Rosa 2016, p. 290) suggests that the confluence of our *corporeal, mental* and *immersive* practices and structures allows for the emergence of resonance.

Work as Part of *Diagonal* Axes of Resonance

Rosa distinguishes three main *axes of resonance,* to which he also refers as axes of world-relation and spheres of resonance: besides *horizontal* axes like family, friendship and politics as spheres of community there, and *vertical* axes of resonance like religion, nature, art and history as more transcendent spheres of engagement, Rosa describes *diagonal* axes of resonance. The last includes objects, work and consumption. The diagonal orientation conveys a connection between horizontal and vertical lines through the pursuit of purposive practices, especially when acting upon reality in a goal-orientated fashion. Here, also the *objective* world of things obtains a voice, reflecting the species-generative role of human actors' capacity to define their place in the universe by constructing and reconstructing both the material and the symbolic conditions of their existence. *In some ways, and for many people, work* constitutes one of the primary spheres of *resonance*, enabling humans – unless they are dominated by relations of alienation – to develop their purposive, cooperative and creative potential. In terms of a *politics of labour,* the quality of work should then not be measured exclusively in terms of efficiency and productivity, let alone in terms of the profits and profit-maximising imperatives derived from it.

The *contents* of the aforementioned axes of resonance vary not only between *individuals* but also between *cultures.* Axes of resonance are *contingent* insofar as they differ in terms of the ways in which they are experienced, valorised and problematised by individuals and cultures. However, to avoid an ethnocentric Western orientation comparative, cross-cultural, intersectorial and global analysis is required to account for the wide range of axes of resonance that emerge in different historical and cultural contexts. Relatedly, there will be a need for a distinction between *universalisable* (objective) and *non-universalisable* (subjective or normative) aspects of resonance. Seeing the latter in their socio-cultural contingency and personal variability is seeing them as serving as sources of differential pathways for human agencies.

Being aware of both their contingent constitution and their universal nature, a critical theory of life and new working practices needs then to examine the social conditions that facilitate or obstruct the formation of axes of resonance. For there are no emancipatory realms of existence without individually and collectively empowering axes of resonance. The silencing of all axes of resonance designates 'the extreme form of individual or cultural alienation at an existential level' (Rosa 2016, p. 297). Just as all variants of personal and social empowerment presuppose the activation of resonance, the repression of resonance by internal or external factors leads to human alienation. Thus, the sociology of world-relations is inconceivable without 'a critique of historically realised *conditions of resonance*' (ibid, p. 36). It has to explore the extent to which particular sets of social constellations foster or impede the emergence of resonance-laden practices that those involved in them experience as meaningful.

Importantly, for Rosa 'resonance' is not synonymous with 'consonance' or 'harmony' or state of 'sterile perfection', just as 'alienation' is not identical to 'dissonance' or 'disharmony'. Simulating or instrumental 'false' forms of ideologically appropriating resonance give a misleading impression that the good life may be achieved through the superficial assemblage of 'harmony on display' or through the accumulation of socially relevant resources. Yet, resonance can never be found in 'pure harmony' or depend simply on 'resourcefulness'; nor does it imply the mere 'absence of alienation'. Rather, it is *'the flaring up of hope for world adaptation and response in a difficult world'* (Rosa 2016, p. 321) it is the emergence of *'a connection to a source of strong evaluations in a predominantly mute, and often also repulsive, world'* (ibid, p. 317). Such moments may involve a deep sense of disharmony and resourcelessness, while entailing the latent presence of alienation.

Resonance – especially those forms of resonance that are derived from the purposive, cooperative and creative potential inherent in human work – can be (re-)appropriated by the economy, business or institutions when they are instrumentally used, into the cycle of material, financial or symbolic valorisation. Thus, resonance can be converted into an instrument of a reifying world. In such reification of resonance of capitalist societies, in which it is strategically employed in the labour market, for example by economising 'empathetic and enthusiastic capacities as productive resources' (ibid, p. 741). On the other hand, forms of creative resonance may emerge out of profound experiences of alienation, oppression and repulsion. Despite pervasive force of quasi-ubiquitous commodification processes in advanced capitalist formations, human beings continue to have a strong desire for experiencing genuinely enriching modes of resonance, whose authenticity transcends the limited horizon of systemic immanence.

Paradoxically, alienation can be both an obstacle to and a reason for resonance-laden practices, such as creative work. Just as 'resonance is possible only against the background of another that remains alien and silent' (Rosa 2016, p. 325), alienation occurs only against the background of another that provides a dynamic counterforce of resilience and empowerment.

Not only can relatively stable axes of resonance may lead to overly habitualised levels of repetition, expressed in experiences of dullness and boredom, turning towards alienation. Also, highly unstable axes of resonance – although, in the long term, they cannot produce sustainable social relations – may be a major source of inspiration, creativity, enlightenment and emancipation, notably in moments of personal or social crisis, obliging actors to call a particular order of things into question. A mainly implicit, unconscious, and antecedent 'dispositional trust in resonance' (ibid, p. 325) is a precondition for people's capacity to relate to, to interact with, to work upon and to transform their existence in accordance with their needs, reflections and desires. The species-constitutive search for depth-resonance is a *sine qua non* of all human encounters with the world, including those that may be characterised as 'mute', 'repulsive' or 'alienating' for a world adaptation. The latter implies the possibility of both the renewal and the transformation of subject and world and, hence, also: the possibility of a genuine encounter with the other and the stranger. This resonant adaptation of the world presupposes the contingency of reality, including the constant negotiation and renegotiation of positions.

Resonance is about openness, inclusion and empowerment, while allowing for the possibility of contradiction, dissent and opposition. To move from the mechanical sphere of *echo* to the contingent realm of *resonance* means to accept the power of unpredictability emanating from human agency. Overall, through Rosa's plea and defence for a resonance-theoretic sociology of world-relations manifestly speaks as a diagnostic voice of a Zeitgeist that reveals and renders important normative implications. Descriptively, modern organisation and society are out *of tune* as conditions for resonance are distorted, while normatively for Rosa *a different, more resonant thus* meaningful *way of being-in-the-world, alternative forms of better tuned world-relations are possible*. Observing an intensification of a longing for resonance, Rosa's optimistic credo has a fundamental hope for resonance that can lead and manifest itself in the search for a better form of 'being-resonant-in-the-world' as the emancipatory possibility of 'a good life' as transformative project also in relation to organisational lifeworlds. New work as inter-practices is not only about new work but about resonant modes of engagement, including with the future in everyday life (Mandich 2019).

The everyday inter-practising as embodied practice of resonance work is of course different in different settings, depending on specific and concrete conditions, structures, processes, people and purposes. For example, care work is one form of embodied labour in which all resonant relationships need to be arranged and coordinated in a way that supports healing or ameliorating suffering and recovery. Concrete practices, for example in lifeworlds of a hospital, need to be interconnected to form bundles of sequences, synchronisation, proximity in rhythmic resonant patterns, etc. These inter-practices are both constitutive and shaped by multiple relational and resonant registers in ways that matter for when and how practices are enacted and reproduced. For example, the working day in the hospital may consist of some recurring relational-resonant practices and institutional rhythms (Blue 2019). These often include consultant, medicine, and ward rounds, clinic appointments, and surgeries, etc. Each of them has its own time, relations and resonances while each is variously dependent on other practices and cycles, materio-spatio-temporal orders and psycho-social processes, thus being inter-relationally and resonantly co-emerging. Such resonant inter-practice of care is not only bound to nurse–patient or doctor–patient or therapist–client relationships in the medical and therapeutic domain or care work (*Careful vulner-ability – An empirical investigation of the role of being vulnerable for care-work(er)* – personal communication), but may be related to all kinds of other practices also beyond health and coaching/counselling realm.

Critical Reflection and Limitations of the Concept of Resonance

However, some critical reflections and questions emerge concerning the limits and problems of resonance theory and practice (Susen 2019). One critical issue concerns the epistemic authority of critical theorists who are telling ordinary people about alienation and the need to be resonant. Not only who, but also telling them how, is problematic, by defining which forms of resonance are more desirable than others to create a good life. Thus, the challenge will be how to reconcile resonance as both a descriptive and a normative concept. Relatedly, critical questions may be raised concerning how to assess or to measure the quality of world-relations in terms of the quality of axes of resonance that emerge within them. Should critical social scientists rely on *objective*, *normative* or *subjective* criteria, or indeed a combination of these, to make accurate judgements about their quality? In terms of future investigations, how to operationalise resonance for empirical research?

How to account for potential or actual discrepancies between levels of perception and approaches, when seeking to provide a genuinely *comprehensive* understanding of the qualitative differences between 'the good life' and 'the bad life'. Moreover, what if for those resonance is suggested, not only *ignore* the expressed, but also *enjoy* the seemingly disempowering elements commonly associated with alienation and non-resonant, e.g. escapist experiences or the right to resonance denial? What about *highly problematic* practices that may 'resonate' with those performing them, including proto-totalitarian or fascist regimes that use resonance-generating techniques and activities. By this they may provide realms of resonance that their supporters experience as inspiring and galvanising. Thus, one danger of resonance orientations is possible reactionary endeavours with which those immersed in them may identify in a resonant fashion.

Thus, we need to be aware that resonance does not involve always a generally positive form of encounter with the world. Concerning the possibility of 'negative' resonance: What is the status of resonant acts of *violence or repulsion,* manipulation, coercion, domination? What about Machiavellian or pathological misuses of resonance in leadership? These may manifest, instead of the mind, hopeful and compassionate resonant leadership (Boyatzis and McKee 2005), in a bad leadership, ruled in rigid, intemperate, callous, corrupt, insular or violent modes of resonance (Kellerman 2004). Therefore, also for developing new more resonant practices of work in organisation and leadership, the status of plural dimensions of power and politics in relation to Rosa's normative monism of resonance need to be further explored. Finally, occurring primarily in ephemeral processual, and transformative experiences and due to its fragile character and constitutive unavailability, resonance is systematically not a usable resource. It cannot be enforced, retained, or obtained for good and all. Thus, resonance is not a panacea and its theory 'should not be misinterpreted as a doctrine of salvation' (Rosa 2016, p. 750).

Critically, we need to ask about the status of realising resonant work to our contemporary context: What are the 'performance of possibilities' of resonant new work practices in the present neoliberalised economy, characterised often by non-resonant and non-responsive forces (Küpers 2019)? For enacting them, these need to be seen as part of a 'post-capitalist politics of the possible' (Gibson-Graham 2006) that would combine intervention with activism, and citizenship, while reflexively asking questions like:

- Will the resonance-integrating performance of embodied new work practices contribute to an enlightened and involved citizenship?
- Will they disrupt structures that limit freedoms and possibilities?
- Will these practices make embodied performing agents (and researchers/ethnographers exploring with them) rethink questions of identity, representation and fairness, and redesign and redo their daily practice accordingly?

Following these guiding questions and understanding performance as a site of 'inter-practice' or 'inter-practice-as-performance' (Küpers 2017b) it may become a medium of change and transformation of practices and effectuation in favour of those who are or become more just, sustainable and wise. Therefore, new work as inter-practices is not only about new work but about resonant modes of engagement, including with the future in everyday life (Mandich 2019).

Conclusion

This chapter has proposed the interpretation of new practices of work as embodied and inter-relational processes. Contextually informed on the basis of the phenomenology of embodied practice, then interwoven practices were arranged and qualified as a nexus of inter-practice and critically related to the concept of resonance. The discussed perspectives invite political consideration of embodied agency concerning transformation and institutional change. It is through embodied agencies of transformative politics (Coole 2005) that alternative ways of living and co-creative practices of new work in praxis can be re-negotiated and realised via cyclical movements and enactments (Coole 2007, p. 175). Therefore, it might be interesting to explore further the role of embodied agency in such transformative political processes as being situated between passivity and activity as well as between receptivity and innovative praxis in relation to institutions and their legitimation and renewal. Understanding an institution as a temporal and historical movement, for Merleau-Ponty (2010), experiences and meanings of practices are both instituted and instituting. They are instituted in the sense of being sedimented and habituated by the past and dependent upon being exposed to an already meaningful world. At the same time, there exists the possibility of instituting that involves an initiation of the new, the opening of a future as an opening of the new within the existing, familiar institutional arrangements.

It is out of the circulation and dialectical relation between historical sedimentation and the originating establishment that an embodied agency can emerge. This corporeal capacity to act can move on new pathways of creative thinking, acting and living that break with determinism (ibid, p. 11). The entwined active and passive relationships refer not only to material, socio-cultural, historical, gendered, and technological conditions and realities of inter-practices. Rather, the 'active–passive' nexus, mediates possibilities for a spontaneous responsiveness of expressive, co-practising bodies.

For Merleau-Ponty, this institutionalised and instituting active and passive processing is part of an interwoven, post-dichotomous web of 'self-other-things' (Merleau-Ponty 2012, p. 57) and an integral being of Flesh (Merleau-Ponty 1995, p. 84). This Flesh serves as a common and generous source (Diprose 2002) for which the body becomes the measure (*"measurant"*) of things (Merleau-Ponty 2003, p. 217). As a 'measure of being' (Merleau-Ponty 1973, p. 124), the perceiving and performing body is seen as mutually intertwined or entangled 'inter-practically' with the phenomena and co-constituting bodies and environments. Both are co-shaping each other in ongoing processes of differentiation, symbolisms and tools as measuring agencies' (Hoel and Carusi 2018).

In time of an ongoing neoliberalization, the reintegration of praxis, (inter-)practices and actions through embodied agencies gains a new significance, especially also in relation to practical wisdom (Küpers 2019). Neoliberal strategies and their constraining, local and globalised reigns and instrumentalising appropriations of embodied practices may not only abstract from the particular. Rather, they also foreclose possibilities of sensing, feeling, thinking, expressing or enacting differently with regard to how practices and relations to oneself, others and the world are or can become organised.

The reintegration of embodied inter-practices reminds us of the remaining situatedness and location in places. These also include virtual places related to new work as they actualise embodied possibilities that are not yet known. Being situated and emplaced in time is where things truly happen to people and organisations, with effective impact on, and affective, adverse consequences for, all those involved; including the fragile planet and its delicate life, calling for a sustainable and wisely committed '(g)localism' (Kemmis 2012) of practising. Facing an unsustainable Anthropocene (Küpers – personal communication), the reproduction of conventional practices of a business-as-usual would lead to an 'ecocidal' collapse undermining the base for flourishing practices. Given our current perilous situation, embodied, responsive, resonant and responsible inter-practices, further qualified as practically wise ones (Küpers 2013a) are, and will be, more timely.

This is even more apparent, as they contribute to much required, more integrally transformative and sustainable practices in organisational and social lifeworlds with their stakeholders as well as wider economic, political and societal relationships and realities. It is hoped that the conceptualisations proposed here provide opportunities to reassess, revive and further investigate the relevance of embodied forms of practising in and through new work organisations as well as their embodied stakeholders, and to move towards a flourishing and sustainable unfolding.

References

Aroles, J., Mitev, N. & de Vaujany, F.-X. 2019. Mapping themes in the study of new work practices. *New Technology, Work and Employment*, 34(3): 285–299.

Aroles, J., Granter, E. & de Vaujany, F.-X. 2020. Becoming mainstream: The professionalization and corporatization of digital nomadism. *New Technology, Work and Employment*, 35(1): 114–129.

Bailey, C., Lips-Wiersma, M., Madden, A., Yeoman, R., Thompson, M. & Chalofsky, N. 2019. The five paradoxes of meaningful work. *Journal of Management Studies*, 56(3): 481–499.

Ball, K. 2005. Organization, surveillance and the body: Towards a politics of resistance. *Organization* 12(1): 89–108.

Benhamou, S. 2017. *Imaginer le travail en 2030? Quatre types d'organisation du travail à l'horizon 2030*. Paris: France Strategie.

Blue, S. 2019. Institutional rhythms: Combining practice theory and rhythmanalysis to conceptualise processes of institutionalisation. *Time & Society*, 28(3): 922–950.

Boyatzis, R. E. & McKee, A. 2005. *Resonant Leadership*. Boston: Harvard Business School Press.

Carter, C., Clegg, S. & Kornberger, M. 2008. Strategy as practice? *Strategic Organization*, 6(1): 83–99.

Cascio, W. F. & Montealegre, R. 2016. How technology is changing work and organizations. *Annual Review of Organizational Psychology and Organizational Behavior*, 3: 349–375.

Chen, L. & Nath, R. 2005. Nomadic culture: Cultural support for working anytime, anywhere. *Information Systems Management*, 22 (4): 56–64.

Coole, D. 2005. Rethinking agency: A phenomenological approach to embodiment and agentic capacities. *Political Studies*, 53(1): 124–142.

2007. *Merleau-Ponty and Modern Politics after Anti-Humanism*. Lanham, MD: Rowman & Littlefield.

Dale, K. 2001. *Anatomising Embodiment and Organisation Theory*. London: Sage.

Davis, E. 2015. *TechGnosis: Myth, Magic, and Mysticism in the Age of Information*. Berkeley, CA: North Atlantic Press.

de Certeau, M. 1984. *The Practice of Everyday Life*. Berkeley: University of California Press.

Degen, M. 2008. *Sensing Cities*. London: Routledge.

Denzin N. 2016. The Call to Performance. In A. B. Reinertsen (ed.) *Becoming Earth: A Post Human Turn in Educational Discourse Collapsing Nature/Culture Divides*. Otterstad: Sense Publishers, 137–161.

Diprose, R. 2002. *Corporeal Generosity: On Giving with Nietzsche, Merleau-Ponty, and Levinas*. Albany, NY: State University of New York Press.

Ebert, N. 2016. *Individualisation at Work: The Self between Freedom and Social Pathologies*. London and New York: Routledge.

Garrett, L. E., Spreitzer, G. M. & Bacevice, P. A. 2017. Co-constructing a sense of community at work: The emergence of community in cow-orking spaces. *Organization Studies*, 38(6): 821–842.

Gibson-Graham, J. K. 2006. *A Post-Capitalist Politics*. Minneapolis: University of Minnesota Press.

Hansen, M. 2006. *Bodies in Code: Interfaces with New Media*. London: Routledge

2014. *Feed Forward: On the Future of 21st Century Media*. Chicago: University of Chicago Press.

Hancock, P. 2009. Management and Colonization in Everyday Life. In P. Hancock and M. Tyler (eds.) *The Management of Everyday Life*. London: Palgrave, 1–20.

Heidegger, M. 1993. The Question Concerning Technology. In M. Heidegger (ed.) *Basic Writings*. New York: Harper, 307–342.

Hoel A. S. & Carusi A. 2018. Merleau-Ponty and the Measuring Body. *Theory, Culture and Society*, 35(1): 45–70.

Husserl, E. 1970. *The Crisis of European Sciences and Transcendental Phenomenology*. Evanston, IL: Northwestern University Press.

Kaushik, R. 2019. *Merleau-Ponty between Philosophy and Symbolism: The Matrixed Ontology*. New York: State University of New York Press.

Kellerman, B. 2004. *Bad Leadership: What It Is, How It Happens, Why It Matters*. Boston: Harvard Business School Press.

Kemmis, S. 2012. Phronēsis, Experience, and the Primacy of Praxis. In E. A. Kinsella & A. Pitman (eds.) *Phronēsis as Professional Knowledge*. Rotterdam: Sense, 147–162.

Kemmis S., Edwards-Groves C., Wilkinson J. & Hardy I. 2012. Ecologies of Practices. In P. Hager, A. Lee & A. Reich (eds.) *Practice, Learning and Change. Professional and Practice-based Learning*. Dordrecht: Springer.

Kemmis, S. & Smith, T. 2008. Prâxis and Prâxis Development. In S. Kemmis and T. Smith (eds.) *Enabling Prâxis: Challenges for Education*. Rotterdam: Sense, 3–13.

Kemmis, S., Wilkinson, J., Hardy, I. & Edwards-Groves, C. 2009. Leading and learning: Developing ecologies of educational practice. Paper presented at *AARE (Australian Association for Research in Education) International Conference*. Canberra.

Kemmis, S., Wilkinson, J., Edwards-Groves, C., Hardy, I., Grootenboer, P. & Bristol, L. 2014. *Changing Education: Changing Practices*. Dordrecht: Springer.

Kingma, S. 2019. New ways of working (NWW): Work space and cultural change in virtualizing organizations. *Culture and Organization*, 25(5): 383–406.

Kozel, S. 2007. *Closer Performance, Technologies, Phenomenology*. Cambridge, MA: The MIT Press.

Küpers, W. 2011. Embodied pheno-pragma-practice – Phenomenological and pragmatic perspectives on creative 'inter-practice' in organisations between habits and improvisation. *Phenomenology & Practice*, 5(1): 100–139.

2013a. The Art of Practical Wisdom ~ Phenomenology of an Embodied, Wise Inter-Practice in Organisation and Leadership. In W. Küpers & D. Pauleen (eds.) *A Handbook of Practical Wisdom. Leadership, Organization and Integral Business Practice*. London: Routledge, 19–45.

2013b. Embodied Inter-Practices of Leadership. *Leadership*, 9(3): 335–357.

2015a. *Phenomenology of the Embodied Organization – The Contribution of Merleau-Ponty for Organisation Studies and Practice*. London: Palgrave.

2015b. Emplaced and embodied mobility in organizations. *Ephemera-Theory & Politics in Organizations*, 15(4): 797–823.

2016. Phenomenology of embodied and artful design for creative and sustainable inter-practicing in organisations. *Journal of Cleaner Production*, 135(1): 1436–1445.

2017a. Inter-Play(ing) – Embodied possibilities of serious play at work. *Journal of Organisation and Change Management*, 30(7): 993–1014.

2017b. Embodied performance and performativity in organizations and management. *M@n@gement*, 20(1): 89–106.

2019. Reintegrating prâxis, practices, phrónêsis & sustainable action for processing systemic constraints in the business and society relationship. *Society and Business Review*, 14(4): 338–359.

Leder, D. 1990. *The Absent Body*. Chicago: University of Chicago Press.

Lips-Wiersma, M., Haar, J. & Wright, S. 2020. The effect of fairness, responsible leadership and worthy work on multiple dimensions of meaningful work. *Journal of Business Ethics*, 161(1): 35–52.

Lips-Wiersma, M. & Morris, L. 2017. *The Map of Meaningful Work: A Practical Guide to Sustaining our Humanity*. Milton Park, Abingdon, Oxon, UK: Routledge.

Lupton, D. 1995. The Embodied Computer/User. In M. Featherstone & R. Burrows (eds.) *Cyberspace, Cyberbodies, Cyberpunk: Cultures of Technological Embodiment*. London: SAGE, 97–112.

Lysova, E. I., Allan, B. A., Dik, B. J., Duffy, R. D. & Steger, M. F. 2019. Fostering meaningful work in organizations: A multi-level review and integration. *Journal of Vocational Behavior*, 110(B): 374–389.

Mandich, G. 2019. Modes of engagement with the future in everyday life. *Time and Society*. DOI: 10.1177/0961463X19883749.

Merleau-Ponty, M. 1973. The Algorithm and the Mystery of Language. In C. Lefort (ed.) *The Prose of the World*. Evanston, IL: Northwestern University Press.

1995. *The Visible and the Invisible*. Evanston, IL: Northwestern University Press.

2003. *Nature*. Evanston, IL: Northwestern University Press.

2010. *Institution and Passivity*. Evanston, IL: Northwestern University Press.

2012. *Phenomenology of Perception*. London and New York: Routledge.

Merry, P. 2019. *Why Work? Economics and Work for People and Planet*. Minneapolis, MN: Amaranth Press.

Müller, A. 2016. The digital nomad: Buzzword or research category? *Transnational Social Review*, 6(3): 344–348.

Nicolini, D., Gherardi, S. & Yanow, D. 2003. *Knowing in Organizations: A Practice-Based Approach*. New York: M. E. Sharpe.

Petriglieri, G., Ashford, S. J. & Wrzesniewski, A. 2019. Agony and ecstasy in the gig economy: Cultivating holding environments for precarious and personalized work identities. *Administrative Science Quarterly*, 64(1): 124–170.

Rosa, H. 2016. *Resonance. A Sociology of our Relationship to the World.* Translated by James C. Wagner. Cambridge: Polity Press.

2019. *Resonance. A Sociology of Our Relationship to the World.* Cambridge: Polity Press.

Rosa, H., Dörre, K. & Lessenich, S. 2017. Appropriation, activation and acceleration: The escalatory logics of capitalist modernity and the crises of dynamic stabilization. *Theory, Culture and Society*, 34(1): 53–73.

Sandberg, J. & Dall'Alba, G. 2010. Learning through and about Practice: A Lifeworld Perspective. In S. Billett (ed.) *Learning through Practice.* Dordrecht: Springer, 104–119.

2009. Returning to practice anew: A life-world perspective. *Organization Studies*, 30(12): 1349–1368.

Scott, J. 1985. *Weapons of the Weak: Everyday Forms of Peasant Resistance.* New Haven, CT: Yale University Press.

Susen, S. 2019. The resonance of resonance: Critical theory as a sociology of world-relations? *International Journal of Politics, Culture, and Society*, 1–36.

Symon, G. & Whiting, R. 2019. The sociomaterial negotiation of social entrepreneurs' meaningful work. *Journal of Management Studies*, 56 (3): 655–684.

Waldenfels, B. 2008. The role of the lived-body in feeling. *Continental Philosophy Review*, 41(2): 127–142.

Wendland, C., Merwin, C. & Hadjioannou, C. 2018. *Heidegger on Technology.* London: Routledge.

Yakhlef, A. 2010. The corporeality of practice-based learning. *Organization Studies*, 31(4): 409–430.

Yeoman, R., Bailey, C., Madden, A. & Thompson, M. 2019. *The Oxford Handbook of Meaningful Work.* Oxford: Oxford University Press.

2 | Wherever I Lay My Laptop, That's My Workplace

Experiencing the New World of Work in a Hotel Lobby

FIZA BRAKEL-AHMED

Introduction

Whether it is the lack of job opportunities or the strong desire for freedom, it cannot be denied that the number of self-employed workers is growing tremendously (Stravens 2017). In the Netherlands, each year around 50,000 people register as a 'self-employed entrepreneur, without staff' and in 2017 there were more than one million self-employed individuals in the Netherlands, most located in the Amsterdam area (Central Bureau of Statistics 2018). The need for flexible co-working spaces and hot desks has led to a booming business in Amsterdam. Co-working spaces, such as WeWork, Spaces, TQ and Seats-to-Meet are increasing rapidly. Self-employed workers rent a hot desk or office for a daily/weekly/ monthly fee, which incurs costs whether they use the work space or not. Parallel to these developments, there is a large group of self-employed workers who create their own work space in (semi-)public places that are not, at least not initially or primarily, designed as co-working spaces (Boothby 2017).

The rapid development of digital technology and the spread of Wi-Fi make it no longer necessary to physically be present in a fixed office space (Colbert, Yee & George 2016; Torten, Raiche & Caraballo 2016). Therefore, workers, both employees and self-employed, are no longer bound to office buildings. Digital devices such as laptops, tablets and smartphones make it possible to 'set up camp' anytime and anywhere, as long as there is electric power and Wi-Fi. Software and apps, such as Skype, Slack, Zoom and Facetime, make it possible to hold meetings with one or more people all over the world while showing presentations. Possibilities to meet virtually are paramount.

With so many choices, an increasing number of workers have the freedom to choose where, when and how they want to work.

As a response to the needs and demands of self-employed workers, and the possibilities to work in any space with electricity and Wi-Fi, the number of co-working spaces has increased exponentially in the last decade (Blagoev, Costas & Kärreman 2019). People who want to work in a co-working space typically pay a daily, weekly or monthly fee in exchange for a hot desk (FlexDesk) or a fixed spot in the building. As co-working spaces are on the rise, and afford an important shift in ways of working, scholars have been researching this phenomenon (Blagoev et al. 2019). There is, however, not a lot of academic literature on unintended co-working spaces, i.e. spaces that are used for coworking, amongst other practices. These spaces were not originally designed as co-working spaces, yet the practices of the self-employed workers, together with the affordance of Wi-Fi, have transformed the spaces – at least partially – into co-working spaces. These spaces could be seen as *unintended* co-working spaces. Although there may be some similarities with Oldenburg's (1999) concept of 'Third Places', 'unintended co-working spaces' are a relatively new phenomenon. The similarities and differences between unintended co-working spaces and Third Places will be discussed later in this chapter.

In this chapter, the focus lies on unintended co-working spaces. In many cases, the designers or managers of the space respond by embracing this shift to (partially) a co-working space, and turn it into a successful business model. This study of unintended co-working spaces is based on ethnographic fieldwork in hotel lobbies in Amsterdam (the Netherlands), which spanned a period of three months. This chapter aims to give the reader a sense of 'being there' (Geertz 1988) and 'experiencing the new world of work' in hotel lobbies. In this study, I focus on 'self-employed workers without staff' who do not rent a coworking space or an occasional hot desk. The emphasis of the research lies in the processes and practices underlying the creation of offices space in (semi)public places (such as coffee shops and hotel lobbies) through the agency of the workers, and how eventually designers and managers of these places respond to these 'unintended co-working spaces'.

In the next section, the concept of co-working spaces and new ways of working will be reviewed. Subsequently, the research methods used in this study will be discussed. This will be followed by presenting the findings of the study. Finally, in the concluding section, findings will be analysed and implications for future research will be laid out.

Theoretical Framework

In this section, I will focus on the phenomenon of co-working spaces and how they facilitate workers to perform work practices 'on-the-go' without being constrained by space and time. In the last decade, co-working spaces have become a field of research for scholars from different fields. The fact that workers are no longer bound to an office, and can create a mobile office anywhere, has implications for the economy (Waters-Lynch, Potts, Butcher, Dodson & Hurley 2016; Waters-Lynch & Potts 2017), architecture, the way organisations are organised (Bizarri 2010; Halford 2005; Kingma 2019), and how people make sense of these New Ways of Working (Gold and Mustafa 2013; Halford 2005). Workers have more autonomy and flexibility in how they divide their working hours (Gajendran & Harrison 2007).

In this study, the focus does not lie on employees being able to work from home, or elsewhere, nor does it look at (self-)employed workers who make use of a paid hot desk in a co-working space, such as WeWork. The groups of self-employed workers studied here are those workers who choose to work from 'unintended' co-working spaces. These are spaces that were not intended as co-working spaces, yet have (partly) become such through the (work-)practices of the actors. These unintended co-working spaces include coffeeshops, museums and hotel lobbies. The coffeeshop chain Starbucks was one of the first to respond to the work practices of its patrons by providing adequate furniture, fast Wi-Fi and framing itself as 'a Third Place between work and home'. Starbucks state its mission is to be a *'third place, where every-one is welcome and we can gather, as a community, to share great coffee and deepen human connection'* (www.starbucks.com).

The concept of 'Third Places' was coined by Roy Oldenburg (1999), as places that are neither work nor home, where people meet, socialise and feel at home, the way churches used to be, and possibly still are, in small cities and villages. This phrase was coined before people had access to the Internet wherever they go, with their laptops, tablets or smartphones. Even though Starbucks wants to frame its image as a Third Place where people have conversations and 'deepen human connection', the whole concept of Third Places seems to be somewhat outdated in today's digital society.

Studies have shown that workers go to co-working places mainly in order not to be disturbed by the distractions at home; yet they do not want to engage in long conversations with each other as they work side-by-side in the space (Gandini 2015; Spinuzzi 2012; de Vaujany & Aroles 2019). The non-engagement in conversations, together with the lack of an intention to actively engage in and form a community, does not correspond to Oldenburg's concept of a Third Place, nor does it reflect the utopian view of 'deepening human connection' that Starbucks puts forward. With an increasing number of self-employed individuals and the blending of work and private selves (Goffman 1973), the 'Third Place' seems to have become a *mix* between work and home, rather than a place that is neither work nor home. In other words, rather than being a 'Third Place', (un)intended co-working spaces seem to be a blend of 'First and Second' Places.

As mentioned previously, this study focuses on unintended co-working spaces, like coffeeshops and hotel lobbies. Unintended co-working places are often furnished like a living room that also offers features needed for work, such as Wi-Fi, electric sockets and some (high) tables. It is worth mentioning that recent official co-working spaces, where workers need to pay a fee and/or become a member, are also adopting the living-room atmosphere in their premises (www.mindspace.me; www.workzoku.com) with comfortable sofas and chairs with fluffy pillows. Alternative places are being 'transformed' into unintended co-working spaces, such as libraries, museums and hotel lobbies (Bilandzik & Foth 2013; Stravens 2017).

Self-employed workers who 'roam the city' and set up camp in unintended co-working spaces want to feel at home, yet still be inspired and facilitated to work. Atmosphere and a 'living-room feeling' are important features (Balakrishnan, Muthaly & Leenders 2016; Merkel 2015). There are always comfortable sofas with coffee tables. Lighting is mellow, and pictures and low-key art are hanging on the walls. Soothing colours, organic materials such as wooden floors and wool carpets, enhance the feeling of comfort and being in a living room. Another important feature is the use of magazines, newspapers and photos and art on the wall. These give the place a 'lived-in feel' rather than the feeling of 'being in a showroom'. Yet there are long tables that serve as working desks, many electric sockets, Wi-Fi, and coffee being served, which are important components of a work place.

In this study, the phenomenon of co-working in hotel lobbies has been researched. Different components (good service, Wi-Fi, cosy atmosphere, ...) make hotel lobbies attractive to use as unintended co-working spaces. The Shoreditch, in which I did the largest part of my fieldwork, even started to frame itself as an ideal place in which to 'co-work'.

Methodology

In 2017, I spent three months doing fieldwork in hotel lobbies. I moved between four different hotel lobbies located in Amsterdam. For ethical reasons, and privacy issues, I will use fictional names to refer to these locations. One of the most important features for working in the lobby of a hotel is the atmosphere and furnishing. The four different hotels I alternated in my fieldwork all had possibilities to sit in, charge digital devices and offered free Wi-Fi. Yet the atmosphere was quite different in each hotel. One hotel, the Vivaldi targeted both business people and tourists. It offered conference rooms, with the possibility to hold a conference for a few hundred people. The Hamilton, from the same chain as the Vivaldi, also targeted business travellers and tourists, without conference possibilities. Each hotel had a lobby that was minimalistic and design-orientated. Furnishings were more about a modern, minimalistic appearance, rather than comfort and cosiness. Hotel Greenwoods targeted mainly business guests and had a lobby with a simple, yet cosy, living-room design with soft lighting, and neutral pictures on the walls – similar to the way large furniture stores exhibit their furniture, recreating a living room, to let the visitors feel what it could be like, without it looking 'lived in'. The Shoreditch had a lived-in atmosphere – second-hand furniture, battered sofas, wooden floor.

As time went by, one of the locations, the lobby of the Shoreditch, proved to have all important features for creating an unintended co-working space, and even a sense of community, and a feeling of belonging. This lobby proved to be the ideal field for 'experiencing the new world of work' as all important features and components were in alignment. Therefore, I decided to spend the latter part of my field work in the Shoreditch lobby. Table 2.1 gives an overview of the fieldwork locations.

Table 2.1 *Overview of fieldwork locations*

	GREENWOODS	SHOREDITCH	VIVALDI	HAMILTON
Location	Amsterdam-South	Amsterdam- Centre	Amsterdam- Centre	Amsterdam- Centre
Star rating	****	****	*****	*****
Target guests	Business / leisure	Leisure / local urban workers	Business / Conference / Leisure	Business / Leisure
Decor	Simple living room	Lived-in urban living room	Minimalistic design living room	Minimalistic design living room with grand piano
Coffee	Yes, get at bar and drink in lobby	Yes, served in lobby	Yes, get at bar and drink in lobby	Yes, get at bar and drink in lobby
Free Wi-Fi	yes	yes	yes	yes

During the course of my fieldwork, I focused on the practices and routines of those using hotel lobbies, by watching closely how they interacted with the space (Nippert-Eng 2015). I found myself 'zooming in and out' of the field (Nicolini 2009). Sometimes I would be observing in a rather detached, fly-on-the wall manner, which could be classified as non-participant observation. On other occasions, I would be more actively engaged in the activities observed, as I would practice co-working myself, herewith bodily, mentally and emotionally becoming a co-worker myself. In a way, I became a research object myself, which gave my research an autoethnographic dimension. After a few weeks in the field, I developed a good understanding of the practices of the people working in the lobby, the sociomateriality of the space as well as the affect of the space and its furnishing. Importantly, by watching the practices of the lobby dwellers closely, I could get a good sense of what kinds of lobbies were more likely to give rise to co-working practices, and to what extent hotel management and designers would embrace the co-working practices. This phase of the research led to the emergence of many different themes, such as the importance of feeling at home, digital technology, good coffee and the tacit culture of non-interaction with each other.

In order to explore further the themes that emerged from the observations conducted in hotel lobbies, I decided to engage in some casual spontaneous conversations and conduct a small series of semi-structured interviews. Engaging in completely spontaneous conversations, without an official interview appointment proved to be difficult and a breach of the tacit culture of non-interaction. Therefore, I made an appointment with interviewees who fit the profile of being 'workers on-the-go'. In the interviews, I asked the interviewee to take some pictures of whatever they saw fit in the lobby. On the basis of this loosely adapted photo-voice technique, I let some of the topics in the interviews emerge from the interviewees. I conducted five interviews. The interviews each lasted about 1.5 hours. They were held within my field work period (February through April 2017) at various locations. Two were held at Hotel Greenwoods, two were held at Hotel Shoreditch and one was held in a coffee shop at my university.

All interviewees were frequent lobby workers, without the means to rent a hot desk in an official co-working space. The main reason was not necessarily to gather new data, but rather to check whether my observations gathered from taking field notes, and my personal experience, corresponded with experiences of other lobby workers. As it was crucial for me not to unintentionally prompt the interviewee or project my findings on him/her, I (loosely) followed the photo-voice method as proposed by Vince and Warren (2012). As I met the interviewee, I would tell them I was getting them a cup of coffee, and if, in the meantime, they could take between six and ten pictures of the lobby (with their phone) of anything they found worth noticing. As I did not want to influence them, I gave no further instructions, and went to get coffee so as to physically distance myself from them as they took pictures. During the interview, I would let them talk about the pictures, and ask them why they took that particular picture. This made the interviews based around their themes, rather than topics imposed by me. Later in the interview, I would show them some of my own pictures (visual field notes) and ask them to comment on whatever they found remarkable. By using this applied photo-voice method, space was created for the interviewees to let topics emerge, rather than a premeditated topic list constructed by the researcher. The interviews proved helpful in getting more depth in my observational data on atmosphere, space, co-working practices and attitudes, rather than solely relying on my own observations and interpretations.

As I was researching my topic, I stumbled upon books that were set in hotels. In the first instance, I read these books mainly to relax, yet still be connected to my research. Some were fictional, others were texts on the hotel experiences of the author. They all added to the richness of my data, and in the end, gave me a clearer multifaceted picture of the phenomenon studied. Although it was not me who conducted interviews with these authors, their stories provided me with their practices, experiences and reflections concerning their time spent in hotel lobbies.

Overall, my ethnographic data contained fieldnotes from (non-) participant observation of practices, artefacts and symbols, visual fieldnotes (pictures taken to capture the atmosphere), photo-voice, semi-structured interviews, newspaper and magazine articles, hotel-review websites such as TripAdvisor, in which people offer their opinions on the hotel, and hotel websites that give an idea of how the hotel wants to frame and position itself. This allowed me to gain a more holistic understanding of the phenomenon studied.

Hotel Shoreditch as an Unintended Co-working Space

As described before, out of my four fieldwork locations, the Shoreditch proved to have the most successful 'co-working lobby', as both the agency of self-employed workers and the agency of the furnishing, combined with the hotel managers and designers providing the ideal features and service, (co-)created an untended co-working space *par excellence*. The Shoreditch therefore became my main field work location, as it was a perfect example of the phenomenon I intended to research.

The Atmosphere of the Place

The Shoreditch is located in a former mayor's mansion along one of Amsterdam's main canals, right in the centre of the city. On their website, the hotel frames itself as '*once the Mayor's home, now your home*'. It is part of a chain of hotels. After entering the sliding doors, the lobby stretches out as a large open space with large windows. The front desk is not visible at first glance, but on closer look there is a long cabinet, stuffed with knick-knacks, on the right of the sliding doors, in between the entrance and the open café/restaurant part. Here is where hotel guests check in and out. Here my first impressions are described in the form of a vignette.

As I enter the sliding doors that separate the street from the hotel lobby, I enter a space with large windows. Throughout the lobby, sofas are arranged with low coffee tables. The floor is wooden, and every sofa-corner has its own square carpet. In the middle of the left half of the space is a large table with chairs around it. Four people, one male and three females in their late twenties or early thirties, are fully concentrated behind their silver-coloured laptops. The four lit-up Apple logos show me that they all have MacBook laptops. They are not the only ones. I glance around to see at least nine other people with laptops on their laps, sitting on the sofas and lounge chairs.

Waiters in blue shirts and jeans and waitresses in blue dresses are scurrying around, taking orders and clearing tables of people who have left and/or finished their drinks. I sit down at the short end of the long table in the middle and start unpacking my laptop, which happens to be a MacBook too. Just as I am pondering about how smoothly I fit in with my Apple laptop, a waitress has already approached me and asks me in English what I want to drink. Somewhat startled, as I am not used to getting served this quickly in Amsterdam, I order a cup of coffee in Dutch, assuming that she has mistaken me for a foreign tourist, as I am, after all, in a hotel lobby. She then tells me she does not speak Dutch, so I order a cup of coffee again, this time in English.

I open up my laptop, look for the Wi-Fi, and feel relieved that it is free and does not even require a password. The connection is fast, and as I open my Mail-programme, forty-three new e-mails come flooding into my inbox. I ignore all advertisement e-mails and newsletters, and read the e-mails that are work- and study-related. In the meantime, my coffee has arrived by yet another non-Dutch speaking waiter. From his accent, I presume he is British. Sometimes, I can feel annoyed if staff in restaurants and shops do not speak Dutch – we are in the Netherlands after all – but in this international urban setting, I feel like a global citizen and find it quite 'cool' to be speaking English with the international staff.

As I nibble on the biscuit I got with my coffee – the latter still being too hot to drink – I notice a fireplace in the middle of the space where the sitting area and restaurant borders meet. The far-right corner of the space has a few Apple desktops on tables with chairs for people to use. In front of the computer area are a few more sofas. Next to the area, bordering the part that is the restaurant, is the front desk. The high desk top of the front desk blends in discretely with the rest of the interior. Perhaps to create more of a living-room feeling in the lobby.

Community, Shared Space and Work

Throughout the months of fieldwork, I notice how people work on the high tables with their laptops, or comfortably snuggled up on one of the battered sofas. I observed people having business meetings with peers and clients in the lobby. There are also some hotel guests in the lobby, and people who just drop in to have a drink with colleagues, friends or on their own. Even though they are (probably) not working, they always seem to be completely focused on their smartphone or tablet.

From my observations, interviews and own personal experience, I discovered that the idea of being 'home away from home' in a lobby that resembles a living room seems to be of utmost importance to the self-employed workers. Being 'home away from home' gives a sense of 'going to work' in a loosely coupled community where, even though nobody is watching, it feels like 'working alone together' (Spinuzzi

2012). Going to work in the lobby creates a sense of purpose, discipline and community. Not having a boss means the self-employed workers have to perform work practices fuelled by self-discipline. No boss is waiting for them in an office, there are no office hours to respect and there is not even an official office for them to go to. Self-employed workers have to find their own work suppliers, do their own advertising, send their own bills, and, most importantly, deliver satisfactory work within the agreed deadlines.

Working in a space where others are engaging in similar practices seems to motivate the self-employed urban digital nomads to work, instead of being distracted by objects and chores in the house. Being present in the lobby also has a disciplinary effect on the lobby dwellers. Even though they know the others are not *really* watching what they do, various lobby workers I interviewed feel motivated to work as all the other people in the space are working. Being surrounded by other people working creates some sense of discipline and community. Even though the others are strangers and by no means colleagues working for the same company, they are of utmost importance. If the lobby is empty, lobby workers will prefer going elsewhere, even though they are not inclined to interact with fellow lobby dwellers. Having a sense of purpose, getting work done 'together', creates a communal goal.

Urban digital nomads prefer not to be working in a very quiet space, like a (university) library, as they feel these spaces are '*uninspiring*' and '*too quiet*'. A lived-in living room feeling where the atmosphere is *cosy* with battered furniture, seems to be the ideal work space, eliciting a sense of community, creativity and productivity. The lobby of the Shoreditch caters to the wishes of its co-working visitors by offering furnishing that is both practical and gives the feeling of being in a living room. The 'living room' has different zones for different moments and practices. Sofas to relax or meet network contacts, work suppliers or friends, high tables to work with full concentration, a restaurant area to have lunch and a bar to have drinks after work. Some lobby dwellers get so comfortable in the lobby that they start taking off their shoes, putting their feet on the coffee tables or sofa. I have often witnessed people having a nap, while sitting in a slouchy posture in the sofa. This kind of behaviour could be seen as 'backstage behaviour' (Goffman 1963). The set-up of the 'living room', however, blurs the lines between a public space, a living room and an office. The space, battered furniture, lighting have the agency to make people feel they are at home and move their bodies accordingly. It could be said that the slouchy sofa's affordance is slouchy behaviour.

Hotel Lobby – A Different Type of Workspace

As mentioned before, not only is the idea of 'Working Alone Together' important to the lobby workers but also the idea of belonging to a community. Self-employed workers have no organisation they work for as an employee. Creating a routine in the lobby makes them feel like they belong to some kind of 'organisation', where the 'organisational culture' is very laid back, without fixed hours and obligations. The other 'co-workers' come and go, and are almost like supporting actors who are around yet do not interact.

The work routine in unintended co-working spaces is more flexible than in co-working spaces where people pay membership to use the space. This creates more of an incentive to use the space, since money has been invested in the membership. These 'intended' co-working spaces are even furnished in a more 'official' way although, as mentioned before, the latest official co-working spaces are recreating a living-room feeling in (parts of) the premises. Sometimes there are lounges attempting to recreate a living-room feeling, perhaps to give the intended working space an 'unintended' feel. In hotel lobbies, such as the Shoreditch lobby, it is the other way round. It has first of all an 'intended' living-room atmosphere, which has been partly morphed into an unintended co-working space by the practices of the people using it as such. As a response to this, the Shoreditch provides comfortable furniture, both sofas and high tables for working, ample electric sockets, reliable, free and fast Wi-Fi. Together with waiters proactively taking orders for drinks, attracting lobby co-workers is a business model for the hotel to generate money from an otherwise 'useless' liminal space where people check in and out of rooms.

Hotel lobbies have to find a way to attract 'regular' co-workers, as nothing officially binds them to the lobby. They could easily choose another unintended co-working space if they are inclined to do so. The Shoreditch has waiting staff who are always friendly and seem to be quite good at recognising regular customers. Although I am not aware whether this is something that the hotel management has asked them to do as part of their training, it does create a feeling of being involved in a community and feeling at home. It gives them an edge on those other hotel lobbies that are not actively taking orders with a smile. This was a clear difference compared to the lobbies of the other hotels that had a lobby bar: there, I had to get up and get the order myself, which I was less inclined to do, especially as I did not want to leave my laptop unattended.

In order to work, all the technological amenities that a professional office building provides should be present. All the interviewees stressed the importance of fast Wi-Fi and electric sockets. Without this, working in the lobby would be impossible, no matter how cosy the living-room atmosphere. Hotels realise this is a crucial feature and will advertise their fast Wi-Fi and possibilities to keep digital devices charged. Hotel Shoreditch explicitly targets people who dwell in the lobby to work, specifically advertising with their extensive possibilities to charge devices. They are not an exception – most hotels with similar living-room lobbies specifically mention their fast Wi-Fi, electric sockets and freshly brewed coffee. Not only the feeling of being in a living room with like-minded co-workers, but also fast Wi-Fi and charging stations are important. By far, most of the work done requires a fast Wi-Fi connection, and the devices used, such as laptops, tablets and mobile phones need to be kept charged. Coffee seems to have multiple meanings for the workers. Interview data, observations, and data from blogs and books show that coffee is associated with work, cosiness and comfort.

Another incentive is the special treatment of regular customers, which is obviously a management decision. In the lobby of the Shoreditch, regular patrons get a special 'coin', which gives them discounts on lunch. This creates a feeling of belonging to a community for the regular Shoreditch co-workers and at the same time leads to more revenue for the hotel. In the months that I have been doing my fieldwork, often fully participating in the practices of working in the lobby, I noticed the Shoreditch is not a place where you can spend all day working on one or two cups of coffee. The waiters scan the lobby frequently and come up to the patrons often enough to get another order. The prices for beverages like coffee are relatively high, but the lobby workers do not seem to mind. Spending all day buying beverages regularly is not a deal breaker. Interviewees see paying for a couple of cups of coffee as paying for a free working spot, and therefore 'part of the deal'. On TripAdvisor, some guests comment on how the lobby is a great place to hang out in cosy sofas, feeling at home and not even minding paying for an overpriced drink in the lobby bar.

Having the possibility to purchase beverages, preferably being served by waiters, is a very important feature of a good unintended co-working space. From my own experience working in the lobby, from interviews, and data from books and magazines, coffee is a crucial factor. Wi-Fi and coffee in lobbies are an important reason to spend time there, even if not working. Some interviewees associated coffee with cosiness and the 'living-room-feeling'. Others just wanted to be sure that they could drink something while in the lobby. When spending hours working in the lobby, being comfortable with a laptop and having the possibility to replenish themselves with snacks and drinks is considered important. All interviewees see friendly service as an added bonus, as it makes them feel noticed and taken care of. Although they are in the lobby alone, it gives comfort being around people engaged in the same activities, and getting served coffee by friendly staff adds to the feeling of feeling at home. The lobby seems to be a living room where work and private lives blend and everything is possible.

My own experience of hanging out in the lobby was not much different from the experience gathered from my data from interviews, books and articles. During my fieldwork, I realised that lobbies were becoming a comfortable place for me to hang out, relax, and get work done. It was not so much that I was trying to identify myself with the lobby workers, or to 'go native', but more of a revelation as I engaged in the same practices while being a participating observer. In the following vignette, I describe my thoughts, feelings and practices as a co-worker in the lobby, espousing both my work and private selves (Goffman 1978).

Hotel lobbies have become my new hangouts. I go there to relax, charge my phone, check e-mail and Facebook. Often, I have my MacBook with me, so I can take field notes and/or get some work done. I browse the digital university library and Google Scholar for literature, check my e-mails, drink specialty coffee and have lunch.

Today my MacBook stays at home. I am travelling light, as I am going to catch up on my social-media accounts, and I also need to read some academic articles that I printed out. I go to my favourite living-room lobby and sit down on one of the leather sofas. I choose a battered one, with a coffee table next to it. I have planned a semi-day off, and in a couple hours I am meeting a friend for lunch in the hotel café.

As soon as I lean back in the Chesterfield sofa, a blue- dressed waiter magically appears. I smile and say: 'Hi Alex, I will have a latte, please.' To be honest, Alex is the only waiter I know by name, and it feels nice to be served by someone familiar. He recognises me, which is a good sign, as it makes me feel at home and hopefully it is one step closer to getting the 'regular customer discount coin'.

The girl opposite me has taken off her shoes and is sitting cross-legged in a huge five-seater sofa by herself. She looks very comfortable indeed. I think of when I was ten years old. We had a brown leather sofa in front of the TV. As I would curl up to watch my favourite show, I can still here my Mother's voice yelling: 'Sit down properly!' I get woken up out of my reminiscing daydreams, or perhaps youth nightmares, by Alex with my latte.

People seem to like to work in a lobby that feels like a living room, yet offers all the features needed to work, such as Wi-Fi, electric sockets and coffee. Various interviewees told me that the fact that other people are also working in the lobby motivates them to work, rather working from home, and getting distracted. They find it stimulating to see others working, and it gives them a self-imposed incentive to work too.

Sense of Community without Interaction

The hotel lobby is a place to meet others but also to avoid the look of others; a place of seeing and being seen – but also of reserve and, as such, lounging in a lobby qualifies as a paradigmatic urban experience

(Tallack 2001, p. 146)

One of my envisioned data-collection methods was engaging in casual conversations with other people working in the lobby. When I tried this, I found people working in the lobby were not responsive. When I engaged in conversations with fellow lobby workers, these were typically cut off within a few minutes. Lobby workers want to be around others, but they do not want interaction. Apparently, I had accidently breached tacit rules. Although I felt rejected, it made me learn a lot about the tacit lobby culture. People working in lobbies are not that social, at least not 'offline'. They display *civil inattention* by acknowledging the existence of others in the public space, yet not wanting to interact or be interacted with (Goffman, 1963). Even friends can spend hours sitting next to each other while not exchanging looks or words, each person fully taken in by their own computer and or smartphone screen. At other times, they talk about things on their screens: a picture, a document, another person via apps such as Skype, FaceTime or WhatsApp. Even though (un)intended co-working spaces want to foster knowledge exchange, a feeling of community and (work)friendships, different studies show that people want to literally 'work alone together' (Spinuzzi 2012) in silence (de Vaujany and Aroles 2019).

Van Dijk (2011) refers on various occasions to this behaviour in his book. He wrote of his experience spending a year sleeping in different hotels in Amsterdam. He feels lonely, yet when people want to talk to him, he avoids them or behaves in a somewhat unfriendly manner, so that they will leave him alone. His observations are similar to the data from my interviews. Other people in the lobby are a pleasant back-ground noise, and their presence is comforting as long as there is no real interaction. Lobby workers like to see human beings around them, as being self-employed without colleagues can be a lonely business. Yet, all of my interviewees were quite adamant about not wanting to engage in actual interaction. The purpose of the others in the lobby is for them to '*just be there*'.

Some interviewees purposefully use their earbuds and headphones in order to create a barrier to interact with them. They tell me that this way they know they will not be bothered. They use the headphones to communicate and demonstrate that they are busy working. It was unexpected to find that people in lobbies purposefully seek a place of comfort where they can work, so that they feel less alone in their endeavours, and yet there is a strong reluctance to engage in conversa-tions with the other lobby workers. Before going into the field, I expected the lobby to be some kind of Third Place (Oldenburg 1999), neither work nor home but a communal space where people meet and interact. The lobby is more of a communal space, filled with people, each in their own virtual bubble, not inclined to socialise, at least not 'offline'.

There seems to be a paradoxical phenomenon. The self-employed choose to work in places such as lobbies and coffee shops, yet seem to want to be anonymous in the crowd and not be disturbed by others. They prefer to be alone while being together (Simon 2009). It would be too easy to conclude that the self-employed are not in contact with others. The influence of the Internet is not to be neglected in this matter. Although the self-employed may seem anti-social in the physical space, they are more social and communicative than ever in virtual space. Being connected to the World Wide Web seems to enlarge one's social space virtually, while at the same time causing a decrease in social interaction in physical space. People are physically in one place, yet not fully aware of their direct, physical surroundings as they carry their Portable Private Personal Territories (PPPTs) around (Hatuka & Toch 2016) around. In these PPPTs actors constantly switch between their work and private lives. The authors see the PPPT as a social and not a physical territory, but as 'a social condition that comes into being by the individual in a space'. This implies that the physical space is inhabited by people in their own individual virtual, social bubbles. It could be said that workscapes have become 'liquid' as people flow in and out of their private and work-lives, and the physical world, and the online world.

Throughout my fieldwork sessions, I came to realise I display the same distant behaviour. I feel comfortable working in the lobby, but I am there to work, not to socialise. It is almost as if the other people there serve as background actors to make me feel I am not alone, and this communal energy motivates me to work. In the following tale, I attempt to portray the feeling of wanting to be surrounded by others and yet to be left alone.

It is a rainy and cold day. Cursing the rain, I go through the sliding doors and walk to the long table in the middle of the lobby. I see that a 'young bearded hipster' is sitting at my preferred spot by the electric sockets. He has huge headphones, which reminds me of a pilot in the cockpit of a plane, imagining his laptop to be the dashboard. Luckily my MacBook is fully charged, so I should be okay for a few hours without juice. I 'set up my work space' across from him at the long table. Today I want to read some articles on ethnographic methodology. 'The pilot' suddenly turns to me and asks me what the password is for the Wi-Fi, and I tell him there is none and that the Wi-Fi is pretty fast and free.

Before I have taken off my coat, a blue-dressed waitress asks me what I want to drink. I have not even thought about that, but before I realise it I have ordered a latte. I am not used to this speed of service in Amsterdam. As I open up my laptop, I check my e-mail and Facebook birthday notifications. I see that today is Wendy's birthday. I post a happy birthday message to her timeline and make a mental note that I should order a gift for her and have it sent to her home. My latte arrives, and I warm my hands on the cup. I type 'ethnographic methods' in the Google Scholar search window and just a mouse click later I get a lot of search results. I browse through them and download the most promising articles. As I am reading my first article, and highlighting the PDF-document for interesting passages, I feel a tap on my shoulder. The 'pilot' asks me if I could watch his laptop/dashboard as he uses the restroom. I tell him 'yes' and smile.

When he comes back a few minutes later, he asks me what I am doing and I tell him I am in the process of writing an article. I change the subject, because I don't want to reveal my lobby-research, nor do I want to lie. This is where I feel I am flirting with the boundaries of ethics. So, I change the topic and ask him what he does. Not surprisingly he is not a pilot, but a freelance graphic designer. 'My main customers are advertisement agencies. I used to work for one, but I quit, because I wanted to start for myself and have more freedom.' He then starts talking about the different projects he has been working on. By this time, I am feeling impatient; this is turning into too much of a conversation, and I find myself saying: 'Hey, sorry, I need to send an important e-mail within ten minutes. Good luck with your agency; your work sounds really cool.' We both turn back to our own laptop screens, and I start checking my Facebook posts.

In hotel lobbies people prefer to not to be disturbed while working or just being in the same space (Simon 2009; Spinuzzi 2012). They 'colonise' the (semi-)public space by using it for their own private purposes, such as chatting virtually, e-mailing, working and updating their social-media accounts. They indulge in backstage behaviour, which I have observed in the way the actors sit (sloppily), laze around, eat and drink (Lofland 1985). Even though people are aware of the fact that they are around others, they respect the privacy of others and claim their own. By displaying this behaviour of 'civil inattention', privacy is made possible in a public place through 'self-distancing' (Goffman 1967). Being connected to a virtual space with Wi-Fi, while physically being in the lobby at the same time, has created a seemingly paradoxical situation of being in two places simultaneously. Höflich (2005) refers to this phenomenon as being in a situation of 'absent presence'. People are physically in the lobby, yet enclosed in their 'Portable private- personal territory' (Hatuka and Toch 2016). Hotel lobbies are like physical places, accommodating lobby workers to be in their own virtual bubble.

In conclusion, my findings are that people working in the lobby feel at home in the living-room lobby with their Wi-Fi and coffee. Within their virtual bubble, they work, play and actively engage in virtual contact with people who are not present physically. Lobby frequenters make a conscious choice to spend time in the lobby. They want to feel part of a like-minded community and be surrounded by other people. Yet, unspoken, the following words linger in the air: '*Please do not disturb*'. Even though people choose the lobby to feel part of a community of urbanites, working hipsters, or worldly citizens, there is no community behaviour in which the actors in the lobby partake. Even friends and couples sitting next to each other are engrossed in their own smartphones, occasionally commenting on something on their phone screen to each other. The only constant interaction is with the waiters, who are paid to do so with a smile. The smiling waiters and the comfort of a good cup of coffee literally and figuratively cater to the lobby workers' needs of being noticed, cared for and nourished.

Revisiting the Lobby as a Co-working Space

As discussed in the introduction of this chapter, the number of self-employed workers is growing. Co-working spaces are catering to these needs, yet many self-employed may not have the means or desire to rent a desk and pay a monthly fee. Others may be travelling a lot, and need geographical flexibility in finding and creating work space 'on-the-go'. In theory, work could be done anywhere as long as there is Wi-Fi; in practice, it has become clear that there are other components that are considered crucial and conducive to co-working 'on-the-go'.

My findings show that space influences the practices of the people in the lobby as much as their practices, in turn, influence the space. Non-human actors, such as the furnishing, Wi-Fi, electric sockets, create an environment people want to come to in order to work, and to feel as though they were at home. Simultaneously, the human actors create a 'workscape' by their practices in the lobby. These findings show the concepts of sociomateriality (Orlikowski 2007; Orlikowski & Scott 2008) as technology, (work) space and human interaction are inter-linked in the (work) practices in the lobby. Moreover, I found that there is a performative approach to space, as space is 'performed' through bodies, actions and non-human actors. (Beyes & Steyaert 2012). In the lobby the self-employed practice 'work', as if they were at home away from home, hotels start providing coffee, electric sockets and fast Wi-Fi.

Hotel lobbies have become a valid option for urban digital nomads. There are, however, some crucial components that should be present in order for the lobby to become a successful unintended co-working space. Obviously, a fast and reliable Wi-Fi connection is an essential feature for workers with laptops and other digital devices. As they are spending hours at a time working, it is important to provide enough electric sockets to be able to charge the digital devices. What makes a hotel lobby outstanding is a comfortable, cosy atmosphere with lived-in furniture and soft lighting. Different zones, for different work, and breaks during or after work, add to the attractiveness. High tables to work with full concentration, cosy sofas to work on matters that require less concentration, and corners with sofa and a coffee table to have (network) meetings. The Shoreditch provides it all, and on top of that has a lobby bar and an open restaurant area. This makes the Shoreditch an attractive unintended co-working space.

In the case of the Shoreditch, the hotel has actively responded to the practices of lobby workers by providing furnishings that improve possibilities to co-work in the lobby. The waiters, dressed in a cool and casual uniforms that do not look like uniforms, blend into the living room. They treat the regular co-workers as friends and provide them with small talk, smiles and coffee. Whether this is an 'act' or not, it does generate income from an otherwise liminal space. The Shoreditch has created an atmosphere of a community of cool, urban people in a casual friendly space, where one can work, relax and 'live', surrounded by like-minded people, without being disturbed in one's work practices.

Unintended co-working spaces like to portray themselves as a Third Place, with close-knit community of co-workers and other patrons. It is important to note that there are some differences. A Third Place is a place that is neither home nor work (Oldenburg 1999). Unintended co-working spaces are where both work and home practices are performed. Moreover, there is no interaction as one would expect in a 'Third Place', as defined by Oldenburg (1999), where people gather to socialise and interact with each other. In the lobby, however, the self-employed do not show any inclination to do so. When observing the practices of the self-employed in a coffee shop there is clearly a tacit culture of 'civil inattention'. As I engaged in conversations, at various occasions during my fieldwork, with self-employed in hotel lobbies, these were cut off within a few minutes. Apparently, I was breaching tacit rules. The semi-structured (planned) interviews I had with self-employed from our network, confirmed the existence of the tacit rule of 'civil inattention' (Goffman 1963, 1967), where people are aware of the fact that they are around others, yet respect the privacy of others and claim their own. By displaying this behaviour of 'civil inattention', privacy is made possible in a public place through 'self-distancing' (Goffman 1963, 1967).

Finally, I would like to end on a side note. Spaces like the Shoreditch lobby may be ideal for digital urban workers who cannot afford, or do not want to be committed to, an official co-working space such as WeWork. Yet, there are many self-employed people in today's gig economy who can barely survive, and most certainly not afford to drink expensive coffee all day in a hotel lobby. I would like to stress that working in hotel lobbies is not affordable for everyone, just like renting a (hot) desk in an official co-working space is not within the means of all self-employed workers. It would be interesting to look at the urban inequality that is being created amongst self-employed workers in today's world of work.

References

Balakrishnan, B. K., Muthaly, S. & Leenders, M. 2016. Insights from Coworking Spaces as Unique Service Organizations: The Role of Physical and Social Elements. In L. Petruzzellis & R. Winer (eds.) *Rediscovering the Essentiality of Marketing*. Cham: Springer, 837–848.

Beyes, T. & Steyaert, C. 2012. Spacing organization: Non-representational theory and performing organizational space. *Organization*, 19(1): 45–61.

Bilandzic, M. & Foth, M. 2013. Libraries as coworking spaces: Understanding user motivations and perceived barriers to social learning. *Library Hi Tech*, 31(2): 254–273.

Bizzarri, C. 2010. The Emerging Phenomenon of Coworking, a Redefinition of Job Market in Net-Working Society. In K. Müller, S. Roth & M. Zak (eds) *Social Dimension of Innovation*. Prague: Linde, 195–206.

Blagoev, B., Costas, J. & Kärreman, D. 2019. 'We are all herd animals': Community and organizationality in coworking spaces. *Organization*, 26(6): 894–916.

Boothby, A. 2017. Er is weer leven in de lobby. *Metro*. 18 April 2017.

Central Bureau of Statistics (Centraal Bureau voor de Statistiek) 2018. www.cbs.nl (accessed 20 November 2019).

Colbert, A., Yee, N. & George, G. 2016. The digital workforce and the workplace of the future. *Academy of Management Journal*, 59(3): 731–739.

de Vaujany, F. X. & Aroles, J. 2019. Nothing happened, something happened: Silence in a makerspace. *Management Learning*, 50(2), 208–225.

Gajendran, R. S. & Harrison, D. A. 2007. The good, the bad, and the unknown about telecom-muting: Meta-analysis of psychological mediators and individual consequences. *Journal of Applied Psychology*, 92(6): 1524–1541.

Gandini, A. 2015. The rise of coworking spaces: A literature review. *ephemera*, 15(1), 193–205.

Geertz, C. 1988. Thick Description: Toward an Interpretive Theory of Culture. In T. Oakes & P. L. Price (eds.) *Readings in the Philosophy of Social Science*. Routledge, 213–231.

Goffman, E. 1963. *Behavior in Public Places*. Glencoe, IL: Free Press of Glencoe.

    1967. *Interaction Ritual: Essays in Face to Face Behaviour*. Garden City, NY: Anchor.

    1973. *La mise en scène de la vie quotidienne*. Tome 1. La présentation de soi. *Paris: Editions de minuit*.

    1978. *The Presentation of Self in Everyday Life*. London: Harmondsworth.

Gold, M. & Mustafa, M. 2013. 'Work always wins': Client colonisation, time management and the anxieties of connected freelancers. *New Technology, Work and Employment*, 28(3): 197–211.

Halford, S. 2005. Hybrid workspace: Re-spatialisations of work, organisation and management. *New Technology, Work and Employment*, 20(1): 19–33.

Hatuka, T. & Toch, E. 2016. The emergence of portable private-personal territory: Smartphones, social conduct and public spaces. *Urban Studies*, 53(10), 2192–2208

Höflich, J. R. 2005. A Certain Sense of Place. In Nyiri, J. K. (ed.) *A Sense of Place: The Global and the Local in Mobile Communication*. Passagen Verlag, 159–168.

Kingma, S. 2019. New ways of working (NWW): Work space and cultural change in virtualizing organizations. *Culture and Organization*, 25(5), 383–406.

Lofland, L. 1985. *A World of Strangers. Order and Action in Urban Public Space*. New York: Waveland Press.

Merkel, J. 2015. Coworking in the city. *Ephemera*, 15(2): 121–139.

Nicolini, D. 2009. Zooming in and out: Studying practices by switching theoretical lenses and trailing connections. *Organization Studies*, 30 (12): 1391–1418.

Nippert-Eng, C. 2015. *Watching Closely: A Guide to Ethnographic Observation*. Oxford: Oxford University Press.

Oldenburg, R. (1999). *The Great Good Place: Cafes, Coffee Shops, Bookstores, Bars, Hair Salons, and Other Hangouts at the Heart of a Community*. Boston: Da Capo Press.

Orlikowski, W. J. 2007. Sociomaterial practices: Exploring technology at work. *Organization studies*, 28(9): 1435–1448.

Orlikowski, W. J. & Scott, S. V. 2008. 10 sociomateriality: Challenging the separation of technology, work and organization. *The Academy of Management Annals*, 2(1): 433–474.

Simon, B. 2009. *Everything but the Coffee: Learning about America from Starbucks*. Berkeley, CA: University of California Press.

Spinuzzi, C. 2012. Working alone together: Coworking as emergent collaborative activity. *Journal of Business and Technical Communication*, 26 (4): 399–441.

Stravens, M. 2017. Aantal zzp'ers afgelopen tien jaar verdubbeld, vooral in de steden. *De Volkskrant*. 13 December 2017.

Tallack, D. 2001. 'Waiting, Waiting': The Hotel Lobby, in the Modern City. In N. Leach (ed.) *The Hieroglyphics of Space: Reading and Experiencing the Modern Metropolis*. London, New York: Routledge, 139–151.

Torten, R., Reaiche, C. & Caraballo, E. L. 2016. Teleworking in the new milleneum. *The Journal of Developing Areas*, 50(5): 317–326.

van Dijk, V. 2011. *Amsterdam Slaapt*. Amsterdam: Hbmeo Publishers.

Vince, R. & Warren, S. 2012. Participatory Visual Methods. In G. Symon & C. Cassell (eds.) *Qualitative Organizational Research: Core Methods and Current Challenges*. London: Sage, 275–295.

Waters-Lynch, J., Potts, J., Butcher, T., Dodson, J. & Hurley, J. 2016. Coworking: A transdisciplinary overview. Available at SSRN 2712217.

Waters-Lynch, J. & Potts, J. 2017. The social economy of coworking spaces: A focal point model of coordination. *Review of Social Economy*, 75(4): 417–433.

3 'So Many Cool Things to Do!'
Hacker Ethics and Work Practices

MICKAEL PEIRO

Introduction: So Many Cool Things to Do!

'So many cool things to do!'[1] This line is used by Mitch Altman to invite people to visit Noisebridge hackerspace, and is also a slogan that is part of the statutes of the Montpellier hackerspace named the Boat in a Bag (BIB). The motto indicates that the organisation and its activities focus on two values: doing things and having fun. Hackerspaces could then carry all the alternative potential of organisations by embodying alternative means and ends.

In modern societies, omnipresent technologies represent new symbols that lie at the heart of capitalism. High-tech organisations are among the most profitable companies, connected devices are taking control of physical bodies, governments are being accused of mass surveillance[2], global corporations are seizing markets and user data as well as developing their own precarious work[3]. Technologies are fascinating, sometimes objects of fantasy in dreams of artificial intelligence, improved bodies and society without crime. They are also objects of fear, when sceptics imagine increasingly wild examples of data capture, database crossing and technology alienation. In this new digital age, hackers represent an alternative proposition to technology privatisation and the dominant circumvention and standardisation practices. To accomplish their projects, hackers have recently gathered in local hackerspaces to propose different ways of working and making

---

[1] See, for example, Mitch Altman's Ted Talk about 'The Hackerspace Movement', November 2012, or his conference presentation during the world's free software meetings in July 2014.

[2] Concerning this topic, see '*Citizen Four*' (2014), Laura Poitras' documentary on Edward Snowden, and '*The Great Hack*' (2019) by Jehane Noujaim and Karim Amer Aon, Cambridge Analytica.

[3] The DipLab report (Casilli et al. 2019) on micro-work in France particularly highlights platforms designed to train artificial intelligence in large digital companies. See http://diplab.eu/

decisions. In addition, they resist the dominant order, not by protest, reforms or the creation of a new global order but by creating local initiatives capable of demonstrating the advocated values of hacking while being appropriated by the greatest number possible. Finally, hackerspaces could be seen as a popular means for people to experiment with local production techniques and to make decisions about the relationship between economic and social issues. In this chapter, we explore the spirit and experience of resistance as they emerge in the context of hacker communities and hackerspaces.

Theoretical Background: Ethics, Work and Space

Since the advent of the Internet, major technology groups have steadily increased their power as well as the number of controversies about their hegemony. In addition to technological giants and among the mass of users, hackers are becoming more and more an important stakeholder. Hackers have also generated many fantasies in the collective imagination, and are often caricatured by non-specialist media. Journalists tend to report extraordinary exploits against governments and private organisations, sometimes praising hackers as wizards and heroes, sometimes denigrating them as villains and geeks. Many fictions since the 1980s have contributed to shaping the image of hackers. They are depicted in famous fictional characters, such as David Lightman, Stanley Jobson, Motoko Kusanagi and Edward, Neo and Morpheus, and, more recently, Elliot and Mr Robot. In our universe, they are represented mainly by people who have publicly defied global institutions. This is the case for such famous personalities as: Edward Snowden and Julian Assange, who have revealed government secrets; Aaron Swartz and Alexandra Elbakyan in the fight against intellectual property; and the large masked movement under the name of Anonymous[4] (Coleman 2016).

Hackers have never been part of the mainstream, but have always been seen as talented programmers, often marginalised when dealing with bureaucratic rules and conventional ways of being. The 1980s made hackers the heroes of the computer revolution, able to overcome

---

[4] I confess that the non-exhaustive selection of characters is indicative of some of my inspirations and admirations.

all kinds of obstacles. Subsequently, the police and judicial crackdown on famous hackers, such as Kevin Mitnick and Aaron Swartz, permanently anchored 'the hacker as a national security threat and a threat to intellectual property' (Halbert 1997, p. 369) and changed the associations with the hacker label (Hafner & Markoff 1995; Hannemyr 1999). The demonisation and criminalisation (Chandler 1996; Hollinger & Lanza-Kaduce 1988) of hackers slowly changed their status from 'technical hero' to 'parasite' (Gunkel 2001). This shift has to be examined in the popular conception of hackers as deviant and transgressive because of their ability to embody resistance to the dominant governance of technologies (Nissenbaum 2004) and to challenge capitalist and bureaucratic organisations (Starr 2000).

Hackers' Stories and Diversity

Hackers are often associated with and represented by computers. However, their origin dates back to a period largely preceding the birth of the Internet. In the 1950s, a group of students from the Massachusetts Institute of Technology (MIT) formed the Tech Model Railroad Club (TMRC) to build impressive and complex model train tracks. Many students have participated in the activities of the club, which was gradually structured into divisions according to those who wished to paint, create buildings or take care of communications (Levy 1984). The club allows students to express their creativity using custom tracks, signal systems and other amenities that were not commercially available. Most creative members of the TMRC receive a hacker badge (Baichtal 2011; Raymond 1996), and a 'project undertaken or product built not solely to fulfil some constructive goal, but with a wild pleasure taken in mere involvement, was called a hack' (Levy 1984, p. 10). If hackers emerged from the university culture and academic principles, amateur practices and technology enthusiasts such as phreakers[5] also played a crucial role in the construction of the hacker figure (Dagiral 2008).

It is still very difficult to provide an exact definition of hackers. One portrayal restricts their activities to computer domains, whereas another extends the definition to any type of intervention. According

---

[5] From phone and freaks, the term refers to people hijacking phones to improve or divert an operation (Dagiral 2008, p. 487).

to the new hacker dictionary[6] edited by Eric Raymond (1996), the hacker is a person who likes to explore details of programmable systems to extend these capabilities. It is also a person who programs with enthusiasm and knows how to appreciate the value of a hack. He or she can be an expert or an enthusiast of any type, keen to take up the intellectual challenge of overcoming all forms of limitation. The characterisation of a hacker finally extends beyond the technical and computer fields to represent a mode of reasoning against standards and codes. A broader portrayal, then, makes it possible to envisage any field involving social problems. According to Emmanuel Goldstein,[7] 'It doesn't have to be a computer. It doesn't even have to be technology. A hacker is someone who figures out how to get around barriers, won't take "no" for an answer, asks an insane amount of questions, and believes in sharing the information he or she discovers' (quoted in Baichtal 2011, p. 9). Richard Matthew Stallman, founder and initiator of the free software movement, finally defined a hacker as 'someone who likes to exercise his ingenuity in a fun way', thus integrating a fundamental component of hackers: the value of the hack as a purpose and pleasure as a factor of their identity.[8]

Paul Taylor's work summarises hackers' specific denominations and associated behaviours. According to him, the term 'hacker' tends to be used by those who are more or less in the institutionalised computer world and are sympathetic to their values, while the term 'cracker' is often used by the defenders of computer security who oppose hacking (Taylor 2005). People are increasingly using their skills in the service of growing commercial or industrial organisations, and the use of computer skills in security or commercial fields has led to the creation of Microserfs[9] (Taylor 1998, 1999), while other individuals have joined the open-source movement in the belief that computing should be free. Finally, some hackers embody a more explicit political stance through

---

[6] New hackers dictionary, available online: http://hackersdictionary.com/

[7] Nickname used by Eric Corley, founder of the famous magazine *2600: The Hacker Quarterly*.

[8] Definition given in an interview with Tere Vaden. www.gnu.org/philosophy/rms-hack.fr.html

[9] Phenomenon described by Douglas Coupland in his novel *Microserfs* (1995). The name combines the company Microsoft and the term serf (the lowest level of a feudal society).

hacktivism[10], in which politics becomes the *raison d'être* of their activity (Taylor 2005).

Hacker Ethics and the Value of the Hack

It is impossible to define hackers without talking about hacking and, more specifically, the experience surrounding all activities performed by hackers. Over time, hackers have developed a particular work ethic (Lallement 2015). Work for hackers is 'not prescribed by hierarchy, without separation between design and execution, with direct cooperation' (Giffard 2007, p. 20). Hackers have never had much respect for bureaucratic organisations, and every rule and norm becomes an arena for hackers to test their mischievous intelligence (Raymond 1996). To qualify as a hack, 'the feat must be imbued with innovation, style and technical virtuosity' (Levy 1984, p. 10). The new hacker dictionary defines hacking as both an 'appropriate application of ingenuity', whether it is a quick adjustment or a meticulously crafted piece of art, and a 'creative joke' (Raymond 1996). The value of a hack is thus gauged as much by the results obtained as by the conditions of obtaining it. In his book *The Hacker Ethic and the Spirit of the Information Age*, Himanen Pekka (2001, p. 23) reports that for Linus Torvalds, creator of the free kernel called Linux, 'the computer is a pleasure in itself. He suggests that programming is an exciting activity and a source of joy. He explains how the Linux kernel was born from small experiments carried out with the computer he had just acquired and that the distribution was born from a pleasure to work on the project'.

Thus, fun appears to be an ever-present motivation among hackers. Process is more important than outcome, travel is more important than final destination. The idea that the hack is its own purpose is also highlighted in Michel Lallement's observation of Noisebridge. He notes during his participatory observation that 'hackers work only on the condition of being able to assign to the task to which they devote themselves a status of end and not of means' (Lallement 2015, p. 123). When collecting the hackers' testimonies and observing their

---

[10] Stuart Millar defines hacktivism as a 'highly politicized underground movement using direct action on cyberspace to attack globalization and corporate domination of the internet' (Millar 2001, p. 4).

activities, he also notices that they do not 'work in the traditional sense, but play' (Lallement 2015, p. 132). The value of the hack and hackers' ethics, then, is embodied in the hackerspace organisation through the principle of do-ocracy,[11] meaning that almost all actions carried out within the hackerspace are directed by the goal of 'doing'. Beyond its own characteristics, hacking is also a form of resistance to the dominant order. According to Richard Stallman, 'hacking is not initially a matter of ethics. It's an idea that gives meaning to life. But there may be reason to say that hacking could cause a significant number of hackers to think of ethical questions in a certain way'[12]. The idea of a general ethics of hackers was therefore formulated for the first-time by Steven Levy (2010):

---

1. Access to computers – and anything that might teach you something about the way the world works – should be unlimited and total. Always yield to the Hands-On Imperative!
2. All information should be free.
3. Mistrust Authority. Promote Decentralisation.
4. Hackers should be judged by their hacking, not bogus criteria such as degrees, age, race or position.
5. You can create art and beauty on a computer.
6. Computers can change your life for the better.

(SOURCE: LEVY 2010, PP. 40–45)

This ethics gives an important place to the means of hacking and highlights challenges regularly made by hackers towards organisations and dominant social relations and protests mainly focused on freedom of information and free work. Indeed, the Internet can be a space for free speech, but it can also be used as a monitoring instrument. Many hackers have acted to prevent these abuses by defending respect for personal data, and whistle-blowers have revealed governments' and private organisations' tendency to practice mass surveillance and data commercialisation (Pekka 2001). As Big Data and artificial intelligence trends have pushed companies to collect massive user data to facilitate

---

[11] Founding principle of Noisebridge. It is embodied in such mottos as 'If you want something to be done, do it', 'Be excellent one for each other' and 'So many nice things to do'. www.noisebridge.net/wiki/Do-ocracy

[12] Source: Interview with Tere Vaden. www.gnu.org/philosophy/rms-hack.fr.html

targeted advertising and monitor all traffic, hacker activity has been part of the defence of freedom of speech and respect for privacy in order to preserve the autonomy of all users. When hackers have collectively organised themselves, their contributions outside the market and the dominant order have been considerable. For example, Richard Stallman and the free software movement have posed a major challenge to the hegemony of intellectual property, and other hackers have questioned privileged access to technology by launching 'in the 1990s internet service providers allowing access to the masses' (Raymond 1996, section 7). In their most political version, hacktivists have supported freedom and autonomy, especially in 1998, when they helped the Zapatista rebels by organising denial-of-service attacks[13] on Mexican President Ernesto Zedillo. More recently, other hacktivists have drawn attention to the increasing presence of video surveillance technologies in private and public spaces and 'offer in an anonymous website tips to disable surveillance cameras' (Nissenbaum 2004, p. 211). Finally, hackers warn against the centralisation and globalisation of power, including the fact that the economic system subordinates all other interests to those of business.

Hackerspaces and Hacker Practices

Hackerspaces are community-operated physical locations where people share their interest in tinkering with technology by meeting to work together on projects and learn from each other. In 2005, there were fewer than 20 hackerspaces in the world, while there are more than 2,000 active or planned in 2019.[14] Hackerspaces spread in the second half of the 2000s,[15] and hackers began to create physical spaces in which they could express themselves and work as they wish. Without reaching consensus, members of the hackerspace community

---

[13] A denial-of-service (DoS) attack is a technique generally used by hackers to temporarily or permanently suspend the activity of a server.

[14] Source: collaborative website https://hackerspaces.org.

[15] The first hackerspace, and one of the most famous, is the Chaos Communications Club (CCC), founded in Berlin in 1981 with five computer user members and no specific location. In 1984, the CCC became popular when it made the first e-banking robbery and returned the money the next day.

have highlighted some criteria of what a hackerspace is. According to the researcher and hacker Jarkko Moilanen (2012, p. 95):

The hackerspace is first managed by its members in a spirit of equality. Second, it is non-profit and open to the outside world on a (semi-)regular basis. Third, people share tools, equipment and ideas without discrimination. Fourth, it places a strong emphasis on technology and invention. Fifth, it has a shared space (or is acquiring a space) as the centre of the community. Finally, it has a strong spirit of invention and science, based on trial, error and free sharing of information.

Hackerspaces are therefore open to all skill levels and areas of interest. In the late 1990s, hackers began to develop and initiate theoretical reflections on hacking spaces. This new wave of hacker-spaces was thus rooted in 'proving hackers could be perfectly open about their work, organise officially, gain recognition from the govern-ment and respect from the public by living and applying the hacker ethic in their efforts' (Moilanen 2012, p. 95). Thus, they decided to build places that would bring members of the community together around common goals and means. The Noisebridge hackerspace is a good example of the desire to intertwine alternative ends and means and the difficulties of maintaining hacker ethics over time. Members who refuse to comply with the hierarchy and pre-established rules must face the issues of sustainability over time as well as the smooth oper-ation of the organisation (Lallement 2015).

Different hacker communities use different names to describe them-selves: fablab, techlab, techshop, garage, repair-coffee, sharing plat-form, garage, third-places, etc. The diversity of new hacker communities expresses the variety of this movement. Empirical works that attempt to clarify the differences between various hacking and do-it-yourself (DIY) communities are still rare (Moilanen 2012). Not all groups can be or want to be labelled hackerspaces, in some cases because of the political resonance of such a denomination and the consequences in terms of openness or even financing. Others proudly claim this name, giving the organisation all the values associated with hackers. It is in the very claiming of this name, its ethics and its political power that the Montpellier hackerspace, the BIB, was built. Hackers grouped together to organise themselves on a daily basis and to offer a space for free technology promotion as well as a new form of work organisation.

An Embodied Ethnography of a Hackerspace

Brief Description of the Hackerspace

The BIB was founded in 2013 in the city of Montpellier by three hackers and their friends. During my involvement, the place relied for its operation on fifteen hackers, almost exclusively white men, who set up workshops in areas ranging from data encryption, electronics, 3D printing, conferences and debates to computer coding, digital health, astronomical observation, sound production and sea navigation.[16] The same fifteen hackers took care of the daily management of the place, including financing, activities and communication. After an informal assembly, the hackers formed an association in 2015 with the aim of promoting 'technological emancipation, in particular through access, practice and sharing of open and free media, tools and techniques.'[17] The members welcome children and teenagers who are curious about new technologies to tinker with electronic objects or play their own games. In the same space are activists who use the hackerspace to benefit from free printing and data encryption advice. Members regularly provide squats with computer equipment. Finally, other members work on their own computer systems and personal projects.

Qualitative and Ethnographic Methodology

The ethnographic posture makes it possible to embody the researcher in his field, removing him from hypothetical control and confronting him as an actor in his own research (Lofland 1974): a position that appears essential in the study of alternative organisations in order to access, hear and show rich and complex data. According to the 'Sherlockian prescription' illustrated by Van Maanen, the design of ethnographic case studies is also powerful in order to build a new theory. In other words, 'less theory produces better facts, more facts produce better theories' (Van Maanen 1979, p. 539).

Our empirical research is based on an ethnographic study (Van Maanen 2011) of/within a hackerspace based in southern France. During our fieldwork (Van Maanen 1979), we combined direct participation with a

[16] For the complete list of workshops set up by the hackerspace, see: https://lebib .org/
[17] Source: Article 2 of the association statutes, 'The BIB', drafted in 2015.

long-term presence in the communities to collect basic facts that allow us to construct an analysis based on representations but also to go beyond speeches. Therefore, we participated in the majority of meetings and decision-making activities, set up a free digital library workshop, attended conferences, participated in many social movements, engaged in a debate in a college around issues of data protection, organised two projects on social movements and property within a cultural squat, and shared many friendly exchanges with hackers. Finally, like every ethnographer engaged in long-term immersion, we adopted some of the ways of thinking, feeling and acting typical of our new community (Wacquant 2005). Even if we had not necessarily been sensitive to issues of free software or net neutrality before passing the door of the hackerspace, the many hours spent with hackers undeniably changed the way we understand research and our general vision of work and society.

The researcher does not reveal but represents, and his or her success depends on the ability to make robust representations. This robustness requires the establishment of equipment and tools that make the represented entities sustainable, i.e., terms, images, idioms, phrases, sentences and stories (Van Maanen 2011). Our fieldwork within these collectives occurred from March 2016 to November 2018 and constituted more than 400 hours of direct observation, participation in more than 62 meetings and events in line with these initiatives, and years of archived exchanges through intranet or email and press articles. We recorded our observations on a daily basis in an ethnographic notebook, both digital and paper (Mbodj-Pouye 2008). Both the factual verbal and non-verbal elements of analysis were annotated in the journal as well as the feelings of the apprentice researcher within the field. To complete this ethnographic study, we had the opportunity to interview the whole set of hackers involved in this initiative, i.e., sixteen non-directive interviews and one recorded 'work meeting', which enabled us to understand the aims of their movement as well as the daily functioning of the community. We chose to conduct informal interviews to collect as much information as possible without directing individuals in their responses. The non-directed interviews were all conducted face-to-face in informal settings (restaurants, cafes, hackerspaces, squats) and lasted on average 1.5 hours. We recorded and transcribed the interviews and the secondary data gathered during the period (IRC, forums, wiki, blogs) in the MAXQDA encoding software so that they could be coded and analysed.

Experiencing 'Do and Fun' as Work Practices

The BIB took its name from the 'Boat in a Bag', a life raft deployed in case of a ship sinking. The hackerspace features a logo representing a double black tyre to capture heat and an orange protective tent for visibility.

> A citizen research laboratory. It is the possibility of having an open friendly meeting place around the digital question, dedicated to technological emancipation, in a perspective of real education. Who wants to teach teaches, who wants to learn learns and everyone shares. (Source document: 'The BIB: a hackerspace in Montpellier')

The BIB supports reflections on technology's social impacts, such as data protection, recycling issues and programmed obsolescence. Hackers invite users to consider their behaviour in relation to technological abundance and its consequences. Actions implemented within the BIB range from the organisation of conferences on freedom of speech, data encryption workshops and machine tool design to the implementation of 'hackpéros'.[18] The hackerspace was founded by three hackers who visited the Toulouse HackerSpace Factory (THSF), an event recognised by the French and international hacker community, in March 2012. The event provided an opportunity for the three founders to participate in conferences and workshops, where they met one of the founders of the */tmp/lab*,[19] who was involved in setting up a hackerspace.

> He made a summary on how to set up a hackerspace and gave us lots of advice. He was unseating a lot of ideas we had, firstly, how to finance it. He told us, you find a place, you settle down and do things. Don't ask for permission to do anything stupid; do something stupid, and then ask for apologies. I liked the radical part. (Source: interview with hacker).

---

[18] A contraction of the words hack and apéritif (French word for a convivial moment over drinks).
[19] Hackerspace located in Choisy le Roi, Ile-de-France.

Do-It-Ocracy–Based Organisation

Since its creation, the hackerspace has always had to deal with limited resources, whether technological or financial. This limitation is one of the characteristics of the life raft, where actions are based on existing modest resources. A legacy of the DIY movement, what is embodied within the place is that people continue to offer workshops that are organised solely with the will 'to do'. If a hacker enters the hackerspace with an idea, he or she is encouraged to implement it with a 'Do it!' Hackers want to demystify the technical nature of projects to allow production tools to be appropriated.

> The aim is to demystify technique and technology. Anyone can do radio; it is not only for major channels. The same goes for video, television and information. Meeting everyone on the hackerspace allowed me to theorise a little more what I had inside me. It is important to provide the means to communicate. There is a real aspect of personal and collective freedom by knowing, understanding and mastering technical tools. (Source: interview with hacker).

Hackers want to emancipate themselves from industrial practices that are sometimes too focused on programmed obsolescence and, above all, instil the idea that technology must be understood and can be modified. The objective is to take ownership of production and consumption tools that are the property of others. Workshops are conducted within the hackerspace to open computers and understand how hundreds of electronic components and multiple physical processes work. Other workshops are offered for people to learn how, for example, to manufacture their own shampoos or develop autonomous farming practices. Other workshops are offered for children to understand the basics of video games through algorithms and codes. The hackerspace, by opening black boxes, wants to be the place where possibilities are imagined and re-appropriated.

> There is a loss of people's autonomy, especially in production tools. Wait; we're selling peeled oranges – I don't want to live on this planet anymore. Of course, I'm kidding, but under these conditions, setting up a hackerspace is interesting. We're going to do workshops to learn how to peel fruits; it stings a little sometimes, but it's just a bad time to go through. (Source: interview with hacker).

Projects are developed according to everyone's wishes. The hackerspace, by proposing an organisation based on will rather than skills, redefines the notion of work. In the context of this approach, which is far from a traditional vision, members operate on a daily basis with the resources they have. Hackers want to make work an unconstrained process in which everyone can participate. They break with a work-vision based on reflection, past experiences and skills to offer a work-vision based on doing. They embody an ethic in which the doing is at the centre of the organised process as much as any political issue. Anyone who does something has the right to do it, which in turn becomes a collective organisational principle: the one who does it is always right. This value tends to favour emancipation of what hackers want to do but also of what they can do. This strong belief in doing re-envisions the boundaries between work and idleness to propose a model in which performance is linked to action rather than its outcome. The BIB is a place without positions and hierarchies, where some members willingly improvise their roles: electrician, manager, teacher, software or hardware engineer, projectionist, accountant, financier, cook, philosopher, artist, etc. The place and its operation become the responsibility of all those who pass through its doors, and the workshops are organised in the same way. During meetings, you will hear 'Who is in charge?' or 'Who wants to set something up?'. Some hackers set up Python coding workshops, others perform 3D printing or circuit-bending, and others work on film screenings. All workshops are individual initiatives; members simply inform themselves so that they can participate and communicate on the collective agenda.

> We really wanted to have a horizontal operation. We do not have a president and treasurer because it does not suit us. It is not the treasurer who is in charge of the accounts at all, and I believe it is me. It is like the direction action principle, an anarchist functioning of the 1970s. We don't wait for the hierarchy approval. If we want to do something, we do it, organised or not. If you want to do something, you do it. (Source: interview with hacker).

The general organisation follows the same principles. It is difficult to see it as a collective division between a hardware team, a network team and a software team on one hand and an accounting team, a communication team and a storage team on the other. The organisation occurs mainly at the individual level by people who wish to become involved. When they want to set up an event, they summon 'All hands on deck!' to specify the need for a large effort. All hackers are then mobilised to set up workshops on what they are passionate about, and to tidy up the place.

> It's always worked in an organic way because we were inspired by the do-it-ocracy idea, which is: you want to do something, do it. You're not gonna piss someone off because you want to do something. It would be a good idea to do that: well, you have a good idea; do it! (Source: interview with hacker).

Hackers contest a structure based on hierarchy to propose a place where only the doing guides action. They experiment and build a model in which they would like to operate. Hackers gather in a place where they try things, with and sometimes without success. Members constantly ask themselves what they want to put in place before even asking whether they have the skills or availability. This was the case when Winter decided to set up a coding workshop while he was still a student himself. His desire to transmit his first acquired knowledge exceeded his lack of pedagogical training and his shyness. Thus, the BIB reveals the ability to do and break the barriers between knowing and learning.

> One of the interesting things of the hackerspace is that there are people who are not teachers, who are sometimes barely competent in their field, that take the teaching role. That is a popular education, an emancipation and empowerment of learners who become experts themselves. It has to be a little wobbly for us to get started. (Source: interview with hacker).

Project 1. The Bib-uton. The Bib-uton was a project carried out within the hackerspace between 2014 and 2016. The objective was to build a button linked to the hackerspace website in order to indicate when it was open or closed. The step-by-step construction of the software-hardware system revealed the particular qualities of the BIB organisation based on doing.

> Doing it isn't just doing it; it's a potential. I remember something pretty funny. Be careful and behave yourself; on paper, it's a stupid thing I'm about to tell you. One day (in April 2014), a hacker came up with a small network card that sent a signal to the website in order to indicate whether it is open or closed – the Bib-uton. He tried that thing and said: it doesn't work. Another hacker connected it to the website, and I said to myself, I have hard and soft plastic; let's make a real button. It is something we didn't finish. It is still a big, disgusting plastic, and the electronic part was ripped off. Nevertheless, at that moment, I am doing 3D printing on a button that a guy had coded that could indicate if the BIB is open or closed. In the end, it was useful; there was a problem before; it was never reported that the hackerspace was open or closed, and there was no more after that. Well, the thing dragged all over the place and broke up; we coded quite a few times. I don't know where it stands anymore. (Source: interview with hacker).

When I arrived at the BIB in March 2016, the 'open or closed' issue still existed. A user still had to connect to the hackerspace internet relay chat and ask if anyone was at the BIB. One hacker then decided, two years after the first version of the Bib-uton, to work again on the project. When I had the opportunity to tell the hacker who worked on the genesis of the Bib-uton that it worked two years later, he told me that this was not exceptional. The BIB is ultimately a place where things happen daily and where daily things happen and accumulate. The hackerspace then becomes a place where the only organising principle is to do things.

> That's great! I am very happy. You see, typically, that's how the BIB should move forward in a fairly natural way. You don't need to ask for rules for that; no one's asked themselves any questions. We just put something down, and at the end we said, it works [laughs]. It's a punk spirit! To achieve this, in my opinion, the easiest way is to do things. (Source: interview with hacker).

Fun-Based Organisation

Hackers gathered to fight against proprietary technologies and promote free culture. To do so, they decide to organise and embody hacking in a real and physical place. This place and its organisation in turn became the reasons for their involvement by making alternative work organisation a collective aim. We now analyse fun as a way to protest against dominant practices and the alienation of work. One of the BIB's founding principles is that hackers attribute a status of end and not of means to the tasks they undertake. This paradigm shift changes the relationship between hackers and work. Work must then be characterised by pleasure, and the place becomes the scene of playful projects with the goal of always questioning digital practices.

> Curiosity is the main driving force, and fun is the engine. This is what no one finds in their usual job anymore because of credit anxieties or social status. People you find in hackerspaces don't care about that. It is difficult to talk with politicians or companies because those guys come in and put money on the table and say, 'I need you to do that for me'. If no one's amused, they're not going to find anyone. If it's an idea that amuses people, he will be able to hire them for nothing, almost free. (Source: interview with hacker).

Fun within the hackerspace claims a political aspect. While values are defended, and hackers' protests are very serious, actions under-taken within the place are based on pleasure and humour. This association is apparent as soon as the first connection to the hacker-space is made. When first-time users ask for the password, the response is a smiling 'Cestpascompliquéputain'.[20] Once you under-stand that it is the password, the multiplication of specific charac-ters, capital letters and numbers makes the task more complicated than it seems. It is a fun way for hackers to show the need for a strong password that is easy to remember. Additionally, hackers have often thought of limiting the internet connectivity of Apple devices. Teasing Apple and Windows owners is common in the hackerspace to denounce private software and data capture. Hackers also demonstrate this sense of fun when addressing serious subjects. For example, when hackers set up a first aid workshop, they could not help making references to pop culture, personal jokes

[20] In English: 'Itsnotfuckingcomplicated'.

and targeted mockery even though they were working on discomfort, unconsciousness, inhalation of foreign bodies, external bleeding, thermal burns and cardiac arrest.

> Okay, guys: you're welding your office chair to a jet pack, and you accidentally burn your tongue: what to do? Your little brother no longer has any UHU to snort; he throws himself on the first poppers pot; too bad you put your screws in it. He chokes: what to do? Don't panic! The BIB offers you a first aid training session.
>
> On the programme: a presentation of some anatomical notions to understand the important gestures to perform – a practical part (no, there will be no jet pack or poppers) – and an exchange part where you can ask the questions that are bothering you. (Source: BIB project – Stay Alive or Die Trying).

Humour in the hackerspace serves to denounce the dominant order or to develop skills. It is the favourite communication mode of hackers in order to desacralise technique but also to prevent boredom or defuse dramatic situations. Finally, and primarily, it is the main driver of collective action. Hackers are always wondering how to get around the established system in a fun way. The fun is both the result of the actions implemented by the hackers and the conditions of their emergence. Hackers wish to fight against pragmatism and managerialism by offering a place where actors do not work but have fun building, creating, making music, or engaging in additional digital or other forms of creativity. Humour and pleasure are then the means of fighting against pragmatism. The BIB organisation is itself a hack according to this process. The idea of naming the hackerspace after a life raft rather than a ship includes the desire to be constantly patched up. Consequently, the BIB was first set up in a garage, reproducing the original computer culture, and then was re-established in an old bank with a start-up, which satisfied the imaginations of the hackers. The hackers finally moved it to an underground dojo that was once a clandestine technobar owned by anarchists and now looks like a fight club. As the founders says, '*If this is your first night in the hackerspace, you have to hack*'.

Finally, the notion of work is questioned. Hackers often associate work with constraint, a task that must be done owing to financial or cultural obligation. They want to move away from this alienated vision of work and talk about pleasure or simply do things. The hackerspace is thus a place where hackers can spend days thinking about raising awareness about IT security in high schools. They can spend hours repairing electricity, tiling toilets and repairing printers or computers, but they will never want to hear about work.

> It's funny; members fight a little bit on this, but there is a relationship to work that is very strange. They are all hard workers; they do things, but it's never about work. (Source: interview with hacker).

Project 2. O.O.P.S Software. We have seen that hackers use fun to hack dominant organisations' practices. The BIB's participation in a hackathon[21] set up by the city of Montpellier in September 2013 gave hackers the opportunity to exercise their talents and subversive spirit. They presented a software called Original Open Pervenches Statistics (O.O.P.S.), which shows, based on data from the city of Montpellier, where it is possible to park without paying. The application makes it possible to collect the hours and sites of contraventions to constitute a database that can predict the statistical chances of receiving a parking ticket. The objective is clear: the hackers want to denounce Big Data and the very organisation of such a hackathon. Hackers also highlight stereotypes from local governments of the hacker community.

> That we call a hackathon a code competition with money at stake and no incentive to use open-source or free software still passes. That one of the organisation's partners is a private computer school, why not? That at least two of the participating teams come from this school is starting to be a lot. So when we notice that a member of the jury is part of the school staff, we start to see red concerning conflict of interest. And when, finally, the winners of the first prize and the jury prize are the teams of the school in question, that's too much. We're not disappointed; we are in stitches! (Source: hackathon report, leBIB.org).

---

[21] An event that gathered volunteer developers for collaborative projects and programming over several days.

In addition to reflecting on the project and organising a team, the hackers spent two days and two nights organising this event. They spent a huge amount of work and energy to denounce stereotypes and the use of skills for economic purposes. Finally, the creation of the O.O.P.S. software allowed them to challenge the massive use of public or private data but also to employ fun as a way of working.

Conclusion: Experiencing and Regulating Transgression Together?

The BIB provides a different perspective on the functioning of alternative organisations. Indeed, the hackers' activities within the hackerspace make it possible to envisage a new form of organisation, which supervises social relations within the hackerspace. In this chapter, we have shown the relationship between means and ends within the hackerspace. The BIB case is in line with Michel Lallement's observations on Noisebridge. The hackers conduct their actions and founded their organisation according to two values: fun and doing. The O.O.P.S. episode illustrates the resistance as well as the organisation of the members in a work performed over several days and nights with multiple ambitions. The first aim was to protest against the very principle of the hackathon, which symbolised the appropriation of work and creativity and data captation. It was also a way for members to make hackerspace activities visible and at the same time to try to recover a prize and finance the hackerspace activities. It was above all a way to recognise subversion and fun as the full and particular way of working. Fun is the driving force behind hacker inspiration and is part of the hacker ethics studied by Steven Levy (2010) and observed by Michel Lallement (2015). The BIB case also suggests that, far from being confined to an individual principle and attitude, fun represents an organisational principle within the hackerspace.

The study of the Montpellier hackerspace also shows that all the activities carried out, as well as the social relations between members, are based on doing. We first analysed the hackers' ability to organise their projects according to their desires in specific cases, such as the creation of a toilet-paper table, a free library, multiple conferences or the Bib-uton. More importantly, the daily observation of hackers made it possible to see how hackers structure the hackerspace according to the same process. Doing is no longer only a means of guiding social action but becomes the only organisational modality. The ethics of doing is at the heart of the process of including new hackerspace members, which does not depend on political convictions, a priori technicality or 'false criteria such as age, ethnic origin or social class' (Levy 2010, pp. 40–45). The ethics is reflected in the organisational tasks and the constitution of the administrative team in Weber's sense, which is not a matter of rational, charismatic or traditional motives but whose power comes from doing, the do-it-ocracy.

To conclude, hackers within the BIB experiment with technological and digital workshops as much as they experiment with organisational techniques. Doing and having fun regulate work practices, the decision-making process and the projects themselves. The reason for grouping hackers is both the fight against dominant systems and the production of one's own system. Hackers build a model that embodies their values and in which they would like to operate. Finally, hackerspace members and citizens who pass through the hackerspace door do not find in the BIB a clear project, whether against capitalism and private property or in favour of any form of freedom. Instead, they find a place where they can study the project and the place to understand how it works, modify and add elements to it, disseminate it to other users, and make any use of it that they wish.

> At the BIB, we invent the model in which we would like to operate every day. That is a manufacturing job. I don't think we want to say we are the model. We are our own model because we are experimenting. I think we can be against the model without claiming to be the model. (Source: lightning conference 'Organize the Liberty?').

References

Baichtal, J. 2011. *Hack This: 24 Incredible Hackerspace Projects from the DIY Movement*. Indianapolis, IN: New Riders.

Chandler, A. 1996. The changing definition and image of hackers in popular discourse. *International Journal of the Sociology of Law*, 2(24): 229–251.

Coleman, G. 2016. *Anonymous: Hacker, activiste, faussaire, mouchard, lanceur d'alerte*. Montreal: Lux Editeur.

Dagiral, É. 2008. Pirates, hackers, hacktivistes: Déplacements et dilution de la frontière électronique. *Critique*, 6: 480–495.

Giffard, A. 2007. (Sur) Un Manifeste Hacker. *Cahier Critique de Poésie*, 2(14).

Gunkel, D. J. 2001. *Hacking Cyberspace*. Boulder, CO: Perseus.

Hafner, K. & Markoff, J. 1995. *Cyberpunk: Outlaws and Hackers on the Computer Frontier, Revised*. New York: Simon and Schuster.

Halbert, D. 1997. Discourses of danger and the computer hacker. *The Information Society*, 13(4): 361–374.

Hannemyr, G. 1999. Technology and pleasure: Considering hacking constructive. *First Monday*, 4(2).

Hollinger, R. C. & Lanza-Kaduce, L. 1988. The process of criminalization: The case of computer crime laws. *Criminology*, 26(1): 101–126.

Lallement, M. 2015. *L'Âge du Faire. Hacking, travail, anarchie*. Paris: Le Seuil.

Levy, S. 1984. *Hackers: Heroes of the Computer Revolution*. Garden City, NY: Anchor Press/Doubleday.

Lofland, J. 1974. Styles of reporting qualitative field research. *The American Sociologist*, 9(3): 101–111.

Mbodj-Pouye, A. 2008. Pages choisies. Ethnographie du cahier personnel d'un agriculteur malien. *Sociologie et Sociétés*, 40(2): 87–108.

Millar, S. 2001. For Hackers, Read Political Heroes of Cyberspace! *The Guardian* (8 March, p. 4).

Moilanen, J. 2012. Emerging hackerspaces–peer-production generation. In *IFIP International Conference on Open Source Systems* (pp. 94–111). Berlin, Heidelberg: Springer.

Nissenbaum, H. 2004. Hackers and the contested ontology of cyberspace. *New Media & Society*, 6(2): 195–217.

Pekka, H. 2001. *L'Éthique hacker et l'esprit de l'ère de l'information*. Paris: Exils.

Raymond, E. S. (ed.). 1996. *The New Hacker's Dictionary*. Cambridge, MA: MIT Press.

Starr, A. 2000. *Naming the Enemy: Anti-corporate Social Movements Confront Globalization*. London: Zed Books.

Taylor, P. A. 1998. Hackers: cyberpunks or microserfs? *Information Communication & Society*, 1(4), 401–419.

1999. *Hackers: Crime and the Digital Sublime*. Abingdon: Taylor & Francis.

2005. From hackers to hacktivists: Speed bumps on the global superhighway? *New Media & Society*, 7(5): 625–646.

Van Maanen, J. 1979. The fact of fiction in organizational ethnography. *Administrative Science Quarterly*, 24(4): 539–550.

2011. Ethnography as work: Some rules of engagement. *Journal of Management Studies*, 48(1): 218–234.

Wacquant, L. 2005. Carnal connections: On embodiment, apprenticeship, and membership. *Qualitative Sociology*, 28(4): 445–474.

Wark, M. 2006. Un Manifeste Hacker: a Hacker Manifesto Francophone Dans un Design de Gallien Guibert. Paris: Criticalsecret.

4 | Experiencing Making

Silence, Atmosphere and Togetherness in Makerspaces

FRANÇOIS-XAVIER DE VAUJANY AND
JEREMY AROLES

Introduction: Welcome to the New World of Makers

Since the late 1990s, the maker movement has been gaining in popularity and has progressively emerged as a salient aspect of urban environments in many countries. Makerspaces are Do-It-Yourself (DIY)- and Do-It-Together (DIT)-orientated communities and spaces that rely on a principle of mutual help (i.e. *quid pro quo*). In a makerspace, people share a common place and a few tools, and help each other in different ways. Makers can be entrepreneurs, employees or just occasional DIY enthusiasts. These spaces, which have been blossoming since the early 2000s (Anderson 2009; de Vaujany, Dandoy, Grandazzi & Faure 2019; Hatch 2014; Lallement 2015), are expected to favour both horizontal (i.e. between those working in that place) and open forms of collaboration (i.e. beyond the immediate involvement in an open space). New buzzwords, such as DIY, DIT, maker movement, hackerspaces, open-source communities, fab labs, neo-craftsmanship and so on, are increasingly inscribed in our collective imagery of the future of work and collaboration. In the context of the rise of the sharing economy, work in general is depicted as more and more collaborative (Aroles, Mitev & de Vaujany 2019; Bouncken and Reuschl 2018; Sundararajan 2017). Interestingly, these 'new' work-related spaces are also expected to bear some political resonance; this can involve co-producing a commons of skills and knowledge or fostering a broader process of commonalisation for their community and beyond (see Lallement 2015; de Vaujany and Aroles 2019). It is worth noting, though, that this dimension is probably more present in fab labs and third-places than in makerspaces.

In order to make sense of the role played by makerspaces in the contemporary landscape of work and collaboration, we propose the concept of New Collaborative Experiences (NCE), which we define as *new modes of feeling and expressing the self and the world in a context that requires collective production and coordination.* We will explore these NCEs through two ethnographic accounts. The first concerns an artistic makerspace located in France, and the second a makerspace in a large university in the United States. Our analysis of NCE will revolve around three concepts, namely silence, atmosphere(s) and togetherness. Overall, this chapter argues that makerspaces can foster new 'forms of doing' but most of all, new experiences of the world, in which our sensibility is visibly extended to ourselves and others, opening up, we contend, possibilities both promising and frightening.

Theoretical Perspective: A Sensible Ontology of the Experience of Doing

Experience and Reversibility

Merleau-Ponty's work, concerned primarily with the notions of body, corporeity and embodiment (Dale 2005; Küpers 2014), has received growing attention in the field of organisation studies (see for instance Küpers 2014; de Vaujany, Aroles & Laniray 2019; Willems 2018; Yakhlef 2010). His phenomenology questions the obviousness of perceptions and the instantaneity of our experiences in order to show the essential mediation of embodiment, flesh and inter-corporeity under-lying ideas of naturality[1] and taken-for-grantedness. The body is understood as the condition of our experience to the world and its continuity. For Merleau-Ponty (1945, 1948, 1960, 1964), we live in and through a phenomenological body in the sense that we are a continuous flow of sensations and perceptions for ourselves. In turn, we feel mainly in the past: we do not know, we do not perceive, but we mainly 're-cognize' and 're-perceive' forms, shapes, structures, gestures and practices that we have 'already' felt (Merleau-Ponty 1945, 1960). Furthermore, according to Merleau-Ponty (1964, p. 162):

---

[1] For Merleau-Ponty (1960, 2010), nature is not a virgin world expecting human transformation and appropriation. Nature is the legitimation and legitimate flow of our life, what we do not even 'see' but that which is at the heart of our visible life.

there is an experience of the visible thing as pre-existing my vision, but this experience is not a fusion, a coincidence: because my eyes which see, my hands which touch, can also be seen and touched, because, therefore, in that sense they see and touch the visible, the tangible from within, because our flesh covers and even envelops all the visible and tangible things that nonetheless surround it, the world and I are within one another, and from the perciperer to the percipi, there is no anteriority, there is simultaneity and even delay.

This movement is neither purely internal nor external (these are categories that Merleau-Ponty invites us to overcome); it is fully reversible. Drawing from the Husserlian example of the two hands that touch each other, Merleau-Ponty (1960) stresses the fact that these two hands are constitutive of a feeling of both touched and touching or the experience of feeling and felt. In other words, while we think we are on one side or the other (touched or touching), we actually are phenomenologically always in the middle (i.e. in what is expressed). This phenomenon is at the heart of many reversibilities and chiasms (e.g. inside/outside, others/I, ego/alter ego, past/present, etc.). We feel ourselves as individuals only through an experience of alterity: the community is the place and mode of expression of these reversible 'I', 'You' and 'We'. Bodily movements, encounters and everyday activities lie at the heart of reversible experiences. The content of expression is also essential. Expression is more than the emergence of meaning (something 'happens'); it is also and primarily a temporality. This happening was, is or will be meaningful (an embodied perception can become or re-become visible and perceptible later). From a phenomenological perspective, in order to apprehend an expression or a mode of expression, one ultimately needs to be immersed in it, share it and live it.

For Merleau-Ponty (1945, 1948, 1964), visibilities and invisibilities are key dimensions of our everyday activities and the chiasms of these activities. In order to perceive and act, we need certain aspects of our life to be invisible, as we cannot simultaneously face the innumerable sensations conveyed through our embodied experience of the world. According to Merleau-Ponty (1964), visibilities and invisibilities are thus not the opposite of each other; invisibilities are the scaffolding of visibilities and also often what could extend them. Time, which is seen by Merleau-Ponty (2010) as the epitome of an institution, is the process through which visibilities and invisibilities can be balanced out. In order to write, one needs to put aside both nostalgia (a disturbing past) and anxiety (an impeding future) without remaining trapped in the present. These temporal and sensorial invisibilities will then reinforce the visibility of one's activities for oneself. Occasionally, one will draw on extra-temporal structures to make an activity possible. It makes it possible to make visible for oneself (and others) what truly matters. Past, future and present can thus be made invisible or senseless or they can resonate with one another (the past being already present in the felt future in the present, or the anticipation of a future being already felt in what appears as the past felt in the present). The same relation connects the concepts of continuity and discontinuity (Merleau-Ponty 1964), and activity and passivity (Merleau-Ponty 2010); far from being oppositional, they interpenetrate each other.

From Expression to Institution

How do we 'order' and organise continuities and discontinuities, visibilities and invisibilities, and activities and passivities, in our lives? In one of his key lectures at the Collège de France, Merleau-Ponty (2010) returns to the notion of institution. He specifies that 'by institution, we were intending those events in an experience which endow the experience with durable dimensions, in relation to which a whole series of other experiences will make sense, will form a thinkable sequel or a history – or again the events which deposit a sense in me, not just something as surviving or a residue, but as the call to follow, the demand of a future' (foreword of Lefort 2010, in Merleau-Ponty 2010, p. ix).[2] An institution is thus something happening steadily behind a set of events, a happening in the happenings. It is neither an archetypal or modal duration nor the repeated aspects of all events; it is what happens in the multiplicity of what happen(ed)(s).

The link is also clear with the three classical Merleau-Pontian chiasms mentioned, namely visibility–invisibility, continuity–discontinuity and activity–passivity. These three chiasms are not the opposite of each other in our everyday activities or institutions. Passivity–activity chiasms pervade most 'happenings' and institutions.

---

[2] We see some similarities to Ricoeur's (1985) work on narratives and time. Interestingly though, Ricoeur barely quotes Merleau-Ponty (except on pages 41, 57, 415 and 416).

Merleau-Ponty (2010) draws an interesting parallel between this chiasm and the action of sleeping. One does not 'decide' to sleep: one goes to sleep and tries to meet the phenomenon. Once 'in' (i.e. asleep), sleeping is not the opposite of activity. Once asleep, we dream and can sometimes remember our dreams. At some point, I will also wake up without 'deciding' to do so.[3] As such, inside sleep, a kind of activity different from the daily ones emerges, one that enables and makes even more visible the activities of the day. Passivity is just the other face of activity. Clearly, the institutional layer of our lives lies on the side of passivity (as defined here). Institutions make it possible to 'act'; they lie at the heart of what happens and what can happen, in the flow of our everyday activities. An institution is thus a trans-temporal regime of activities–passivities, continuities–discontinuities and visibilities–invisibilities.

Three Sensible Concepts in Merleau-Ponty's Writings: Silence, Atmosphere and Togetherness/Solidarity

Silence and Silencing

Various authors have highlighted the surprising lack of research on the notion of silence in management and organisation studies (see for instance Bigo 2018; Blackman and Sadler-Smith 2009). A significant proportion of the existing literature has investigated the coercive dimension of silence (i.e. 'being silenced') (see Brown and Coupland 2005 or Costas and Grey 2014). Closer to our concerns are researchers who have argued that being silent or silenced in organisational settings is not only a power-invested process, but is linked to various organisa-tional practices (Brinsfield 2014; Grint 2010) and forms of expression in organisational debates (Kirrane, O'Shea, Buckley, Grazi & Prout 2017) and is ultimately a meaningful phenomenon pregnant with possibilities (Bigo 2018; Fleming 2013; de Vaujany & Aroles 2019). This chapter is concerned with the ways in which silence is incorpor-ated into new work practices, with regards to how these are actualised and embodied through everyday practice.

We engage here with the notion of silence through Merleau-Ponty's (1945, 1964, 2010) writings. For Merleau-Ponty (1945, 2010), silence

---

[3] I can delegate this task to an alarm clock. But even if I set it up myself, phenomenologically, in my present, it will not be a decision I made.

is not a passivity, a discontinuity or an invisibility. Silence requires numerous efforts to be maintained and is also the envelope of miscellaneous noisy acts that take place in the phenomenological body and through the embodied practices of workers. For Merleau-Ponty, silence is 'not the mere absence of sound or simply an opposite to language', but 'its other side' that makes meaningful expression possible (Mazis 2016, p. xiii). It constitutes both a rhythm of work and a temporal orientation for collective work. Through Merleau-Ponty's work, we see 'silencing' as a major event in Merleau-Ponty's (2010) sense, a happening inside happenings, something underlying, ordering and giving directions to what 'happens' in collective work activities. Merleau-Ponty's work offers a fascinating angle through which to explore the role played by silence in the context of the embodied practices of workers engaged in new work configurations.

Atmosphere

In his book *Phenomenology of Perception*, Merleau-Ponty (1945, p. 196) draws on the notion of atmosphere in order to analyse sexuality, stating that 'sexuality is neither transcended in human life, nor featured in its centre by unconscious representations. It is constantly present as an atmosphere'. An atmosphere is then simply something that needs to be visibly invisible or sensibly insensible. According to Strati (2009, p. 239), 'Organizations have their own specific materiality made of the corporeality of persons and artefacts, but which also comprises something impalpable and invisible that can be emblematically denoted as "the atmosphere of the organization" – as suggested by commonplace expressions such as "there's something in the air", "a heavy atmosphere", "there's an ill wind blowing", "see which way the wind blows" or "let in some fresh air". The notion of atmosphere is a way to shed light on the unbounded temporal and spatial nature of *experiencing*. Böhme (1993, p. 119) argues that '[a]tmospheres are always spatially without borders, disseminated and yet without place that is, not localizable. They are affective powers of feeling, spatial bearers of moods'. In this way, the notion of atmosphere is related to all organisational phenomena; 'Organization invariably is an atmospheric phenomenon. It takes shape as a swirl of affect, constructed from constellations of objects, stories, technologies, texts, human bodies and their affective capacities' (Beyes 2016, p. 115).

As Pallasmaa (2014) has pointed out, atmosphere is deeply linked to the existent properties of a space as well as its human perception. When we remember that space is a kind of experience, our perception of it becomes key; 'A space or a place is a kind of a diffusely felt multi-sensory image, an experiential "creature", a singular experience …' (Pallasmaa 2014, p. 235). Objects, gestures and space are constitutive of an atmosphere, as are quasi-things and quasi-materiality, such as smells, colours, textures and ephemeral artefacts contained in the embodied memory and activities that make up the 'inside' of a place (Griffero 2017). Thus, bodies, objects and places are all expected to create an atmosphere, which is often described in the literature as a relational and processual concept (Michels 2015).

Management and Organisation Studies (MOS) researchers have been invited 'to examine how affective atmospheres are created and how the affective states are transmitted in the organization' (Borch 2009, p. 224). According to Küpers (2002, p. 32), 'the atmosphere within organising is primarily not what people think about it, but what they live through with their 'operative intentionality (Merleau-Ponty 1963, p. xviii)'. In this respect, the notion of atmosphere is related to how one feels or rather experiences a particular milieu; in other words, as argued by Beyes (2016, p. 116), 'it constitutes a modus operandi and way of seeing or apprehending'.

Togetherness and Solidarity

The third aspect that we wish to explore occupies a significant position in the work of both the early and late Merleau-Ponty. For Merleau-Ponty (1945), we are all involved in inter-corporeity. Just like anyone else, we have our own body, we experience processes of embodiment and we feel the movements of others at our own individual scale through a 'common' of sensibilities, schemes and emotions that constitute our experience of the world. We do not need to think about this enmeshment of inter-corporeity when we walk on the street, drive our car, have a discussion with a friend or simply share a space with others. Beyond conventions, this pre-reflexivity is highly relational, not necessarily normative or highly incorporated.

From this, Merleau-Ponty (1945, 1964) also stresses the importance of felt solidarities (see Mazis 2016). This is a key aspect of his concluding words at the end of *Phénoménologie de la Perception* when he returns to the literary work of Saint-Exupéry and his well-known volume, *Pilotes de guerre* (*Flight to Arras*). In a famous episode, namely the Arras episode, Saint-Exupéry was very close to dying. German soldiers were bombarding his plane as well as those of fellow pilots. The fight was intense. In this context of high fraternity, each member of the team strongly felt the other members as well as the interdependency with and importance of their gestures. In the end, it was not so much about saving one's life; it was really about findings ways of building a common future. An important question in this context is how to cultivate this sense of solidarity in our world. If we translate these concerns to the new world of work, the question becomes how to cultivate, in our societies, the right passivities. Makerspaces could, we argue, offer interesting and insightful answers to this issue. We could first act next to each other, looking in the same direction – which opens the door to true solidarity.

Research Method: An Ethnographical Account of Two Makerspaces

Introducing Our Empirical Sites

To explore NCEs, we chose two different sites: an artistic maker-space (AMS) and an educational makerspace (EMS). AMS opened in 2005 in a major French city, in a former factory. It was established following a riot in front of an artistic squat. Following growing pressure from the local residents, the mayor decided to take measures to clean up the area by experimenting with 'new places' subsidised by the city. AMS accepts both professional and non-professional artists and provides them with several floors to practise their art. The ground floor is devoted to fashion designers, actors and co-workers. The second floor is open to painters and sculptors. The third floor is reserved for painters and photographers and hosts a silver jewellery workshop. Finally, the fourth floor is dedicated to novelists.

EMS is located in a major university in the United States. On its website, EMS is presented as a pioneering space aiming to support and encourage hands-on projects. The space is open to all (e.g. students, staff and faculty). It relies on and fosters new sorts of interdisciplinary teamwork using cutting-edge tools that allow rapid prototyping and digitally driven production. It includes large areas for making and provides training on how to use the tools provided in this space.

Ethnographic Styles of Investigation

Our research started with a series of visits and short stays in eighty-seven collaborative spaces (sixty-eight visits in co-working spaces and nineteen in makerspaces, hackerspaces and fab labs) located in ten different countries (Australia, France, Germany, Greece, Israel, Japan, Portugal Singapore, Spain and the United Kingdom). Hackerspaces are very close to makerspaces; one difference (albeit not systematic) is the political orientation of hackerspaces. Hackers follow a particular ethics (e.g. open knowledge) and as such, hacker-spaces can host particularly engaged activists and activities.[4] Fab labs are part of a global network and operate under The Fab Charter. Fab labs can be seen as makerspaces that rely on a logic of open knowledge, which involves continuously documenting creative and productive processes for the broader community. Finally, co-working spaces, which are geared towards entrepreneurs, innovators, project managers, freelancers and employees, consist of shared spaces focused on mutual help and community building (see Garrett, Spreitzer & Bacevice 2017). These visits provided the opportunity to meet freelancers, entrepreneurs and project managers, to develop our understanding of new work practices (i.e. collaborative entrepreneurship, mobility, freelancing, telework, etc.) and to experience different modalities of collaborative work (as a growing phenomenon). They were instrumental in providing a contextual understanding of the ways in which collaborative workspaces operate. They also allowed us to appreciate some of the key differences between makerspaces and other types of collaborative spaces. In addition, developing a basic understanding of the logic of makerspaces (through visits and on-site discussions) made the start of our ethnographic research smoother.

These visits were followed by ethnographic research conducted in AMS in 2017. The ethnographic research at EMS (which is still in progress) started in early September 2019. By adopting an

---

[4] This stance has been questioned by recent research highlighting the prevalence of the 'community-orientation' of the hacker movement over its political engagement (see Davies 2017).

ethnographic style of investigation, one can explore the complex, messy and contested 'realities' of organisations (Law 2004) and thus produce richer accounts of organisational realities. This part of the research was an opportunity to explore further some of the ideas and themes that emerged through our visits to collaborative spaces, notably the role of silence, atmosphere and togetherness. All the empirical data discussed in this chapter come from the ethnographic research conducted in AMS and EMS.

The data collected during the ethnographic inquiry mainly consist of observations (for AMS and EMS), semi-structured interviews (for AMS) as well as numerous conversations (both for AMS and EMS). In AMS, most of the phases of observation took place on the ground floor. The first author of this chapter was seated in the co-working area, facing the (only) entry point into AMS. This was an opportunity to see all the people coming in and out, how people negotiated their entry and also to socialise. There were also several opportunities to move to the upper floors for coffee, lunch or other breaks. Observations amounted to nine half days within the makerspace, supplemented by three half days of observation of the vicinity of AMS (cafés, neighbourhood associations, etc.). The first author of this chapter took notes of what happened around him and ordered his notes at the end of each day. Seven semi-structured interviews have complemented the phases of observation conducted in AMS. With regards to the second ethnographic research, the first author has been spending three full days per week (from 9th September onwards[5]) in EMS. He was seated in the collaborative working area, from which he could have a panoramic view of the space and the activities taking place around him. He also took part in several events organised or hosted by the makerspace, in particular training sessions organised in the lab area or more general conferences. This was an opportunity to converse with members of this space. Finally, in both cases, photographs, archives and online resources have been used in the early stages of the research in order to develop a better understanding of some of the key issues connected to makerspaces and new collaborative spaces in general.

---

[5] Observations have been interrupted in March 2020 by the coronavirus crisis.

Happenings at AMS

Contextualising Noises and Silence at AMS

Artistic squats are both a model and a counter-model for AMS, a
source of inspiration about what should (and should not) be done.
Prior to setting up AMS, its founder spent a considerable amount of
time observing artistic squats. The majority of AMS members, who are
visual artists, have experienced squats. With this in mind, the founder
of AMS explained that AMS is designed in such a way that it physically
constrains and seeks to avoid 'squat practices': '*Visual artists are
natural squatters. Every bit of space that can be squatted will be
squatted. We have to avoid doors. We need large plateaus*'. Yet AMS
reproduces the structure of squats, notably visible through the presence
of a doorman at the entrance of the place. The doorman is here to both
monitor who gets in and help visitors. One of the worst fears of the
doormen and the manager is to see the place become a squat again. As
a result, each resident has been issued a plastic member card that must
be left with the doorman when entering AMS. When AMS closes for
the day, there should be no card left on the doorman's desk (made
visible to everyone). Nobody is allowed to stay overnight at AMS.
Given that roughly 60 per cent of the residents are on benefits, there is
little doubt that, without this system, it would happen. On one occasion, we heard a phone conversation during which a member explained
that he did not know where he would spend the coming night.
Structurally, AMS is not nicely decorated like some fancy co-working
spaces, or even other makerspaces, we visited; there is no table foot-
ball, table tennis or lounge in AMS. While AMS is primarily geared
toward creative work, it also organises training in management skills
(e.g. sessions about business models, accounting).

Having experienced the culture of squats creates a particular relationship to the noise of the street and to noises alien to creative
activities in general. It produces a very specific phenomenological body
(Merleau-Ponty 1945), extremely sensitised to unusual noises. For
former squatters, much brouhaha coming from the street or brutal
noises within AMS would connote ideas of danger (either the police
violently storming the squat to evict its occupants or dealers fighting
for the territory of the squat and its market), perhaps reminiscent of
certain lived experiences. In that sense, loud noises can thus be

traumatic for some people 'inside'. The founder explained that '*any noise can be frightening. One day, the rumour had it that the place would be transformed into an art centre. They would be evicted. Most of these people are in precarious situations. More than ever, any unusual noise frightens them*'. Unusual noises can be seen as a disruption in the daily flow of activities that give directions and meaning to the work of the residents of AMS. This particular relation to noises is not only very informative of the historicity of the place and its occupants, but also of the conditions under which creation may happen at AMS.

Rhythms, Visibilities, Silence and Events at AMS

Silence was expected in the vast majority of the places we visited and AMS was no exception. For the managers of these various places, silence was a requirement for collective work. In an open or flexible space, phone calls, meetings and discussions need to be avoided, or confined to specific times and spaces. Maintaining silence was a way to optimise both time and space. If users follow these rules, then there is no need for individual offices or compartmentalisation, and therefore less room is required for the co-working space, the makerspace, the hackerspace or the fab lab to operate. Some spaces thus offered time periods without Wi-Fi to make it possible for people to disconnect electronically. Yoga, sophrology, mindfulness or Tai Chi classes were also often silent or quiet times (beyond the open space) available at several spaces we visited. Interestingly, silence was also presented as a service offered by the manager of AMS, an opportunity to disconnect; to be alone (yet surrounded) and to take time to focus on a project or even oneself.

On the workers' side, silence was described in our conversations as a way not to be disturbed by other people (almost acting like an invisible protection) while also feeling other members around (as opposed to feeling lonely at home[6]). Clearly, they wanted to feel alone together (Spinuzzi 2012) and silence was a paradoxical infrastructure that could materialise this possibility. Some people described silence as something

---

[6] Silence was then an opportunity for a 'felt solidarity' between entrepreneurs (Mazis 2016).

shared; one member said '*I can share a long conversation, but I can also simply share silences*', thus hinting at the peculiar expressivity of silence. Indeed, silence appeared as the locus of collective undertaking and invisible attempts and trials to produce artistic visibilities. In his book *Signes*, Merleau-Ponty (1960) observed (by means of a slow-motion picture) that Matisse would often move his hands without touching his painting, and that paintbrushes would often move in extremely quick virtual drawings before actually touching a canvas and drawing; only a part of the movement actually touched the canvas. Most artists in AMS were in the process of producing these invisibilities wrapped by silence. They sat in front of their piece without 'doing' something, feeling what has been or could be done, making gestures around their piece, or experimenting a gesture on a smaller piece, all this producing a fascinating silence wrapping all the invisible activities necessary for the production of visible activities (Merleau-Ponty 1964).

On some other occasions, silence was described as something boring or hard to cope with, especially when one receives great or very bad news to share, or simply feels bad. In this case, silence was perceived as disciplining the space of AMS and limiting possibilities (in the sense of constraining actions). We sometimes saw people leaving their work desk to go to the kitchen, around the coffee machine, or to the informal smoking area (i.e. in some liminal spaces) and spend time there just to have an opportunity to break the silence and start a discussion.

Altogether, this produces a continuous movement 'inside' AMS with people constantly 'in action'. Most of the expressivity of gestures and movements (Merleau-Ponty 1964) is thus about activity and creativity. The place is not expected to be a bubble for disconnection in the creative process or a context for entertainment and escape. Most breaks (e.g. for discussions) we attended took place outside the creative realm of AMS (e.g. in the kitchen, in the corridors, in the internal court, on the terrace or in front of the building). Clearly, these spaces play a role in the continuous flow of creativity and associated practice of learning that give direction to the actions of AMS. Furthermore, they can be seen as an extension of the embodied practices of workers, a necessary moment in time in order to make visible certain invisibilities and invisible other practices.

Silence as a Central Institution and a Meta-event: From Chiasm to Institution

Within AMS, we observed several key discontinuities in the continuous process of maintaining silence by co-workers, designers (on the ground floor) and painters (upstairs). For members, one key interruption is when people would enter or leave the space and simply say hello or goodbye. This was seen as a legitimate noisy practice in the open space. Surprisingly, giving or receiving a phone call was another. We thus often observed people answering phone calls, standing up, and leaving the space while walking in the direction of a liminal area (e.g. a phone booth, the stairs, the internal court, the street). A relaxed posture, eyes not staring at the screen of the laptop or a document, a particular body signal (a simple hello) were also other contexts of (often short) conversations with desk neighbours. These were only possible if the neighbour also sent signals of openness to a conversation. Other opportunities to break a silence included the introduction of a new-comer (with close interests, projects or skills), tours, visits or unex-pected events (e.g. a printer is not working and users require some help). But surprisingly, in places where mutual help, gifts and counter-gifts are expected to be strongly present, silence (as a social process) was quite continuous at AMS (and other collaborative spaces we observed) in the dominant time-spaces constituted by everyday activ-ities. In addition, collective events and liminal times and spaces were opportunities for intense and often rich conversations.

For painters or other makers at AMS, silence was less obvious since their activities and tools would create more noise than those of co-workers. That said, conversations were quite rare. While people might be interrupted by a goodbye or a hello, we noticed that people leaving took care not to interrupt or bother other painters during a key activity. We thus saw people hesitating and realising that it was not the right time to leave, quickly changing their trajectory to not create a sense of obligation to interact. Continuities and discontinuities in gestures and movements were thus tightly related to visibility–invisibility loops and their maintenance (Merleau-Ponty 1964). Advice and sharing of tools and materials could also be another reason to interrupt silence. This was notably the case when one needed a material that was missing (e.g. paint, brush or other tools) or noticed something wrong in the practice of a younger or less experienced painter in the place. Strangely (at least for the non-painters we are), we rarely saw (maybe a longer study would have made it visible) people complimenting each other or evaluating other people's work; we did hear compliments being made in the kitchen but nothing in the main room where the main creative activities occur. Finally, phone calls and collective events were also part of major interruptions of silence for makers.

Behind the shared silence of AMS, in the flow of an activity shared with other people, breaking silence could be a way to extend another continuity: feeling part of the 'becoming of society', getting a sense of 'togetherness' and community, and inscribing oneself in a flow of activities that overtakes one's own bubble. For instance, we witnessed a case that made the presence of silence as an institution more visible. A silkscreen printer, located on the ground floor, had been going through a tough period for several months. It had become almost impossible for him to sell his cards and posters. One day, three interns from the fashion workshop (on the same floor) came close to him to cut pieces of fabric. Suddenly, he stood up, moved towards the big printers and produced a set of posters. Will he sell them? Probably not. Will he learn or test something new through this process? Probably not. But this is obviously not what was at stake. What was at stake for him was to share a legitimate movement, engaging with others, sharing the rhythm of the place, accompanying the sequences of other people's work, constructing an affective relationship in the moment. It was an endogenous process, a co-construction, a shared feeling between the silkscreen printer and the three interns. It represented something they experienced together, or rather, the silkscreen printer experienced it as something that they shared together as the three interns were part of the engagement and pursued it.

Interestingly, we noticed that silence was at the heart of numerous opportunities for encounters and learning (work discontinuities), or contrariwise, strategies to avoid encounters (work continuities). This was particularly true for painters. Body postures, immobility and the position of trestles were sometimes meant to create lasting bubbles of silence. Some artists were thus involved in gestures far from the eyes they could meet or stare at (those of people coming close to them). This was a way to create some focus on gesture itself, being at the heart of reversibility (Merleau-Ponty 1945). In contrast, other artists would put their trestles close to entry points or liminal spaces, be much more mobile and open to cross other people's gaze. For instance, we observed a writer setting up an improvised office in the kitchen and a draftsman locating his trestle in the painters' area. These two people deliberately looked for a provisional openness in their work process, probably for both emotional and work-related reasons. They were looking for discussions, encounters and advice. People involved in such spatial openness were sometimes stuck in critical processes and problems relating to their paintings and simply looking for solutions, or were close to the end of their piece and wanted to share an emotion which could be a source of learning for other people and for themselves.

Most people at AMS worked on their craft and learned their art beyond the time-space of AMS. These discontinuities were paradoxically a way to extend and continue the creative and learning process, enriching it with new times, new inspirations, new associations and new contexts. Continuities and discontinuities could also be seen in a more chiasmic way for those mainly working outside (e.g. in a workshop or in their apartment) and coming episodically to AMS. For them, coming to AMS was a way to break the silence that they may already be facing in their apartments or workshops. This was the case for some professional artists, but also for retired women (fondly called 'the grannies' by other residents) or for 'slashers' involved in other artistic activities than their art in order to survive. For many of them, AMS was a landmark and a 'centre'. For one person we met, we even wondered whether art was not simply a pretext to break loneliness and to create one-off conversations. He explained, '*I come here almost every day. I'm part of the landscape. I like to talk to people here*'. Similarly, some people moved from one floor (and universe) to another in order to have a chat with other people. The discontinuous noise of episodic conversations was thus the heart of a sociality, the opposite of the emptiness of their life outside, which was often made of continuous silence at home. At some point, we realised that we no longer noticed or cared about these whispered conversations, this discontinuous music with its melodies, which had become part of our silence.

Atmosphere and Solidarities: When Making Is also a Passivity

In contrast to AMS, which was very much a stand-alone organisation, EMS is part of a larger organisation that we will call here the Big

University (BU). BU is a private university present in almost all fields of knowledge and with a leading status. EMS came to life in 2016 with the purpose of integrating into the same physical space various projects as well as other spaces that were on different parts of the campus. This was seen as a way of fostering synergies and collaborations across different specialisms. EMS comprises many different areas and activities, including notably a foyer ('social' space for lunch and informal gatherings), a large room for various events (e.g. talks, seminars, panel discussions), a space used for collaboration (e.g. developing and working directly on independent and collaborative projects), an electronics area, a 3D printing area (with a total of twenty-seven 3D printers in use) as well as a laser cutting area.

Our ethnography of EMS has also been an opportunity to cover a broader territory: that of a large American university spawning across many different campuses that are scattered throughout the city. Beyond its makerspace, it comprises numerous other labs, incubators and places devoted to both research and making. EMS is clearly today a leading makerspace; it is a place visited by many institutions that are interested in developing their own makerspace and are looking for ideas (on several occasions, we heard discussion about EMS during our visits and stays in other collaborative spaces in many different countries). It is clear that EMS is fully merged with the pedagogy of both the school and the department. As such, projects, teaching and events often take place here. The welcoming process as well as the main rules regarding the use of this space are fairly straightforward. In a nutshell, these rules concern access (i.e. who is allowed to access the facilities) and include a safety dimension (this takes the form of a mandatory safety orientation), which is related to how to use basic tools as well as 3D printers. Importantly, they also provide a framework for the many internal events that take place on its premises. As such, the place is mostly used for classwork, hobbies, or 'just for fun'.

During an early visit in 2017 (in the context of a study-trip), we were struck by the interface between EMS and the surroundings and the city in general. The makerspace is surrounded by windows that oversee the neighbouring area; it is a highly transparent space. Interestingly, the same applies inside. The collaborative workspace is separated from the liminal space by a window. The main area consists of a large and open space with mainly mobile furniture and no walls. We regularly felt the relationship between making and showing. Both for the institution and the individual here, the place is a way to perform and materialise skills, knowledge and values, to make them visible for participants as well as spectators. During our research, we were surprised by the number of people who would come to EMS without actually making use of the place. In fact, many people would not interact with any of the tools provided by the space or engage in any productive parts of the place during their stay. What were they doing then in EMS? What were they finding and feeling? How were they experiencing this space? At some point, it became obvious. For some, it was just a place like any other in the city. But for many, it was an atmosphere! A vague potentiality for action, which could be their potentiality for action tomorrow. A place with which they could intimately connect; the noises (rather scarce in the morning), the smell, the gestures, the people encountered, etc. This was their place. As such, they would not necessarily come to EMS to engage in discussions or looking for fortuitous encounters – they would come for something that is somehow more essential, more vital. We rarely saw people talking together beyond the bubble of the group or the project in which they seemed to be involved.

Most of all, making in EMS is absolutely everywhere. Explanations are given through diagrams, figures and prototypes. The idea is to experiment, test and try new things. Obviously, this has become part of the aesthetic of the place. Traces of cutters, pens, pencils, furniture moved around, smell of tools used, and laughter after an attempt at doing something are encountered everywhere and at any time. They are part of the fabric of the place. This made us realise that most of the time, as we walk around, we are in a finalised and quite clean world – a world that is very distant from the richness and multifaceted nature of the acts of making and creating. The quasi-objects of our atmospheres are stable and finite. *What defines the atmosphere here and the broader NCE is experimenting, letting matter flow.* Of course, this is full of possible tensions and paradoxes. The institution is always present to remind one of the rules (e.g. do not eat, put tools in their correct place, etc.) and in particular the safety instructions (via recorded messages).

While 'making' is everywhere, 'non-making' is also a key part of the atmosphere of the place. We were surprised by the number of people, in particular in late afternoons, joining the makerspace to study individually, organise a group meeting, have a loud chat or just cross the space. EMS is clearly a friendly place, a bubble in the middle of a BU where it might occasionally be difficult for students to find spaces in which they can focus on their studies. Beyond that, waiting appears to be an important component of the process of making. 3D printers are actually very slow. One needs to wait sometimes for hours in front of the machine in order to get their finished product. Talking is a way to avoid boredom but also to socialise. In front of other machines (such as laser cutters), most members of a group would not be active. All these social, waiting, intermediary times in EMS appeared as very important in the process of making and its temporalities. These non-making times in the makerspaces (spent waiting for a machine to finish, thinking about a new project or dealing with a problem) allowed reflexivity, sharing, conceptualisation, but also the fun, humour and fantasy required for the making process. In short, from a phenomenological perspective, we were struck by how both making and non-making activities were involved in a chiasmatic relationship and, in fact, were two faces of the atmosphere at EMS.

Let us walk a little bit outside, in the area around EMS. As part of a highly gentrified area, the campus of which EMS is part is much more diverse than most other parts of this area. Poverty and homelessness are somehow much more visible, even from the windows of the maker-space. The place is very interesting to contrast with another place belonging to BU: its incubator, which we call BI. If the windows of EMS are full of projects, diversity statements, values, grassroot projects, making-orientated slogans and examples, the windows of BI are much more about successful entrepreneurial projects and money-raising activities (e.g. X has raised ten million dollars in funding for such or such project). Interestingly, the windows are not really transparent and it is not possible to see the internal activities of BI from the outside. This contributes to both creating and cultivating a very different aesthetic and atmosphere. If the atmosphere of EMS, as we have argued, largely spills over to the university and the neighbouring area, BI constitutes a more delimited and confidential time-space (one that cannot be accessed externally).

During his stay there, the first author of this chapter has had the opportunity to feel something important related to the atmosphere of the place, namely light. As the place is open to the inside and the outside, it is covered by windows. For several days, he sat next to the 3D printers, facing the large windows of EMS. At the beginning, he would pay attention to what was happening outside. But quickly, all this just became just light. The place around and the people were not visible anymore. There was no longer something 'going on' in this area, it had just become a light, a natural light that kept connecting him to the rhythms and fluctuations of the outside world. Interestingly, he realised that when he would work more inside the place (in the collaborative space area), he would not see the light of the day. In contrast, he was, somehow paradoxically, more exposed to the atmosphere of the place itself. Whereas he could also feel the smell and the noises when he was seated in front of the window, actually, he did not really pay attention. His orientation, gestures, and body followed, almost naturally, the external light.

Finally, he had the opportunity to go one step further in the exploration of the atmosphere of the place one evening. He was walking outside and it was already dark (he was coming back from the library and on his way home). He decided to take a seat for a couple of minutes outside EMS. He could feel the light of the place spreading outside, illuminating part of the area, melting with it. Whereas the external area was just a light when he was seated inside, the internal light coming outside was obviously part of the atmosphere of EMS, which did not stop at the 'skin' and borders of the place. EMS was obviously part of the broader atmosphere of the public space in front of it.

Conclusion: At the Heart of the Experience of the New World of Work, NCE?

More than ever, making is showing and showing is making. Makerspaces are part of a broader movement, also present in digitalisation (de Vaujany and Vaast 2016), which makes our societies rely more and more on both materialisation and performative processes. Digitality creates a world made of printing, logistics, new forms of currency and values. We contend that the NCEs we explored in this chapter are moving towards this direction. Collaboration, DIY and DIT, which lie at the heart of makerspaces, as well as many other practices that are broadly related to New Ways of Working, rely on numerous processes of materialisation and performativity based on lights, noises, silences, evolving atmospheres, narratives, particular gestures and new temporalities. Quite clearly, this presents some positive aspects: people are more and more incited to collaborate, and feel that what they do contributes to communities and as such, resonates more broadly with society. Yet, there is also a frightening dimension to these processes that we should not overlook. NCEs, which emerge as atmospheric, unbounded and often continuously 'cool', are powerful control practices and devices that become at some point very difficult to interrogate – particularly from within.

References

Anderson, C. 2009. *Makers: The New Industrial Revolution.* New York: Crown Business.

Aroles, J., Mitev, N. & de Vaujany, F. X. 2019. Mapping themes in the study of new work practices. *New Technology, Work and Employment,* 34 (3): 285–299.

Beyes, T. 2016. Art, Aesthetics and Organization. In B. Czarniawska (ed.) *A Research Agenda for Management and Organization Studies.* Cheltenham: Edward Elgar Publishing Limited, 115–125.

Bigo, V. 2018. On silence, creativity and ethics in organization studies. *Organization Studies,* 39(1): 121–133.

Blackman, D. & Sadler-Smith, E. 2009. The silent and the silenced in organizational knowing and learning. *Management Learning,* 40(5): 569–585.

Borch, C. 2009. Organizational atmospheres: Foam, affect and architecture. *Organization,* 17(2): 223–241.

Bouncken, R. B. & Reusch, A. J. 2018. Coworking-spaces: How a phenomenon of the sharing economy builds a novel trend for the workplace and for entrepreneurship. *Review of Managerial Science,* 12(1): 317–334.

Böhme, G. 1993. Atmosphere as the fundamental concept of a new aesthetics. *Thesis Eleven,* 36(1): 113–126.

Brinsfield, C. 2014. Employee Voice and Silence In Organizational Behaviour. In A. Wilkinson, J. Donaghey, T. Dundon and R. B. Freeman (eds.) *Handbook of Research on Employee Voice.* Cheltenham: Edward Elgar, 114–131.

Brown, A. D. & Coupland, C. 2005. Sounds of silence: Graduate trainees, hegemony and resistance. *Organization Studies,* 26(7): 1049–1069.

Costas, J. & Grey, C. 2014. Bringing secrecy into the open: Towards a theorization of the social processes of organizational secrecy. *Organization Studies,* 35(10): 1423–1447.

Dale, K. 2005. Building a social materiality: Spatial and embodied politics in organizational control. *Organization,* 12(5): 649–678.

Davies, S. R. 2017. Characterizing hacking: Mundane engagement in US hacker and makerspaces. *Science, Technology, & Human Values,* 43(2): 171–197.

De Vaujany, F. X. & Aroles, J. 2019. Nothing happened, something happened: Silence in a makerspace. *Management Learning*, 50(2): 208–225.

De Vaujany, F. X. & Vaast, E. 2016. Matters of visuality in legitimation practices: Dual iconographies in a meeting room. *Organization*, 23(5): 763–790.

De Vaujany, F. X., Aroles, J. & Laniray, P. 2019. Towards a political philosophy of management: Performativity & visibility in management practices. *Philosophy of Management*, 18(2): 117-129.

De Vaujany, F. X., Dandoy, A., Grandazzi, A. & Faure, S. 2019. Experiencing a new place as an atmosphere: A focus on tours of collaborative spaces. *Scandinavian Journal of Management*, 35(2): 101030.

Fleming, P. 2013. Common as silence. *Ephemera*, 13(3): 627–640.

Garrett, L. E., Spreitzer, G. M. & Bacevice, P. A. 2017. Co-constructing a sense of community at work: The emergence of community in coworking spaces. *Organization Studies*, 38(6): 821–842.

Griffero, T. 2017. *Quasi-things: The Paradigm of Atmospheres*. Albany, NY: State University of New York Press.

Grint, K. 2010. The sacred in leadership: Separation, sacrifice and silence. *Organization Studies*, 31(1): 89–107.

Hatch, M. 2014. *The Maker Movement Manifesto*. New York: McGraw-Hill Education.

Kirrane, M., O'Shea, D., Buckley, F., Grazi, A. & Prout, J. 2017. Investigating the role of discrete emotions in silence versus speaking up. *Journal of Occupational and Organizational Psychology*, 90(3): 354–378.

Küpers, W. 2002. Phenomenology of aesthetic organising: Ways towards aesthetically responsive organizations. *Consumption, Markets and Culture*, 5(1): 21–46.

2014. *Phenomenology of the Embodied Organization: The Contribution of Merleau-Ponty for Organizational Studies and Practice*. New York: Springer.

Lallement, M. 2015. *L'âge du faire*. Paris: Editions du Seuil.

Law, J. 2004. *After Method: Mess in Social Sciences Research*. London: Routledge.

Lefort, C. 2010. Foreword. In: *Institution and Passivity. Course Notes from the Collège de France (1954–1955)*. Evanston: Northwestern University Press.

Mazis, G. A. 2016. *Merleau-Ponty and the Face of the World: Silence, Ethics, Imagination, and Poetic Ontology*. New York: SUNY Press.

Merleau-Ponty, M. 1945, 2013. *Phénoménologie de la perception*. Paris: Gallimard.

1948. *Sens et non-sens*. Paris: Nagel.

1960. *Signes*. Paris: Gallimard.

1964. *Le visible et l'invisible: suivi de notes de travail*. Paris: Gallimard.

2010. *Institution and Passivity. Course Notes from the Collège de France (1954–1955)*. Evanston: Northwestern University Press.

Michels, C. 2015. Researching affective atmospheres. *Geographica Helvetica*, 70(4): 255–263.

Pallasmaa, J. 2014. Space, place and atmosphere. Emotion and peripherical perception in architectural experience. *Lebenswelt. Aesthetics and Philosophy of Experience*, 1934(4): 230–245.

Ricoeur, P. 1985. *Temps et récit. Tome 3: Le temps raconté*. Paris: Editions du Seuil.

Spinuzzi, C. 2012. Working alone together: Coworking as emergent collaborative activity. *Journal of Business and Technical Communication*, 26 (4): 399–441.

Strati, A. 2009. 'Do You Do Beautiful Things?': Aesthetics and Art in Qualitative Methods of Organization Studies. In D. A. Buchanan and A. Bryman (eds.) *The SAGE Handbook of Organizational Research Methods*. SAGE, 230–245.

Sundararajan, A. 2017. *The Sharing Economy: The End of Employment and the Rise of Crowd-based Capitalism*. Cambridge: MIT Press.

Willems, T. 2018. Seeing and sensing the railways: A phenomenological view on practice-based learning. *Management Learning*, 49(1): 23–39.

Yakhlef, A. 2010. The corporeality of practice-based learning. *Organization Studies*, 31(4): 409–430.

PART II

Digital Platforms and the New World of Work

5 | *Exploring Inequalities in Platform-Based Legal Work*

DEBRA HOWCROFT, CLARE MUMFORD AND
BIRGITTA BERGVALL-KÅREBORN

Introduction

Interest in platform work and the gig economy has expanded significantly as digitalisation and new modes of organising symbolise structural change in contemporary forms of work. Research emanates from various disciplinary areas, including computer science, law, internet studies, anthropology and employment relations, which reflects the heterogeneity of practice. One area that is relatively under-researched is that of inequalities and platform work, which constitutes the focus of this chapter.

In a typically technologically deterministic fashion, much of the attention paid to platforms concerns how technology is driving new forms of working, with commentators suggesting that the transformative effects of platform work represent a new form of capitalist organisation (e.g. Srnicek 2017; Sundararajan 2016). Attributing the scale of expansion of platforms simply to technological innovation is simplistic, since it separates technology from the social world within which it resides, while at the same time arguing it constitutes the mechanism for bringing about change (MacKenzie and Wajcman 1985). Understanding sociotechnical change requires moving beyond the assumption that technology itself determines the organisation of work and so any analysis of platform work should be understood within the context within which it appears, since the same technology may well have very different consequences (Rosenberg 1976). With this in mind, our starting point is that inequalities are embedded within traditional workplaces to varying degrees and in distinct manifestations. If we add to this mix the ways in which economic and technological change can lead to inequalities in new guises (Rubery 2019), it seems apposite that platform work requires further scrutiny. Therefore, this study, which draws on the seminal work of Acker (2006), aims to investigate whether platform work reproduces inequality regimes. Extant research on platform work predominantly focuses on lesser-skilled work with clearly defined tasks; in contrast, this study aims to explore experiences of high-skilled work. Given the multiplicity of platforms, we have elected to concentrate on a specialist area of expertise: the provision of legal services. Existing research on inequalities in law has tended to emphasise the corporate sector and little is known about other areas of law (Tomlinson, Valizade, Muzio, Charlwood & Aulakh 2019).

Our interest lies not in platform work per se, but in understanding the relationship between digitalisation and contemporary developments in work and employment. Research on platforms has largely concentrated on work experiences, interactions and practices that lie *inside* the boundaries of the platform, neglecting situational understanding of the sectoral context from within which platform work is abstracted. The aim is to link the micro-social experiences of platform work with the macro-social context of the legal profession. The relationship between these two levels is dynamic and reciprocal since the experiences of social actors are shaped by the wider occupational setting.

In this chapter, we begin by outlining the context and framing for the study, including the key elements of platform work, Acker's notion of inequality regimes, and summarising inequalities within the legal profession. The research design follows, before the findings are presented, which have been analysed using Acker's practices and processes, which feed into the construction of inequality regimes. Finally, the chapter reflects on the study and outlines the wider contribution.

Context and Framing

Inequalities and Platform Work

Platforms operate as labour-market intermediaries, opening their technology to buyers and sellers in order to provide an extensive range of applications and services. This positions platforms in an orchestrating role as they act as the central hub in a marketplace for the mediation of both physical as well as digital services and tasks. For digital tasks, the entire activity is carried out online from initial instruction through to completion and evaluation; physical tasks are managed and mediated digitally (often via an app) but carried out offline (e.g. transportation, DIY). Platforms vary widely and cover a range of different offerings, yet although there are differences with regard to skill levels, task complexity, remuneration, as well as levels of autonomy and control, there are several defining features. A common tendency is the decomposition of work, standardisation of tasks and the use of low-cost labour that is available on-demand and drawn from a global workforce. Much of the initial research has focused on microwork, with Amazon Mechanical Turk being emblematic of low-cost platform work. More recent research has been extended to 'higher-skill' platforms where it could be assumed that greater levels of control and self-management are prevalent. Conversely, the limitations to control and autonomy and the dependence on online ratings are remarkably similar to microwork platforms (Schörpf, Flecker, Schönauer & Eichmann 2017).

Despite the growing attention devoted to working in the gig economy, it represents a relatively small share of the workforce[1], as full time employment remains the norm. Nonetheless, the expansion of platform work has led a number of optimists to suggest that this form of work provides new job opportunities, offering flexibility for those with care obligations, which may support the construction of flexible and more sustainable work. Platforms could potentially play a role in providing alternatives for those weakly attached to the labour market and with limited access to the formal economy.

When debating the benefits of platforms, it is important to be cautious. Platform work is predominantly a continuation of capitalist enterprise (Srnicek 2017) and augments wider trends in the growth of non-standard employment, an area where women are disproportionally represented. It would be naïve to assume that technologies, which are 'crystallizations of society' (Wajcman 2018, p. 4), have the capability to resolve inequalities, since they bear the imprint of their social context. In terms of gender differences, existing research shows that men are undertaking platform work as an additional source of income to supplement the day job, while for women it is more likely to constitute their primary source of income (ILO 2018). Consequently, the insecure nature of this form of work matters more. Platform work often requires investing time searching for work tasks (Berg 2016) and so for women a higher proportion of their total working hours are

---

[1] The UK has the highest share of crowdworkers internationally at around 3 per cent (ILO 2016).

likely to be unpaid. In terms of rewards, there is a gender pay gap on platforms (Adams and Berg 2017). Some may attribute pay differentials to research that shows men are more likely to solve complex problems and undertake high skills tasks than women (Wood, Graham, Lehdonvirta & Hjorth 2019). However, gender pay differentials operate regardless of feedback scores, experience, occupational category, working hours and educational attainment, which suggests gender inequality is embedded in the operation of platforms (Barzilay and Ben-David 2017). The tripartite nature of platforms has led to the substitution of the traditional managerial function with algorithmic control (Wood, Graham, Lehdonvirta & Hjorth. 2019), but these systems are only as effective as the testimonies, and negative reviews have been associated with race and gender discrimination (Slee 2015).

Inequality Regimes

Integral to our study is Acker's (2006) concept of 'inequality regimes', which can be applied across all types of organisations and is defined as 'systematic disparities between participants in power and control over goals, resources and outcomes; workplace decisions, such as how to organise work; opportunities for promotion and interesting work; security in employment and benefits; pay and other monetary rewards; respect; and pleasures in work and work relations' (Acker 2006, p. 443). Research to date on inequality regimes has focused predominantly on traditional organisations, typically based on bureaucratic spheres of organising and decision making. However, as Acker (2006) notes, inequality regimes are fluid, variable and transform over time. In the context of digitalisation and work, it is apposite that platforms as an emerging organisational form are explored.

According to Acker (2006), organisations vary in the practices and processes that result in inequality regimes. She highlighted five inter-related processes that contribute towards the construction of inequality. First, *organising the general requirements of work* encapsulates how the everyday function is organised. This is predominantly based on the image of the unencumbered worker (Acker 1990) who is dedicated to the organisation and exempt from domestic and social reproduction. Second, *organising class hierarchies* represents the process of classification whereby jobs, tasks and wage categories are assigned. Third, *recruitment and hiring* refers to the process of finding and matching the worker to a particular position: securing the 'ideal worker' with the appropriate levels of competence. In practice, the absence of neutral decision making ensures that patterns of segregation continue. Fourth, *wage setting and supervisory practices* determine the division of surplus between workers and management and also establish who controls the work process and in what manner. Finally, *informal interactions while 'doing the work'* concern the ways in which gender is reproduced in everyday interactions.

At the abstract level, processes and procedures that contribute towards the construction of inequality regimes seem less relevant to platforms. Given the tripartite governance of platform work, unlike traditional organisations with clear lines of authority and responsibility, platform workers are immune from direct supervision, as they are classified by the platform as 'independent contactors' (Berg 2016) with self-employed status. In this respect, they are deemed to have autonomy since, in the absence of supervisors, they choose when and how they will participate on the platform. Inequalities embedded in various forms, such as written work rules, labour contracts and managerial directives, no longer apply to the 'independent contractor'. Platform workers either set their own wage rate or decide which tasks and projects to bid for. The nature of the work is widely perceived as beneficial to those requiring flexibility for family life, enabling work to fit in around domestic rhythms. In terms of interactions between groups that enact dominance and submission, the vast majority of the work is carried out alone with little evidence of team-based working. There is limited exchange between buyers and sellers given the transient nature of task completion, and the likelihood of informal relationships developing is slim. Most of the interaction is fleeting (Howcroft and Bergvall-Kåreborn 2019) and so the more subtle and unspoken inequalities that permeate traditional organisations are unlikely to materialise to the same degree. Furthermore, the transactional logic of platform work complements the hypothetical, unencumbered worker (especially given that platforms such as Amazon Mechanical Turk reference workers by alphanumeric identifier), operating as a gender-neutral abstract category, fulfilled by disembodied workers.

In contrast with inequality regimes which are prevalent, to varying degrees, across organisations, it is tempting to assume that platforms, as an emerging form of work, are gender-blind. However, platforms are premised on a free-market logic of production that celebrates and valorises market competition. It is presumed that those who succeed, do so because of natural superiority and merit, but this is based on an assumption that naturalises inequality. For women, working on remote platforms reflects their labour-market vulnerability, which stems from the gendering of skills and the domestic division of labour.

Equality and Diversity within the Legal Profession

Given our focus on exploring the reproduction of inequality regimes within platforms that provide legal services, in this section we summarise key findings from the wider literature on equality and diversity in legal work in order to facilitate broader contextual understanding of how experiences are shaped. The legal profession has been variously described as a 'bastion of male privilege' (Bolton and Muzio 2008) consisting of 'rambo litigators' associated with hyper-masculinity (Pierce 1995). However, what was once perceived as an exclusively white male profession is undergoing diversification. In the UK, for the first time in 100 years, women now make up the majority of practising solicitors and twice as many women as men are studying for law degrees (The Law Society 2018 – see www.lawsociety.org.uk). However, the increasingly diverse nature of access to the profession is not being reflected in equal distribution of opportunities as presenteeism, sexist practices, and racial stereotyping pervade the culture of the legal profession (Sommerlad, Webley, Duff, Muzio & Tomlinson 2017).

The legal profession is characterised by horizontal segmentation, consisting of variable rewards, career opportunities and working conditions with women and minorities clustering in the least lucrative market segments (Tomlinson, Muzio, Sommerlad, Webley & Duff 2019). Sex segregation across legal specialisms is apparent (Pringle et al. 2017), as men dominate lucrative/high-status areas such as corporate law while women occupy front-line positions and less prestigious areas of practice such as family law, housing and probate (Tomlinson et al. 2013). While some have viewed the incursion of women into male-dominated professions as having a potentially positive impact as their presence 'trickles up' (see Hakim 2006), 'archaic attitudes to gender' (Sommerlad 2016) persist. Vertical stratification results in fewer opportunities for women and minorities to make partnerships compared with their white male counterparts (Tomlinson et al. 2019; Walsh 2012). The widespread perception that promotion is easier for white males (Sommerlad et al. 2017) is confirmed by the evidence. Female barristers account for 37 per cent of the practising bar, but the group of eminent lawyers known as Queens Counsel contains fewer than 14 per cent (The Law Society 2018 – see www .lawsociety.org.uk). Occupational inequities are reflected in pay and rewards: in the UK in 2019, women working at one of the ten largest legal firms are being paid on average 43 per cent less than their male colleagues (Kinder and Narwan 2019).

To be a lawyer requires compliance with norms that sustain 'the valorisation and dominance of masculine characteristics' (Pringle et al. 2017, p. 442) thus marginalising the 'feminine' and devaluing work that women do (Tomlinson et al. 2013). Opportunities for career advancement are principally based on 'the heritage of the past' rather than a willingness to progress social change (Pinnington and Sandberg 2013). Workplace expectations reflect the norm of an abstract job carried out by a disembodied worker who exists only for the work and is unencumbered by outside imperatives such as family and care responsibilities (Acker 1990). The notion of a 'top' legal professional working in a city law firm is based on male models of working with a 'long-hours' culture and a willingness to socialise with clients and colleagues beyond formalised hours (Pinnington and Sandberg 2013; Sommerlad et al. 2017).

Requests for flexible working and an improved work–life balance jar with the traditional indicators of career dedication: motherhood is equated with reduced commitment. Numerous studies (e.g. Pringle et al. 2017; Tomlinson et al. 2013) show that promotion to partner level requires the privileging of work over family considerations, which endorses the stereotype of the male breadwinner and the stay-at-home wife. The dominance of white males at the top of the organisational hierarchy is of concern when future partners are selected on political considerations (particularly informal relations with senior partners) as much as on performance criteria (Pringle et al. 2017; Walsh 2012), which disadvantages those who are dissimilar. As a result, gendered constructions of what it means to be a legal professional result in many talented women (particularly those with caring responsibilities) making do with part-time work or accepting lesser roles that do not match their skills and competences. The perception that there are limited opportunities for promotion influences future decisions such as willingness to stay with the firm and remain in the profession (Walsh 2012), which perhaps explains why women and BME lawyers are over-represented in law firm departures (Sommerlad et al. 2017).

Over the last thirty years or so, there have been a number of changes in the patterns of organisation of the legal profession in England Wales (Ackroyd and Muzio 2007), which has consequences for inequalities. This has led to novel ways of delivering legal services and new types of providers. According to Susskind (2017), there are three main drivers of change. First, the 'more-for-less' challenge has led to increasing workloads in the context of diminishing resources. This has taken place alongside decreases in the provision of public legal aid, which has meant that legal services are inaccessible to poorer clients. Second, liberalisation has led to regulatory change (the Legal Services Act 2007), which has permitted the setting up of 'alternative business structures' (ABSs), allowing non-lawyers to own and run legal businesses, leading to an expansion of smaller firms and start-ups. Finally, Susskind argues that technological change is presenting opportunities to innovate and rethink the ways in which law is practised. Although platforms are not considered in his analysis, they represent a material response to the drivers of change that he documents.

Research Design and Site

Our research aims to investigate whether inequality regimes are reproduced within platform organisations. Given the heterogeneous nature of platform work, the focus was narrowed to legal work and services. We selected People Per Hour (PPH), a well-established platform that offers a broad portfolio of 'high-skill' professional services (e.g. accounting, marketing, consultancy, software development, etc.), including legal services. PPH specifically targets the SME (small- to medium sized business) market on the basis that even the smallest of businesses can source specialist projects and access high-level skills and talent for a fraction of the price.

PPH is an open platform whereby people can register as seekers of work ('freelancers') and/or requesters of work ('buyers'). Freelancers create an online profile that includes broad information on the services they provide, as well as hourly rate. Profile pictures are commonly employed and abbreviations are used as opposed to full names.

Each profile includes average rating (by the declared number of buyers), the number of projects worked on, the number of buyers worked with, the date of last activity, and response time. There are two options available to freelancers seeking work. First, custom projects or tasks are posted by buyers, at which point competitive bids can be submitted. Payment for custom projects are either agreed as fixed price, price per item or as a per hour rate. The second option involves freelancers posting fixed-price services named 'offers', where they provide advice on a particular topic for a set fee. Once a project has been assigned and a 'workstream' created, the details are agreed by the buyer and the freelancer, with little intervention from PPH. When the project begins, the buyer pays funds into an escrow account and the freelancer raises a payment request when the work is completed. Payment is subject to buyer satisfaction and if the invoice is rejected, detailed feedback is to be provided in the workstream and the freelancer is offered at least two further iterations on the deliverables. Unlike the majority of platforms, terms and conditions state that PPH offer a dispute resolution service. PPH deduct commission ('service fee'), which varies by billing amount, but the vast majority of transactions fall below £500 and this incurs a 20 per cent fee. Buyer rating feeds into the overall score of the freelancer, and reviews are attached to individual profiles.

Initial contacts were obtained through PPH using the search criteria of 'legal sector' for industry and 'UK' for location. The UK has three legal systems, which are England and Wales, Scotland, and Northern Ireland. Given the specificity of legal jurisdiction, our study concentrates on workers who specialise in law within England and Wales. The returns were diverse, suggesting search terms were poorly applied to the database, resulting in lists of freelancers offering non-legal services as well as being based outside of the UK. The returns also varied on a daily basis, with some freelancers dropping out of the list and new ones emerging. We regularly accessed the list over a period of six months in order to mine the database as effectively as possible and in the hope that we had captured all of the UK-based freelancers offering legal services. We contacted participants directly via the platform by inviting them to discuss their experiences of providing legal services on PPH. We contacted fifty-five people and received replies from 21. Checking against the patterns in the dataset, we made a deliberate effort to recontact and invite for interview women with a high number of projects and hourly rates and men with a relatively low number of projects and hourly rates, so that we were sampling across the full range of experiences.

An online participant survey collected demographic information in advance of the interview, in order to help provide focus (Table 5.1). Two of the researchers carried out semi-structured, in-depth interviews, all of which were digitally recorded and transcribed verbatim. We began each interview by asking the respondent to summarise their careers to date in order to provide an account of their early aspirations and their subsequent career history through to current employment. The interviews then focused on three main areas: what attracted them to platforms; experiences of carrying out work on the platform; and how platform work fits into their career and personal plans. All of the participants had undergraduate law degrees. All but four had further postgraduate or professional legal qualifications; some were 'fully insured solicitors' with recognised professional indemnity insurance, as stipulated by the Solicitors Regulation Authority (SRA).

A careful reading of the transcripts led to identifying issues relating to the experience and practice of working on PPH, in the context of knowledge and understanding of the wider legal profession. We adopted an abductive approach (Blaikie 2000) as opposed to a series of planned phases, moving back and forth between empirical observations and theory. Although coding was primarily shaped by Acker's framework of inequality regimes, we remained alert to uncovering other elements. In order to remain sensitive to the distinctive and holistic experience of participants, excessive categorisation was avoided (Holloway and Jefferson 2000). In accordance with the provision of research participant anonymity, unique identifiers are used throughout this chapter.

Research Findings

In this section we present the data analysis that draws on the intersection of Acker's (2006) practices and processes, which combine to construct inequality regimes.

Organising the General Requirements of Work

This process encapsulates the organisation of the everyday function. In the context of platform work we took this to include motivations for

Table 5.1 *List of interviewees*

ID	Age	Ethnicity	Employment status	PPH as source of income	Time category	Hourly rate	PPH rating	No. of projects*
F01	20–29	White (other)	Self-employed	Secondary	6–12 months	£20–30	5.0	<16
F02	30–39	White British	Self-employed, legal & non-legal services	Secondary	1–2 years	£120–130	5.0	<16
F03	40–49	White British	Full time employed in legal profession	Secondary	<6 months	£60–70	5.0	>16
F04	30–39	White (other)	Self-employed	Secondary	<6 months	£30–40	-	0
F05	30–39	White British	Full time employed in legal profession	Secondary	<6 months	£30–40	-	<16
F06	20–29	Asian/ Asian British	Unemployed / student	Main source	<6 months	£10–20	5.0	<16
F07	40–49	White British	Self-employed	Secondary	>5 years	£10–20	5.0	<16
F08	20–29	White (other)	part-time employed, non-legal	Secondary	<6 months	£20–30	5.0	<16
F09	20–29	White British	Full time employed in legal profession	Secondary	<6 months	£0–10	(not yet rated)	<16
F10	30–39	White (other)	Full time employed in legal profession	Secondary	1–2 years	£100–110	5.0	<16
F11	40–49	Black African/ British / Caribbean/	Self-employed	Main source	2–5 years	£40–50	4.9	>16

Table 5.1 (*cont.*)

ID	Age	Ethnicity	Employment status	PPH as source of income	Time category	Hourly rate	PPH rating	No. of projects*
F12	40–49	White British	Full time employed in legal profession	Secondary	2–5 years	£100–110	5.0	>16
M01	50–59	White British	Self-employed	Secondary	>5 years	£250–260	4.7	<16
M02	30–39	Asian/ Asian British	Self-employed	Secondary	2–5 years	£70–80	4.9	>16
M03	30–39	Asian/ Asian British	Full time employed in legal profession	Secondary	<6 months	£40–50	–	0
M04	50–59	White British	Self-employed	Main source	>5 years	£120–130	4.7	>16
M05	60+	White British	Self-employed	Main source	>5 years	£150–160	4.9	>16
M06	40–49	Asian/ Asian British	Self-employed	Secondary	6–12 months	£20–30	4.8	<16
M07	30–39	Black British/ African/ Caribbean	Full time employed, non-legal sector	Secondary	1–2 years	£60–70	5.0	<16
M08	60+	White British	Self-employed, legal & non-legal services	Secondary	>5 years	£40–50	4.9	>16
M09	20–29	White British	Self-employed, legal & non-legal services	Secondary	<6 months	£120–130	5.0	<16

*To anonymise the data, we have categorised interviewees on the basis of hourly pay rate categories and in terms of being lower or higher than the average number of projects for women participants (see below).

working on the platform as well as day-to-day experiences and practices. The data analysis revealed that female participants were inclined to use PPH in two main ways. First, around half of the women respondents are employed as full time 'offline' legal professionals, often based in the public sector or commercial sector as in-house counsel as opposed to traditional law firms, and they were drawn to PPH as a supplementary source of income. They were loosely bound to the platform and it served a purpose in providing *'additional money'* (F01PPH) or being *'useful for the luxuries'* (F03PPH).

One participant who was also utilising PPH for extra income, described the challenge of building a career in the legal profession, especially during the process of qualification when income levels are low: *'When you think that we studied equalities and discrimination and all the human rights, when it comes to the practice, it is the jungle and you need to survive'* (F01PPH).

The second category of female participants were using the platform to build a career based on flexibility and self-employment, and viewed PPH as a stepping stone in the process. The majority had struggled to break into the legal profession, but having invested in their education and training, they were determined to carve out a role for themselves. Some had managed to establish themselves as solo self-employed legal professionals, only resorting to PPH *'when I'm really desperate'* (F07PPH), while others were having to combine their activity on PPH with lesser-skilled service work such as jobs in hospitality or call centres in order to generate income. For the majority who had taken the self-employment route, it represented a response to the difficulties experienced in accessing a traditional law firm, as expressed by a research participant from Turkey: *'My main consideration [for rejecting a traditional law firm] was my nationality, . . . a lot of the time they would turn me down before they even looked at my qualifications because I have the wrong name'* (F08PPH).

For others, PPH served a purpose as an enabler as they strive to establish themselves in a profession that is beset with inequalities. One participant commented on the challenges posed by her experiences working as an intern and with work visa problems:

I first worked in the law firm as work experience for six months, without pay, and it was quite difficult in London when you're not being paid. And then they offered me a job and I worked with them as an employee for four months, but because of my visa, I had to change, I had to convert my visa to a self-employed business person visa. That's why I'm working as a self-employed person and for PPH too. (F01PPH)

One female participant explained why she had rejected the long-hours culture associated with working in a law firm and resorted instead to contract work and PPH:

When I trained I was working very long hours, I was working until midnight, and I thought this is not the life for me ... so I thought I cannot keep doing this, it's actually draining me and I just don't enjoy it ... I prefer having flexibility which is why I contract and why I do these sorts of projects. I prefer controlling my time rather than being one of many employees in a department and having to stay there all hours. So that's the main driver. (F10PPH)

While much is written about the benefits of flexible working, particularly for those with caring responsibilities, only one woman (F10PPH) was actively and unambiguously choosing this type of career because it provided greater flexibility: '*I had my son in 2015 and I just wanted to be around a bit more, and working in the city and working to somebody else's timetable didn't really work for me anymore*' (F02PPH).

PPH served as a more substantial source of income for male participants. They were predominantly solo self-employed and, over time, PPH had provided a significant revenue stream. For example, for one participant who had been using PPH for around ten years, the platform consistently represented between 60 and 70 per cent of his income (M05PPH). Most had accumulated significant expertise based on working within the traditional legal profession and were far less likely to have experienced barriers to access. Compared to female participants, they were generally older and far more inclined to have exited the profession having built their expertise in legal practice (male average age of 47; women average age of 34). For the majority of male respondents, those occupational experiences had been largely negative and this had partially shaped their search for alternative ways of working: '*With traditional law firm partnerships, if you think of the structure as very akin to how a Mafia family is organised you won't go far wrong. It's deeply unpleasant. They're very aggressive places to work*' (M01PPH).

This sense of unpleasantness was echoed by another participant commenting about his experience of working for a high street solicitor:

'*I wish I'd known that there was this market [PPH] beforehand because I don't think I'd have ever gone and worked for a firm ... it feels like I'm giving two fingers to the normal legal profession*' (M02PPH).

One participant discussed how technological change within the legal profession represented a 'big shift' that had enabled former high street solicitors, such as himself, to work with a far wider range of clients: '*so it's kind of opened up a whole new world in that respect*' (M08PPH). Numerous participants remarked on the sense of enjoyment associated with self-employed legal work and PPH, after having had a traditional legal career based in an office environment: '*I'm really happy ... I'm enjoying myself in the profession for the first time*' (M05PPH).

In terms of organising the everyday function, much of the work was based on bidding for projects, where timeliness was vital. Here the distinction between users who are loosely or tightly bound to PPH is critical, since the former category often loses out, having invested in unpaid labour. For female participants who had full time jobs, they were disadvantaged by constraints on their inability to respond quickly. Their 'day job' also limited their capacity to react to larger projects as well as projects with tight deadlines. There was a common perception that it was futile to bid for projects that had been posted for some time and had already received a number of applicants:

Sometimes you just get so overwhelmed with crap basically ... if I see fifteen or eighteen other people have bid for a job already, I won't bid for it, even if it looks like a great job, and that's a shame because actually twelve to thirteen of those people might not be suitable anyway, but it's putting me off bidding. (F02PPH)

Given the challenges of the immediacy of bidding for projects, women's structural constraints meant that they were more inclined to design 'offers' with a set price as a way of standardising a relatively discrete, simple job and leaving clients to contact them. This also reduces the amount of unpaid job search time.

By contrast, organisation of the everyday function for male participants often centred around timely routines for bidding.

I'm bidding for jobs all day ... once you build up a profile and if you can do it regularly and bid on jobs very quickly you tend to get the work. (M02PPH)

I have a morning routine, so the first thing I do is look through the correspondence I've got through the PPH system, and then I will have a look at the work types and put a bid in for anything that I fancy, and then it takes me five, ten minutes to write a bid. So it's part of my routine, it's not a problem. (M05PPH)

This reflects their prioritisation of PPH activity since it constitutes – to varying degrees – a reliable stock of work. In this study, the period of time using the platform ranged from a few weeks to ten years, with men far more likely to have used PPH for longer and self-identify as 'veteran PPHers'. Many were able to draw on their experience and leverage a stock of templates:

[T]here's an element of cut and paste, of standard blurb and the description of what's needed to do the job is generally no more than a paragraph, put a price on it and bang, off it goes. It works that way, because a lot of jobs that come in can be quite similar in content. (M08PPH)

Organising Class Hierarchies

This represents the process of classification whereby jobs, tasks and wage categories are assigned. While the brand and reputation of platforms remains pivotal in attracting a critical mass, the transactional nature of platform work means that a reliable workforce is measured in classification systems based on digital ratings. These processes are seen to operate as an 'invisible hand' that rewards good producers while punishing poor ones (Goldman 2011, p. 53). Consequently, in the gig economy literature, reputation, ratings and managing one's online profile is seen to be critical since these determine access to future work (Gandini 2019; Schörpf et al. 2017). Such is the importance of ratings that algorithmic control is claimed to be central to the operation of online labour platforms (Wood et al. 2019).

On PPH, both buyers and freelancers are obliged to leave qualitative feedback and a rating ranging from 1 to 5. In fact, if a freelancer wants to access a review of their performance and have it displayed on their profile page, they are required to also submit a review of the buyer. In contrast to the literature, the vast majority of interviewees seemed unconcerned with ratings, explaining that they had performed well and been recognised accordingly. That is not to say that they were unaware of the consequences of poor ratings: '*One bad review will actually cut off all the possible future projects that you have'* (F01PPH). Nonetheless, most were unable to articulate how their rating fed into the ranking algorithm and their position in the search process. That aside, one area where the importance of ratings does feature heavily relates to new freelancers with zero projects and zero ratings. There was a common assumption that when starting out on PPH, it was important to bid low in the first instance in order to generate a positive review. This had the effect of reducing wage levels, as explained:

Because I'm a fairly new profile and don't have a rating, it's unlikely that people want to select you unless you've put in probably the cheapest bid, so I started to try and put in as low a bid as I could possibly accept or else I'll never get chosen. (F09PPH)

This participant chose to offer her services at £6 p/hour (which is below the national minimum wage) in order to secure an initial project and a positive rating. A similar experience was relayed by a male participant (M03PPH) who was new to PPH. He also opted to bid low, but for him the fee was £40 p/hour.

As Table 5.1 shows, research participants had generally received very positive reviews. However, one experienced PPH user was scathing of the capability of clients to provide informed reviews:

They all get four, five star reviews because the client doesn't know what they're getting. If you put a few wherefores and hereafters in a document you can make it look really good and it can be the biggest load of rubbish that you've ever seen, but as a client you wouldn't understand that because you're not used to looking at legal documents. So the rating system doesn't take into account the qualifications of the work that's been done, and so the rating system just doesn't work.'(M05PPH)

Recruitment and Hiring

The traditional employment relationship is based on the process of finding and securing the 'ideal worker' with the appropriate levels of competence (Acker 2006). In contrast, the 'independent contractor' classification that is widely applied to platform work suggests that recruitment and hiring processes are of limited relevance since individuals effectively make a choice as to whether or not to sign up for the platform. In this regard, there is equal access to the platform, but the ways in which participants may benefit from the platform varies.

Registering on PPH involves the creation of a personal profile, which the overwhelming majority of our research participants described as being fairly straightforward. PPH has a profile policy offering guidelines that encourage users to highlight their skills and credentials, upload a professional image, and strongly discourages the use of full name or contact details ('This rule is first and foremost to protect you').

While images on PPH are static, they nevertheless have the potential to influence perceptions and hiring. Generally speaking, there was a far greater tendency for male self-employed legal professionals to use a company brand and logo (even though PPH state that personal photos rather than logos make a significant different to success). One participant explained the benefits:

Initially on PPH I was under my own name and then I see other people who are selling their legal services having a corporate type name and sometimes people wanted a letterhead typed and a website. So then I realised that I may as well put a corporate identity to it, to put a front on the services I'm offering, there's a website, there's an email address. I suppose it gives the impression to clients that you're a lot bigger than you are. (M02PPH)

Given the tripartite nature of platform operations whereby freelancers bid for work with clients via the platform, the process of matching also seems relevant under this thematic category. The data analysis revealed a variety of filtering approaches by freelancers, ranging from a 'scatter gun' approach of bidding for many projects where '*you do have to kiss an awful lot of frogs to find a prince*' (M01PPH) to the more discriminating with interviewees being selective about the types of working relationships they were willing to engage in. A recurring problem was that clients often lacked adequate understanding of the complexity of the project which could result in overspill. One participant explained: '*I tend to look for people that come across as quite professional and quite savvy at what they want. So that knocks quite a few people out*' (F04PPH).

Others explained the challenge of dealing with clients who seemed unaware of the cost of legal services, for example: '*There are those who think that they are God's gift and you are lucky to have the opportunity to jump through their hoops for, frankly, a fee where you'd be paid less than the national minimum wage*' (M01PPH).

Wage Setting and Supervisory Practices

In traditional organisations, wage setting refers to the division of surplus between workers and management. With PPH, the income disparities are stark (Table 5.2). In terms of income generated, women's earnings ranged from zero to 10K (81 projects), averaging out at £1,860, while men's earnings ranged from zero to 130K (635 projects), averaging out at 33K. This partly reflects the number of projects completed, and can also be accounted for in the distinct approaches to PPH as a generator of either a primary or secondary income stream. There is also evidence of a significant gender pay gap. The Hourly Rate ranged from £6 to 120 for women, averaging out at £48. The figure ranged from £25 to 250 for men, averaging out at £99. The median hourly rate for a woman (£30) was only slightly higher than the lowest hourly rate for a man (£25); that is, almost half of the women had a lower pay rate than the lowest paid man. These hourly rates operate in the shadow of the offline market, where women earn less than men.

As Rubery (2019) points out, while pay gaps are of concern, the range of pay inequalities and the conditions that create this is of greater interest. This could arise from women's undervaluation of their competencies and skills, even though some were well aware of this: *'I'm massively underselling myself"* (F02PPH). While a couple of highly experienced female participants who had previously worked in law firms justified their acceptance of lower pay rates as being a trade-off for flexibility, others attributed this to lack of experience or simplicity

Table 5.2 *Employment and income figures for women and men*

	Women	Men
Number of projects completed (range)	0–81	0–635
Number of projects completed (average)	16	143
Total income generated overall	£0–10,000	£0–130,500
Average income generated	£1,860	£33,000
Hourly rate (range)	£6–120	£25–250
Hourly rate (average)	£48	£99

of the work: '*I think when the [PPH] bubble comes up to say you're bidding a bit low, I probably would increase it, but not necessarily to the price point that they recommend because I've never done consultancy before so I always think that I'm ripping people off*' (F05PPH).

This contrasts starkly with the self-evaluation of male participants who were confident that they were deserving of higher hourly rates, as illustrated below: '*You have to be clear that you are doing it as a solicitor under your insurance and in accordance with SRA rules and so forth. You always cost stuff, you have to follow what the job deserves or what the job is worth*' (M01PPH).

According to Acker (2006), supervisory practices establish who controls the work process and in what manner. Given the tripartite nature of platform operations, the independent contractor status, and the fleeting nature of transactions, employment relations cannot merely be classed in terms of a simple binary of control versus autonomy. For platforms to be deemed successful, developing a reputation as a provider of quality services is critical. As a consequence, indeterminacy of outcomes (Caves 2000) cannot be solved though hegemonic or neo-normative forms of control connected to lifetime of service to a company (Thompson et al. 2007), as is more typical of traditional organisations. In order to ensure provision of a quality service, PPH have devised a number of interventions aimed at ensuring certain levels of quality are achieved in communication practices. For example, penalties are applied to personal rankings for late delivery or cancellations, freelancers are required to respond within one working day to messages from buyers, and, if the buyer is not satisfied with the product, the freelancer is obliged to offer a further two iterations.

Given PPH has limited capacity to control freelancers, it attempts to bind users to the platform through the WorkStream process. Terms and conditions specify that the WorkStream is the key point of communication to be used by buyers and freelancers and keeps both parties protected in case of a dispute. PPH post regular reminders stating that communication should take place through the platform with Skype, email, or phone numbers only permitted as part of the service. Every message posted in the WorkStream, requires users to click a tickbox agreeing to the following: 'I acknowledge that all billing regarding this Project (including follow on work) has to be conducted through PPH in order to comply with PPH policy'. One participant described how

PPH attempts to minimise direct communication with the client and the potential to carry out work outside of the platform.

At one time, if you put a telephone number in there, it wouldn't let you ... It used to be quite funny, because you'd think, well there really needs to be conversation here, and you'd think of ways of inputting your telephone number, writing it in words rather than numbers, just so it wouldn't get screened out. You couldn't put an email address in, because they would screen that out. And therefore it wouldn't accept the communication. (M08PPH)

In spite of PPH recognising the validity of communication outside of the platform and adopting a more flexible approach, control of the interaction process still remained problematic for some: *'I take all of my correspondence off the PPH platform because it's confidential. So probably four or five times a year I get a message to say that they've sent a deposit back to a client when I'm halfway through a job'* (M05PPH).

In terms of evaluations of the contract with PPH, there was general consensus that the 'service fee' was excessive and that the comparatively low rates of pay are disappointing. One participant (M05PPH), who had developed an excellent reputation over a number of years and had been a good fee earner, described the service fee deductions as *'absolutely disgusting'*, particularly the increase in rates over time. While female research participants expressed dissatisfaction with the service fee, this was the only real area of complaint. Male participants were far more critical of PPH and its operations, presumably because remuneration levels were of greater significance and also, having generally been on the platform for longer, they had experienced changes in terms and conditions. One exasperated participant remarked: *They are killing their own goose ... they are reverse auction sites* (M01PPH).

Informal Interactions while 'Doing the Work'

While a significant literature exists on the reproduction of inequalities (particularly gender) in everyday interactions in organisations, the interaction practices are often subtle and difficult to identify and document (Acker 2006). They can include assumptions regarding whom one chooses to interact with, which can result in exclusion. For the most part, platform work is transient, with a predominance of one-off projects and the work tends to be individualised with little scope for team-based work (Howcroft and Bergvall-Kåreborn 2019). The sense of isolation was a recurring theme and was summed up as follows:

You sort of feel like you're putting a bid in and you read a bit about what the work is, but other than that, there's not really much to engage with. You know other people have bid but you don't know who they are or what they said or anything. (F09PPH)

However, when interviewing male participants, it emerged that an informal network of PPH freelancers had evolved:

The one thing that PPH has done over the years, is it's created a network of like-minded individuals ... We tend to use it as a referral network because we know who we trust on there in certain areas ... And there are probably three or four other people in there that I would describe as worth having in my network, from the legal perspective, because we've all got certain specialities ... And so we've traded stuff. And I'm happy to refer people, not within People Per Hour, outside of People Per Hour, because I know them. (M08PPH)

This network enabled the exchange of work among a group of solo self-employed professionals and was described as '*a nice little support network for me, it's also a nice support network for them*' (M05PPH). This was more widely beneficial since if a client request went beyond the boundaries of individual specialist knowledge, it facilitated access to other specialists and created a network of reciprocity. This suggests that the norms of the traditional legal profession, which are based on a hierarchy of male networks, are also evident on PPH.

Conclusions

The aim of this chapter has been to investigate whether platform work reproduces inequality regimes. In contrast to research on platforms which considers lesser-skilled, microwork activities and tasks, this study has examined higher skilled work, which is ordinarily assumed worthy of 'professional' status. We have drawn extensively on the work of Acker (2006) and applied her theoretical framework that maps the practices and processes that co-create inequalities in organisations. This has been utilised to analyse the practice and experience of providing legal services on PPH. These experiences have been situated in the context of inequalities within the traditional legal profession, in order to shed light on what draws well-qualified legal professionals to offer their services on a platform.

As high-skilled, highly educated workers with an identifiable profession, our research participants seemingly experience far more control over their work processes than evidenced by research examining platforms such as Amazon Mechanical Turk (Irani 2015) or Uber (Peticca-Harris, deGama & Ravishankar 2020). In this respect, some of the wider concerns of algorithmic control, for example, which is indicative of power asymmetries and inequalities, do not apply to the same extent. The heterogeneity of platforms is not simply based on the diversity of services being offered, but on the operation of different production logics, so that what might be efficient and capital-generative for one platform might not necessarily apply to PPH. For PPH operating as a platform that is marketed as offering high-skilled services to business, a large freelancer base is critical. As Hyman (1989) argues, the more complex and sophisticated the workers knowledge, the more difficult it is to monitor performance and prescribe tasks. This poses particular challenges for platforms, given they are not functioning in the role of an employer.

Situating the study in the wider literature on inequalities in the legal profession has enabled consideration of the structural disadvantages that lead workers to consider platform work. Structural inequalities which are embedded in the offline legal profession are not simply mirrored, but amplified in platform work, contesting any claims that platform work has the potential to act as a leveller, as disadvantages persist. The empirical findings show that legal practice on PPH is most suited to the simpler, standardised tasks and activities with seemingly clear boundaries, which are usually based on a fixed fee. In relative terms, although the hourly rates are far higher than the majority of platform work, there are few opportunities for career progression or for developing knowledge of the practice of law.

The study shows how gendered inequalities in traditional law firms are played out on PPH. The nature of platform work means that it is difficult to pinpoint precisely who is enacting discriminatory practices; it is more interesting to understand why structural disadvantages lead people to use platforms and how such inequalities are being reproduced in practice. Women's experiences in the legal profession, in terms of salary differentials and the challenge of progression, have led them to seek additional income on the platform. Yet juggling full time employment with platform work hinders their ability to participate effectively in such a competitive environment. For many it served as a filler as opposed to a long-term option. For others who are unable to access the legal profession through traditional routes, despite their investment in qualifying, their commitment to a career in law has led them to pursue alternative modes of entry. Their lack of professional experience in a firm serves as a disadvantage in terms of demanding higher pay levels and generating the confidence to do so. By contrast, male participants were far more inclined to operate as solo self-employed with PPH work providing a decent proportion of their income. Generally older, their experience of working within a traditional legal practice is reflected in the ways in which they organise their work (e.g. focused and well-timed bidding), the hourly rates that they charge, and income earned. Often at different life stages, male participants were fairly contemptuous of law firms and welcomed the opportunity provided by platform work to forge an alternative career. Their experience and expertise enabled them to be selective about the work that they do and the rates that they charge. They also benefited from longevity on PPH, which over time had enabled the formation of a network of support and work exchange, reminiscent of the traditional legal profession.

Finally, the impetus for this study was to gain broader understanding of the relationship between digitalisation and contemporary forms of work. Popular claims with deterministic tendencies suggest that new ways of working, driven by digital technology, are fundamentally transforming working life. Despite the rhetoric of autonomy, flexibility and self-determination associated with new forms of work organisation, these are rarely boxed off from work as we know it. As our study shows, structural inequalities that are embedded within traditional, offline work environments, are not only replicated, but augmented in online environments. Concomitantly, the wider landscape of workplace change sees the rise of deregulation, insecure employment, in-work poverty and flexibilisation, which leads people to seek alternative sources of income. Consequently, platform work continues to attract workers and will continue to do so until a fundamental overhaul of workplace inequality is realised.

References

Acker, J. 1990. Hierarchies, jobs, bodies: A theory of gendered organization. *Gender & Society*, 42(2): 139–158.

2006. Inequality regimes: Gender, class, and race in organizations. *Gender & Society*, 20(4): 441–464.

Ackroyd, S. & Muzio, D. 2007. The reconstructed professional firm: Explaining change in English legal practices. *Organisation Studies*, 28(5): 729–747.

Adams, A. & Berg J. 2017. *When home affects pay: An analysis of the gender pay gap among crowdworkers*. Available at SSRN: https://ssrn.com/abstract=3048711 or http://dx.doi.org/10.2139/ssrn.3048711

Barzilay, A. & Ben-David, A. 2017. Platform inequality: Gender in the gig-economy. *Seton Hall Law Review*, 47(2): 393–431.

Berg, J. 2016. Income security in the on-demand economy: Findings and policy lessons from a survey of crowdworkers. *Comparative Labor Law & Policy Journal*, 37(3): 543–576.

Blaikie, N. 2000. *Designing Social Research*. Cambridge: Polity.

Bolton, S. & Muzio, D. 2008. The paradoxical processes of feminisation in the professions: The case of established, aspiring and semi-professions. *Work, Employment and Society*, 22(2): 281–299.

Caves, R. E. 2000. *Creative Industries: Contracts between Art and Commerce*. Cambridge, MA: Harvard University Press.

Gandini, A. 2019. Labour process theory and the gig economy. *Human Relations*, 72(6): 1039–1056.

Goldman, E. 2011. Regulating Reputation. In H. Masum and M. Tovey (eds.) *The Reputation Society: How Online Opinions are Reshaping the Offline World*. Cambridge, MA: The MIT Press, 51-62.

Hakim, C. 2006. Women, careers, and work-life preferences. *British Journal of Guidance & Counselling*, 34(3): 279–294

Holloway, W. & Jefferson, T. 2000. *Doing Qualitative Research Differently*. London: Sage.

Howcroft, D. & Bergvall-Kåreborn, B. 2019. A typology of crowdwork platforms. *Work, Employment and Society*, 33(1): 21–38.

ILO 2016. *Non-standard Employment around the World: Understanding Challenges, Shaping Prospects*. Geneva: ILO.

2018. *World Employment and Social Outlook – Trends 2018*. Geneva: ILO.

Irani, L. 2015. The cultural work of microwork. *New Media & Society*, 17(5): 720–739.

Kinder, T. & Narwan, G. 2019 Gender pay gap widens at law firms, The Times, April 08 2019, available at: www.thetimes.co.uk/article/gender-pay-gap-widens-at-law-firms-7kmrrwvmf#:~:text=The%20gap%20for%20staff%20employed,partners%2C%20between%202017%20and%202018.

Mackenzie, D. & Wajcman, J. 1985. *The Social Shaping of Technology.* Buckingham: Open University Press.

Peticca-Harris, A., deGama, N. & Ravishankar, M. N. 2020. Postcapitalist precarious work and those in the 'drivers' seat: Exploring the motivations and lived experiences of Uber drivers in Canada. *Organization,* 27(1): 36–59.

Pierce, J. 1995. *Gender Trials: Emotional Lives in Contemporary Law Firms.* Berkeley, CA: University of California Press.

Pinnington, A. H. & Sandberg, J. 2013. Lawyers' professional careers: Increasing women's inclusion in the partnership of law firms. *Gender, Work and Organization,* 20(6): 616–631.

Pringle, J. K., Harris, C., Ravenswood, K., Giddings, L., Ryan, I. & Jaeger, S. 2017. Women's career progression in law firms: Views from the top, views from below. *Gender, Work and Organization,* 24(4): 435–449.

Rosenberg, N. 1976. *Perspectives on Technology.* Cambridge: Cambridge University Press.

Rubery, J. 2019. Joan Acker and doing comparable worth. *Gender, Work and Organization,* 26(12): 1786–1793.

Schorpf, P., Flecker, J., Schönauer, A. & Eichmann, H. 2017. Triangular love–hate: management and control in creative crowdworking. *New Technology, Work and Employment,* 32(1): 43–58.

Slee, T. 2015. *What's Yours Is Mine: Against the Sharing Economy.* New York: OR Books.

Sommerlad, H. 2016. 'A pit to put women in': Professionalism, work intensification, sexualisation and work-life balance in the legal profession in England and Wales. *International Journal of the Legal profession,* 23(1): 61–82.

Sommerlad, H., Webley, L., Duff, L., Muzio, D. & Tomlinson, J. 2017. *Diversity in the legal profession in England and Wales: a qualitative study of barriers and individual choices.* Available at: www.legalservicesboard.org.uk/what_we_do/Research/Publications/pdf/lsb_diversity_in_the_legal_profession_final_rev.pdf

Srnicek, N. 2017 *Platform Capitalism.* London: Polity Press.

Sundararajan, A. 2016. *The Sharing Economy: The End of Employment and the Rise of Crowd-based Capitalism.* Cambridge, MA: MIT Press.

Susskind, R. 2017. *Tomorrow's Lawyers.* Oxford: Oxford University Press.

Thompson, P., Jones, M. & Warhurst, C. 2007. From conception to consumption: creativity and the missing managerial link. *Journal of Organizational Behavior,* 28(5): 625–640.

Tomlinson, J., Muzio, D., Sommerlad, H., Webley, L. & Duff, L. 2013. Structure, agency and career strategies of white women and black and minority ethnic individuals in the legal profession. *Human Relations*, 66(2): 245–269.

Tomlinson, J., Valizade, D., Muzio, D., Charlwood, A. & Aulakh, S. 2019. Privileges and penalties in the legal profession: An intersectional analysis of career progression. *The British Journal of Sociology*, 70(3): 1045–1066.

Wajcman, J. 2018. Digital technology, work extension and the acceleration society. *German Journal of Human Resource Management*, 32(3–4): 168–176.

Walsh, J. 2012. Not worth the sacrifice? Women's aspirations and career progression in law firms. *Gender, Work and Organization*, 19(5): 508–531.

Wood, A., Graham, M., Lehdonvirta, V. & Hjorth, I. 2019. Good gig, bad gig: Autonomy and algorithmic control in the global gig economy. *Work, Employment and Society*, 33(1): 56–75.

6 | Workers Inquiry and the Experience of Work

Using Ethnographic Accounts of the Gig Economy

JAMIE WOODCOCK

Introduction

The gig-economy and platform work have become increasingly popular topics of research – as well as public discourse – in recent years. This is due, in part, to the highly visible nature of these new forms of work. Rather than having to delve too far into the 'hidden abode' of work (Marx 1976, p. 279), many gig workers can be found delivering food, providing transport or waiting outside across the city. The drastic changes of work that food delivery and private hire transport can be experienced through the customer experience and the fleeting interactions with workers. This, as Ticona and Mateescu (2018) have noted, risks an overemphasis on these visible and male-dominated forms of gig work – with relatively little attention paid to the historically hidden care and domestic work that is increasingly being mediated by platforms.

Despite the initial claims that these workers were atomised through digital platform technologies and therefore likely to be 'unorganisable', it is relatively easy to access these workers. This has led to a proliferation of journalistic and academic research – with no need to negotiate with traditional gatekeepers of the workplace for access. However, despite this increased access, the voices of workers in the gig economy have remained notably absent in many accounts. There is a tendency towards emphasising the new technological methods of control and surveillance – as well as the well-worn claims about the coming automation of work. However, as I have argued elsewhere, there is a range of preconditions that shape the gig economy. These include technology, but also social factors and political economy, as well as combinations of each (Woodcock & Graham 2019).

This chapter reflects on a three-year project of co-research with workers in the gig economy. It started in London with Deliveroo workers, just before the strikes in August 2016. Over the following years, it has grown to include Uber drivers in London, as well as stints of fieldwork with platform workers in South Africa and India. The original intention of this chapter was to present another co-written piece in the experience of the gig economy. However, co-writing is a complicated and unpredictable process. The current group of workers with which I am spending most of my time are engaged in other more immediate concerns – following on from recently co-authoring a piece with one of them (Aslam & Woodcock 2020). This has meant, rather than producing an account with a worker, this chapter is better placed to reflect on the process, drawing out lessons both about working in the gig economy and the role of researchers within this.

The chapter starts with a theoretical and methodological introduction on workers' inquiry, which guides my research practice – with the alternative title of: why do research anyway? This provides an opportunity to motivate workers' inquiry, while also establishing the foundations for what will follow. The next part critically examines the current research on the gig economy – noting the focuses and findings so far. This is then placed into conversation with the findings from the co-research that I have been involved in, drawing out both similarities and differences. The next section critically reflects on the process of co-research – focusing on drawing out lessons. The final part offers some early conclusions on the gig economy, as well as suggesting future research.

Workers' Inquiry – Or Why Do Research Anyway?

Whenever I explain what my own work involves – not always in the backs of Ubers – I shorten it to say: 'my work is researching work'. This is met with a range of responses: sometimes a lack of interest (an important reminder to researchers that while our topic may be the most important thing to us, other people may not care at all), feigning interest ('oh sounds interesting'), a joke about academia (the best involving some kind of comment about how that can be 'real' work), or spark the start of a conversation about how work is changing. However, my work being about researching work is only one part of the story. Social research has the challenge of involving the researcher, being a part of what they are trying to understand. There is no chemistry set of workers and capital that can be objectively experimented with. Instead, researchers interested in work have to make sense of their own work in relation to the work they are researching. This means understanding how their own paid work relies upon other people's work – both the work that supports theirs, as well as that of their 'subjects'. Research on work has the potential to be extractive, making a career out of writing about other people's work. This is a point that will be returned to in later sections.

Work is not an equal relationship. At its core, the capitalist work relationship involves the buying and selling of people's time. There is, of course, a whole range of unpaid work and labour that capital relies upon. However, just as capital could not function without unpaid work, paid work remains a key part of capitalism. This buying and selling of time involves a fundamental indeterminacy between the interests of the buyer and sellers (Marx 1976). These different interests are also an issue of standpoint: either for those who have nothing else to sell but their own labour power or the owners of the means of production – between workers and capital (Tronti 2019). Researching work means researching this relationship, one that involves social and material relations, along with a history of struggle and conflict. This also involves understanding shifts that have taken place, including, for example, the rise of digital labour (Casilli 2017). This means research on work involves taking a side. If someone refuses to take a side (or you do not know which side you, or they, have taken) then it is more than likely supporting the status quo and capital.

Researchers can have a contradictory role in universities under capitalism. If they teach, their role is to train and then sort future workers – often at a high cost and debt for students. This may free up time for research or it might be funded by research councils or other bodies. In the former case, there is more freedom to choose what to research, while the latter comes with both explicit shaping of what research will be funded – but both are subject to implicit, but strong, pressures about what to research. Research (particularly in the United Kingdom with Research Excellency Framework (REF)) is subjected to anonymous peer-review (with all the problems associated with that) and often expected to generate impact (or acceptable forms of value). The material pressures on early-career academics means they may be closer in conditions to gig-economy workers (although still quite far from) than previous generations of academics. This is certainly not the case for senior academics, who increasingly take on direct managerial responsibilities. However, this is not to say that early-career academics will take the workers side – they may see themselves as future professors/managers in the university and not publish research that would undermine that.

As I will argue throughout the chapter, I have attempted to take the side of workers throughout my research through the use of inquiry. The approach of workers' inquiry has a long history (Haider & Mohandesi 2013; Woodcock 2014), although there are lengthy gaps in its use. While Marx originally proposed an inquiry in 1880, it was only seriously taken up again after the Second World War by the *Johnson-Forest Tendency* in the United States and *Socialisme ou Barbarie* in France (van der Linden 1997). One of the most compelling examples is *The American Worker* (Romano & Stone 1946). This piece, co-written with a factory worker, was part of the group 'learning to seek out in the daily life of the workers in the factory the expression of their instinctive striving towards their liberation' (Glaberman 1947, p. 1). This was followed up by *Indignant Heart: A Black Worker's Journal* (Denby 1989), detailing the life of a black worker moving from the south in the United States to work in car factories, as well as *A Women's Place* (Brant & Santori 1953) on the struggle over housework. As Haider and Mohandesi (2013) have argued, this went beyond Marx's postal survey, opening up inquiry as a process to allow 'workers to raise their own unique voice, express themselves in their own language'. This is then later developed from the 1960s onwards in Italy, through a tradition that became known as *Operaismo* or Workerists. In these cases, the methods became part of the initial understanding of how work was changing, but also tied specifically to political organising. Gigi Roggero (2010, p. 4) has argued, 'Alquati' – one of the formative theorists of Workerism – 'taught us that the problem is to grasp the truth, not to describe it. For the capacity to anticipate a tendency is not an intellectual artifice but the compass of the militant and the condition for the possibility of organization'.

There are two key developments that can be identified here. The first is the method of co-writing as both co-production of knowledge and organising, initiated by the *Johnson-Forest Tendency*. The second is the development of the concept of class composition in Italy. This involves a focus on the experience of workers, developing it into an analysis of the way that capital attempts to 'incorporate the working class within itself as simply labour power', while the 'working class affirms itself as an independent class-for-itself only through struggles which rupture capital's self reproduction' (Cleaver 1979, p. 66). Class composition provides a framework through which these individual inquiries can be analysed, as well as generalised into a wider account.

Following *Operaismo*, there have been some individual projects, like the call centre inquiry by Kolinko (2002), but there exists another gap until the wave of recent inquiries starting in the 2010s. For my own research, this started with call centres (Woodcock 2017), videogame workers (Woodcock 2019) and the gig workers discussed later. This involves taking up the project of co-research as part of workers' inquiry, connecting the process of knowledge construction to organising with workers.

In particular, the projects discussed in this chapter have been guided by my involvement in the journal *Notes from Below*, which has taken up the method and developed it into a contemporary method and analysis of class composition. For *Notes from Below* (2018) this means projects that focus on understanding class composition as 'a material relation with three parts: the first is the organisation of labour power into a working class (technical composition); the second is the organisation of the working class into a class society (social composition); the third is the self-organisation of the working class into a force for class struggle (political composition)'.

The pieces of co-research discussed in the chapter were attempts to make sense of the changing class composition in different kinds of gig work. This starts with the experience of the labour process and work (technical composition), exploring how workers relate to each other and society (social composition), and experimenting with forms of resistance and organising (political composition). In these two examples, the co-research involves an adaptation of the 'full fountain pen' method, in which 'intellectuals would be paired with workers ... they would listen as the workers recounted their story, write them down on their behalf, and then have these workers revise the written documents as they saw fit' (Haider & Mohandesi 2013).

In summary, workers' inquiry is not just another way to do research, but rather a way to use research as part of an organising project. It is therefore an explicitly partisan approach, not only interested in finding out (in this case) about platform work in the gig economy, but supporting workers to transform their conditions. Workers' experiences are therefore not an interesting addition or an insight, but a core part of the co-research process. After all, without workers and their experience there can be no organising in the gig economy.

Researching the Gig Economy

The gig economy has become an increasingly fashionable topic of research. As of 22nd January 2020, Google scholar lists 13,300 articles on the 'gig economy' – that is, more articles than there are words in this chapter. However, (and without actually having read all of these articles) there are some general trends in the literature than can be observed. The early research in the gig economy had a tendency to be overly optimistic, particularly when the term 'sharing economy' was still popular (cf. Sundararajan 2017). This led to early critiques that attempted to place the so-called sharing economy within longer trends of capital accumulation and exploitation (Slee 2015). Research in the computer sciences (and particularly HCI – Human Computer Interaction) focused on crowdwork much earlier than the broader sociology of work literature. For example, Amazon Mechanical Turk became an important site of research (Gupta, Martin, Hanrahan & O'Neill 2014; Hara et al. 2018), with attempts to begin categorising the kinds of work being done online (Holts, 2013), and even attempts at forms of collaborative or co-research connected with organising, particularly Turkopticon (Irani 2015; Irani & Silberman 2013) and Dynamo (Saleh et al. 2015).

This had led to broader debates about the novelty and effect of algorithms in society (Pasquale 2015), as well as the role of algorithms in platform work (Lee, Kusbit, Metsky & Dabbish 2015; Rosenblat & Stark 2016). In some accounts, this has been linked to the rise of platform capitalism (Srnicek 2017) or critiques of specific models of gig work like Uber (Rosenblat 2018; Scholz 2017). The growth of this kind of work has meant that there have been many attempts to map the gig economy (Heeks 2017; Hunt & Machingura 2016; Huws and Joyce 2016; Ojanperä & Graham 2018), but the voices of gig-economy workers are often absent in these kinds of surveys. This mirrors some of the debates on automation of work, like Frey & Osborne (2017), which see changes in work as happening to workers, with little agency on their part. However, there is a growing critical literature that does feature voices of workers (Hill 2017; Ravenelle 2019), as well as some attempt to chart resistance (Wood, Lehdonvirta & Graham 2018), as well as using workers' inquiry as a method (Cant 2019). This chapter is an attempt to encourage more of the latter, centring workers voices and exploring the experiences of those actually working in the gig economy.

Findings from the Co-research

I have been conducting research with Deliveroo and Uber workers, some of whom are part of the Couriers and Logistics and United Private Hire Drivers (UPHD) branches of the IWGB. This has been part of a longer engagement with the union, including the University of London branch (the first part of the union, mainly comprising Latin American cleaners), as well as helping to establish the Game Workers Unite (GWU) United Kingdom branch of workers in the videogames industry. While the latter two are not considered part of the gig economy, there are many similarities relating to issues like precarious work.

The two co-research projects focused on here are deliberately partisan. My engagement with these workers was through involvement with the union. Following the method of workers' inquiry, this has combined the research process with that of organising. In both these cases, this has meant following the lead of the workers involved – both of whom were already actively organising on their respective platforms.

This perspective also means that throughout the piece I refer to the co-authors as 'workers'. This is intended as a critique of the gig economy, as both of them were technically considered to be self-employed independent contractors. This is a legal loophole used to free platforms from the requirements of employment law and protection, including paying the minimum wage, holiday and sick pay, pensions, right to be in a union and bargain collectively, and protection from unfair dismissal. Neither of them felt that they were self-employed, rather that they were campaigning for greater employment rights. In the United Kingdom, this is already possible under the intermediate 'worker status', between employment and self-employment. Therefore, the use of 'worker' is more than just a critique, but fits the identity and status that these workers felt they were.

This use of 'worker' as a term is also part of the process of considering the broader ethics of research. The conventional process of research ethics were followed, including a continuous process of informed consent throughout the entire process; the co-writing ensuring they were not being misrepresented, as well as becoming an active part of the research process; considering my own positionality as a paid academic researcher with a relative position of power; providing anonymity and a pseudonym for the first worker, while ensuring the second worker, who was named, understood the risks of foregoing anonymity.

Further ethical considerations were made that are not often, if ever, part of the institutional process (Badger & Woodcock 2019). The first involves using 'worker' as part of taking a side against the public-relations offensive that platforms have been pushing, whether in the media or courts (Woodcock & Graham 2019). The second is carefully considering, with each worker, whether there are potential issues relating to making some processes or tactics visible. With Deliveroo, workers have often been keen to explain tactics used to ameliorate the worst aspects of their work – which, if the platform discovered, they would likely stop. This involves thinking critically about the politics of knowledge production – particularly for publications that are not stuck behind academic or publisher paywalls.

The third consideration is one that runs through both projects, as well as in my work more generally: What is the benefit for workers of participating in the research? For gig workers, who could be working rather than speaking to researchers, this is particularly pressing. While some people may enjoy the process of talking about their work or getting the opportunity to voice their opinions, too often they do not see the result, whether it is a paper they may not have access to or not. This is definitely not to say that workers cannot read or appreciate the outputs of academic research (see the literature chosen to be included by the Deliveroo worker), but rather that much academic output would be of little interest or use to workers who are organising. Instead, these projects also allow for a reflection on how work in the gig economy can be carried out in non-extractive ways, going beyond just ensuring that no harm is caused, whether direct or indirect, but to actually have a positive impact with gig workers.

Inquiry at Deliveroo

The first co-research piece that will be focused on is 'Far from Seamless: A Workers' Inquiry at Deliveroo' (Waters and Woodcock 2017) that I co-authored with a Deliveroo driver in London. It was published in *Viewpoint Magazine* – a militant research collective that features writing on workers' inquiry and class composition. The article begins by charting the resistance and strikes in August 2016, outlining the key events and processes that were underway at the time. We then explained our method for writing the piece, which is worth quoting again here:

> In this piece, we draw attention to the labor process at Deliveroo and what it is like to work on the platform. It has been collectively written between the Deliveroo driver Facility Waters (a pseudonym), and Jamie Woodcock, who is employed at a university where he researches work. We have experimented with different ways to collect and share information about working at Deliveroo. In particular, we have tried to peel back the black box, emphasising that work on Deliveroo is not seamless, but rather it takes place in specific geographic locations in the city ... we have collaboratively written on Google Docs and augmented our analysis with GPS technology and interactive maps. We encourage readers to explore the interactive map alongside the text.

This meant adapting the full fountain pen method into one mediated by an online app, writing together on Google Docs. This built upon a longer collaboration that Facility and I had, starting before the London Deliveroo strikes in 2016, which had also involved a series of interviews as well as organising together. The writing process itself moved in inconsistent bursts. When the shift work at Deliveroo allowed, Facility and I would meet to discuss the piece, adding notes and sometimes paragraphs to the Google doc. This provided the basis for both of us to then independently contribute to the document, pushing it forward to completion. The majority of the piece was written by Facility – including adding most of the literature – while towards the end of the writing process, my own involvement became more like an editor.

The article itself is split into two parts. The first covers the process of applying for Deliveroo and a typical day of work. This was intended to provide a narrative account of Facility's experience, bringing up issues around contractual status, relationship to the company, as well as to other riders. The 'A Day Riding for Deliveroo' section is written from their first-person perspective, introducing the material and geographical dimensions of the work. Throughout this section Facility uploaded pictures of their perspective – whether a dark kitchen in South London or the side entrance to a Nando's that workers are supposed to use. These are interspersed with screen captures from their iPhone that illustrate what the interaction with the Deliveroo app looks like at various points.

The second part of the article moves onto the analysis of the technical composition of work at Deliveroo. This involves introducing the idea of an 'illusion of freedom' and the role of technology in the workplace. Part of this argument came from a long-running discussion that we had about the role of data in the management of Deliveroo. Facility had noted that it would be great to know how much they cycled – or even have an idea of how well they performed in the various metrics. Deliveroo, of course, holds all these data, but refuses to share with workers – unless when informing disciplinary procedures. Instead, Facility decided to self-track their routes around the city, producing a number of graphical representations as part of the article. This became a kind of counter-use of metrics, seeking to uncover the exploitation of the platform, which then fed into a critique of the politics of knowledge.

The creation of data for the article led to Facility researching more about how to make sense of their work at Deliveroo. As Facility chose to end the piece:

A distance becomes absolute and binary, complete or incomplete, delivered or not delivered – the delivery as a commodity in itself, as something to be produced by one and consumed by another. However, the strikes reveal the fragility of this 'perfection'; the movement from dots on screens to bodies in the streets simultaneously alters the visibility of the worker, removing them from the 'God's eye-view' of the commodity, whilst rupturing the seamless, hyperreal space of the city.

While it may have appeared that the academic would introduce the literature, instead Facility discovered a number of different analytical angles to unpick the technical composition of their own work. It is worth noting that Facility was also a recent sociology graduate and the literature is clearly inflected with this. However, this became linked to the worker organising that was taking place, opening up a space to debate the significance of the strikes, for example. Thus, the process of co-research is not only one of producing a co-written article, but of starting conversations and organising that go beyond the written word.

Inquiry at Uber

The second piece was co-written with an Uber driver and organiser, Yaseen Aslam: 'A History of Uber Organising in the UK' (Aslam & Woodcock 2020). The piece was commissioned as part of a special issue of *South Atlantic Quarterly* on worker writing, providing the opportunity (and a deadline) for Yaseen and me to write together, which we had discussed previously. I have known Yaseen since 2017, after he joined the IWGB, so following the co-research with Deliveroo drivers in the previous piece. Yaseen is the co-founder of UPHD, which became a branch of the IWGB. He is the lead claimant against Uber in the landmark case for worker rights, alongside James Farrar. Yaseen has worked in the minicab industry since 2006 and joined Uber in 2013 when they first launched in London. He has been organising drivers for the past five years.

The format of the piece is similar to the former, written in the first person of the worker. Yaseen had worked in the minicab industry since 2006 and started working for Uber when the Uber X service launched in 2013. He had taken extensive notes – some of which had been prepared for evidence in the legal challenges against Uber, while others were to document and try to understand his own organising. In addition to the notes, we also spoke at length about his experiences, both in what would be more formal interviews, with audio recording, as well as many more informal discussions. The process of co-writing involved Yaseen sharing these notes, which I edited into a shorter piece, then co-editing the piece on Google doc. This was much closer to the 'full fountain pen' method, providing support to a worker to tell their own story about work and organising.

One of the differences with this piece is that Yaseen no longer works for Uber. As detailed in the piece, Yaseen came into conflict with Uber at many points, ultimately leading to his 'deactivation' (or firing) from working for the platform. Given Yaseen is named in the legal case for worker status and has appeared in the media, there was no need to anonymise or use a pseudonym. While the piece includes his personal experiences of driving for Uber, the focus is charting the history of organising. It is therefore not only co-writing with a worker, but a worker who has been organising. We agreed to write the piece as part of telling his story of organising, covering the successes as well as the mistakes. In the discussions we had beforehand, we both noted how many people have tried to tell the stories of the successes – as well as interviewing drivers about their bad conditions, but never returning to speak to them again. The theme of engagement with academics is one that Yaseen and I returned to many times during our discussion. As he concluded in the piece: 'Throughout all of this I have learnt many lessons. When we first started organising people said we would never succeed, this included trade unionists, academics, and journalists. So few people believed in us or gave us the support we needed at the time. Instead people talked to us, got what they wanted, and left'.

As research about the gig economy has become increasingly popular, so have gig economy workers become increasingly subjected to research. Yet Yaseen's experience – and it is worth quoting the paragraph here – needs to be repeated and amplified:

When I first started working for Uber, I had not even heard of the words 'gig economy' or know what they meant. Uber claiming that I am self-employed with my own business and that drivers contract directly with customers to provide a driving service. I do not agree with this. Right from when I started working for Uber, I saw Uber as a company which offered a private hire service to customers and I worked for Uber as part of their service. However, Uber later claimed to be a 'tech startup' rather than 'a labor company' (Scholz 2017, p. 44), meaning that I supposedly had a driving business myself. My experience was that Uber had the commercial relationship with the customer, not me: the customer paid Uber, not me (drivers were not allowed to take cash as payment as all customers have to pay Uber electronically for their journey); Uber decided on the fare and cancellation penalties that customers paid, not me; the customer provided all their details to Uber and they had a policy of not giving drivers certain information about the customer. In addition, Uber paid me, including bonuses under various schemes, and Uber set the rules that we drivers had to follow. When changes were introduced, we just had to accept them.

There were only minor editorial changes to make here, as well as adding a citation to Scholz. Another key theme that emerges from the paper is the importance of race and discrimination for Uber. This comes up across the examples of minicabs, Uber, Transport for

London, the courts and even unions like GMB. These are stories that are often missing from accounts of the gig economy, particularly when it is presented as a 'new' phenomenon. Similar to the previous piece on Deliveroo, this piece is part of an ongoing organising campaign. This is both against institutional racism as well as Uber itself. The written piece provided the opportunity for Yaseen to tell his version events. As he explained:

> When people look in from the outside they think that we the organisers are amazing, lucky, or have some sort of special characteristic – but this is not true: organisers are made. Organising at Uber has been a very bumpy ride. We have had to suffer mentally, financially, and our families have suffered too. That is the commitment that it has taken to organise at Uber. This has meant taking on a billion-dollar company, confronting regulators, but also the small victories like helping a driver keep their license and livelihood. While we may lose a battle here and there, we will never lose the war. Our journey continues.

The Challenges of Co-research

The accounts presented here of the two pieces are intended to draw attention to the benefits of co-research – both in terms of the output created, as well as the ongoing relationships and campaigns. However, there are also important issues that arise when conducting projects like this. In this section, four of these will be considered: first, the form of the written output; then the process of producing it; the relationship between researcher and worker; and then a reflection on intervention.

The first challenge is the form that the co-research output takes. The research process is always broader and more widely ranging than the journal article outputs that usually accompany them. The tendency towards dividing findings into as many articles as possible – captured by the somewhat bleak joke of 'Minimum Publishable Unit' – fragments research projects and limits the scope of claims being made. Similarly, co-writing the results of co-research, while hopefully not subjected to the same minimums, inevitably loses large parts of the process. Writing often deliberately (or even inadvertently) loses the nuances, the complexity and the messiness of the experiences of work. Some aspects are deemed not worthy of writing down or cannot be easily expressed in the written form.

For the first piece with the Deliveroo worker, a non-academic, but still academic-related, publication was chosen. This allowed reflection on the theoretical influences of the project around workers inquiry, while also being a venue that published for free online. This was important for both of us, as it would mean that other Deliveroo workers could read it if they wanted to. This format also allowed experimentation with multimedia aspects, including the GPS tracking maps in multiple formats, including photographs. For the second piece, a peer-reviewed academic journal was chosen. In this case, the article was commissioned and published alongside other pieces of co-writing with workers and academics. While this venue has a more limited audience, given it is an academic publication, it fits within a broader collection.

These issues are connected to the second point: the process of writing. Both are short articles, the first at around 9,000 words and the second at 4,000 words. This meant that in both cases, there was much more that could have been said from the process of co-research, with the output only capturing a small aspect of it. When a piece is co-written, or edited, with an academic, this brings with it conventions and expectations of academic writing. Even with the best intentions, academics are shaped by the writing environment in which they spend the majority of their time. The choices about what is interesting or what an expected audience might want to read therefore shape the editing process, both what is included and what is left out. This also requires careful consideration of who the audience is expected to be for the output of co-research. For example, writing up the experiences of the gig economy is of current interest to many academics, as well as more general readership. However, given the writing is intended as part of a process of organising with workers, a non-academic readership among other workers is also an aim. This risks the final piece being caught between contrasting expectations, format and style. For example, each of the pieces makes reference to the academic literature (much more so with the Deliveroo piece, but also with the Uber one too). While worker writing does not preclude the use of literature (which should not just be left to academics), much of the literature does not speak to the concerns or struggles of workers. There is therefore a careful balance to be made in attempting to pose an argument across both audiences.

This contradiction between academic and researcher audiences is also an important part of the third point: the differences between the research and subject. Academics, as university workers, are clearly in a different subject position to workers in the gig economy. While there has been an increase in precarity within universities in the previous decade, most academics have employment contracts, albeit increasingly short-term rather than permanent. I have worked at a range of institutions during the periods of co-research covered by both of the pieces. Like most academics, there is the pressure to publish, but neither of these pieces counted towards institutionally recognised publications. These were, in a way, supplemental to the forms of output needed to continue my own employment. As Yaseen noted, there is often an extractive relationship between researchers and workers in the gig economy, which is something to be particularly mindful of. Despite the reasons discussed above, both pieces required a process of continual reflection on how to ensure this was not reproduced. The workers inquiry approach is one of trying to break down the distinction between researcher and subject, but this does not mean that the power relationships between the two are not important. One way that I have sought to overcome this is to keep the dialogue going after the co-writing, as well as exploring what I can offer to workers from my position as an academic, including volunteering for the union.

Extending the co-research process beyond writing leads to the fourth issue: the problem of intervention. If the role of the academic is limited to only reporting and analysing the gig economy, the kinds of intervention discussed in this chapter would be deemed inappropriate. However, the history of research on work is one of intervention, just often from the perspective of management. For example, Taylor's (1967) *The Principles of Scientific Management* involved an explicit intervention, developing in the Taylorist management of work, seeking out new ways to control and motivate workers. The early Italian Workerists also found that workers could be suspicious of interventions of academics. For example, in Alquati's inquiry at the Olivetti factory, many workers were 'cautious' about engaging, due to the 'contributions made by previous left sociologists to the intensifications of labour' in the factory (Wright 2002, p. 54).

The act of not intervening is also an intervention, as it supports the status quo. Burawoy (1998, p. 14), reflecting on his practices of workplace ethnography, argues that a reflexive approach to intervention means that it does not need to be minimised, but instead can benefit the research process and the participants. For example, he argues that:

> It is by mutual reaction that we discover the properties of the social order. Interventions create perturbations that are not noise to be expurgated but music to be appreciated, transmitting the hidden secrets of the participant's world. Institutions reveal much about themselves when under stress or in crisis, when they face the unexpected as well as the routine. Instead of the prohibition against reactivity, which can never be realized, reflexive science prescribes and takes advantage of intervention.

While the theory of intervention might be quite straightforward, the practical instances of intervention can be more complicated in terms of personal interrelationships. The academic's role involves a position of power, particularly in terms of access to formal knowledge, time and resources. If inquiry places the worker's experience at the forefront, this can then complicate the processes of intervention and debate. With Facility, we had developed a relationship of critical debate about Deliveroo – both the work involved and the organising. There were points of agreement and disagreement throughout the process of writing, but these were worked out through the co-writing. With the Uber driver, this process was harder to work through – as the co-writing involved more editing than negotiating, the process of disagreement was handled differently. Our collaborating involved more than the writing experience, instead taking place within the broader relationships of the union, with all the tactical and strategic disagreements this can often involve.

It is in this way that workers' inquiry can also be placed within the broader traditions of participatory action research, albeit one that often attempts to go further. This involves the aim 'to create participative communities of inquiry' and encourage 'a practice of participation, engaging those who might otherwise be subjects of research or recipients of interventions to a greater or lesser extent as co-researchers' (Reason & Bradbury 2008, p. 1). However, Paul Brook & Ralph Darlington (2013, p. 240) have discussed the possibilities of developing an 'organic public sociology of work' from this starting point, but warn that 'the ebb and flow of struggle 'from below' obviously affects the opportunities'. However, as struggles in the gig economy are rising, the challenge here is finding ways to tie research to workers struggle, with all of the unpredictability that can entail. But despite there still being many variables at play: 'one thing is clear for now, we need to stop talking about resistance as emerging in platform work! Resistance is clearly happening' (Cant & Woodcock 2019).

Conclusions and Future Research

This chapter has been intended as a moment to reflect on co-research and co-writing – however, this time as a single author. Over the past three years I have spent much of my time speaking to workers in the gig economy. This has included Deliveroo and Uber workers in London featured in this chapter, as well as platform workers in Bangalore, Cape Town and Johannesburg periods of fieldwork in 2018, and in the back of many Ubers, Lyfts, Bolts and so on across the world.

The reflection here is an opportunity to consider how and why the experiences of workers are key to making sense of the new world of work – and particularly the gig economy. These two pieces show how research can be put into conversation with workers, uncovering their hidden and lived experiences. The co-writing experience is also one of providing support to workers to speak to their own experiences and introduce their voices to debates about the future of work. The use of workers' inquiry means that this is not just to produce a written output, but tying this to organising and resisting work. However, these examples of co-writing have also drawn attention to four methodological issues with co-research: first, what kinds of written outputs are appropriate; second, how to undertake the process of producing co-writing; third, how to effectively balance the relationship between the researcher and workers; and then also reflecting on what it means to make interventions.

These four issues underpin co-research. However, as the chapter has shown, this is not a short or quick process to engage with workers in this way. My own ethnographic research that provided the introductions to workers, built the trust upon which the relationships could be formed and shaped the nature of the possible interventions. These started over three years ago and have so far produced two written outputs, one of which was relatively short. In a similar timeframe, more conventional academic research would have led to many more articles (which in my case, I have published alongside these kinds of pieces). However, the strength of these kinds of co-written articles is the unique perspective of bringing workers into the debates on work. After all, workers are already experiencing these shifts in work and understand them on a day-to-day basis. What is clearly needed now is more attempts at co-research between researchers and workers, rethinking how research on work is undertaken and why.

References

Aslam, Y. & Woodcock, J. 2020. A history of Uber organizing in the UK. *South Atlantic Quarterly*, 119(2): 412–421.

Badger, A. & Woodcock, J. 2019. Ethnographic Methods with Limited Access: Assessing Quality of Work in Hard to Reach Jobs. In D. Wheatley (ed.) *Handbook of Research Methods on the Quality of Working Lives*. Cheltenham: Edward Elgar, 135–146.

Brant, M. & Santori, E. 1953. *A Women's Place*. New Writers.

Brook, P. & Darlington, R. 2013. Partisan, scholarly and active: Arguments for an organic public sociology of work. *Work, Employment & Society*, 27(2): 232–243.

Burawoy, M. 1998. The extended case method. *Sociological Theory*, 16(1): 4–34.

Cant, C. 2019. *Riding for Deliveroo: Resistance in the New Economy*. Cambridge: Polity.

Cant, C. & Woodcock, J. 2019. The End of the Beginning. *Notes from Below*, issue 7, www.notesfrombelow.org/article/end-beginning

Casilli, A. 2017. Global digital culture| digital labor studies go global: Toward a digital decolonial turn. *International Journal of Communication*, 11: 3934–3954.

Cleaver, H. 1979. *Reading Capital Politically*. Brighton: Harvester Press.

Denby, C. 1989. *Indignant Heart: A Black Worker's Journal*. Detroit: Wayne State University Press.

Frey, C. B. & Osborne, M. A. 2017. The future of employment: How susceptible are jobs to computerisation? *Technological Forecasting and Social Change*, 114: 254–280.

Glaberman, M. 1947. Strata in the working class. *Internal Bulletin of the Johnson-Forest Tendency*, 6. Available at: www.marxists.org/archive/glaberman/1947/08/strata.htm

Gupta, N., Martin, D., Hanrahan B. & O'Neill, J. 2014. Turk-Life in India. *Proceedings of the ACM International Conference on Supporting Group Work* (GROUP 14) Sanibel Island, 9–12 November.

Haider, A. & Mohandesi, S. 2013. Workers' Inquiry: A Genealogy. *Viewpoint Magazine*, issue 3.

Hara, K., Adams, A., Milland, K., Savage, S., Callison-Burch, C. & Bigham, J. P. 2018. A Data-Driven Analysis of Workers' Earnings on Amazon Mechanical Turk. *Proceedings of the 2018 CHI Conference on Human Factors in Computing Systems*, Paper No. 449, New York: ACM New York.

Heeks, R. 2017. *Decent Work and the Digital Gig Economy: A Developing Country Perspective on Employment Impacts and Standards in Online Outsourcing, Crowdwork, etc.* Paper No. 71, Manchester: Centre for Development Informatics, Global Development Institute, SEED.

Hill, S. 2017. *Raw Deal: How the 'Uber Economy' and Runaway Capitalism Are Screwing American Workers*. New York: St Martin's Press.

Holts, K. 2013. Towards a taxonomy of virtual work. *Work Organisation, Labour & Globalisation*, 7(1): 31–50.

Hunt, A. & Machingura, F. 2016. A Good Gig? The Rise of On-Demand Domestic Work. ODI Development Progress, Working Paper 7.

Huws, U. & Joyce, S. 2016. *Crowd Working Survey: Size of the UK's 'Gig Economy'*. Hatfield: University of Hertfordshire.

Irani, L. 2015. The cultural work of microwork. *New Media & Society*, 17 (5): 720–739.

Irani, L. & Silberman, M. S. 2013. Turkopticon: Interrupting Worker Invisibility in Amazon Mechanical Turk. *Proceedings of CHI 2013*, Apr 28-May 2, 2013.

Kolinko. 2002. *Hotlines – call centre, inquiry, communism*. Available at: www.prol-position.net

Lee, M. K., Kusbit, D., Metsky, E. & Dabbish, L. 2015. Working with Machines: The Impact of Algorithmic, Data-Driven Management on Human Workers. In B. Begole, J. Kim, K. Inkpen and W. Wood (eds.) *Proceedings of the 33rd Annual ACM SIGCHI Conference*. New York: ACM Press.

Marx, K. 1976. *Capital: A Critique of Political Economy Vol. 1*. London: Penguin Books.

Notes from Below (editors) 2018. The Workers' Inquiry and Social Composition. *Notes from Below*, issue 1, www.notesfrombelow.org/article/workers-inquiry-and-social-composition

Ojanperä, S. & Graham, M. 2018. *Mapping the Availability of Online Workers — Oxford Internet Institute*. Retrieved 29 October 2018, from https://geonet.oii.ox.ac.uk/blog/mapping-the-availability-of-online-workers/

Pasquale, F. 2015. *The Black Box Society: The Secret Algorithms That Control Money and Information*. Cambridge, MA: Harvard University Press.

Ravenelle, A. 2019. *Hustle and Gig: Struggling and Surviving in the Sharing Economy*. Oakland: University of California Press.

Reason, P. & Bradbury, H. 2008. *Sage Handbook of Action Research*. London: Sage.

Roggero, G. 2010 Romano Alquati — militant researcher, operaist, autonomist, marxist — has passed away, Age 75. fuckyeahmilitantresearch, available at: http://fuckyeahmilitantresearch.tumblr.com/post/502186794/romanoalquatimilitant-researcher-operaist

Romano, P. & Stone, R. 1946. *The American Worker*. Detroit, MI: Facing Reality Publishing Company.

Rosenblat, A. 2018. *Uberland: How Algorithms Are Rewriting the Rules of Work*. Oakland: University of California Press.

Rosenblat, A. & Stark, L. 2016. Algorithmic labor and information asymmetries: A case study of Uber's drivers. *International Journal of Communication*, 10: 3758–3784.

Salehi, N., Irani, L. C., Bernstein, M. S., Alkhatib, A., Ogbe, E. & Milland, K. 2015. We Are Dynamo: Overcoming Stalling and Friction in Collective Action for Crowd Workers. *Proceedings of CHI 2015*, Apr 18–Apr 23, 2015.

Scholz, T. 2017. *Uberworked and Underpaid: How Workers Are Disrupting the Digital Economy*. Cambridge: Polity.

Slee, T. 2015. *What's Yours Is Mine: Against the Sharing Economy*. London: OR Books.

Srnicek, N. 2017. *Platform Capitalism*. Cambridge: Polity.

Sundararajan, A. 2017. *The Sharing Economy: The End of Employment and the Rise of Crowd-Based Capitalism*. Cambridge, MA: MIT Press.

Taylor, F. 1967. *The Principles of Scientific Management*. New York: Norton.

Ticona, J. & Mateescu, A. 2018. Trusted strangers: Carework platforms' cultural entrepreneurship in the on-demand economy. *New Media and Society*, 20(11): 4384–4404.

Tronti, M. 2019. *Workers and Capital*. London: Verso.

van der Linden, M. 1997. Socialisme ou barbarie: A French revolutionary group (1949-65). *Left History*, 5(1): 7–37.

Waters, F. & Woodcock, J. 2017. Far from Seamless: A Workers' Inquiry at Deliveroo. *Viewpoint Magazine*, available at: www.viewpointmag.com/2017/09/20/far-seamless-workers-inquiry-deliveroo/

Wood, A. J., Lehdonvirta, V. & Graham, M. 2018. Workers of the Internet unite? Online freelancer organisation among remote gig economy workers in six Asian and African countries. *New Technology, Work and Employment*, 33(2): 95–112.

Woodcock, J. 2014. The Workers' Inquiry from Trotskyism to Operaismo: A Political Methodology for Investigating the Workplace. *Ephemera*, 14 (3): 493–513.

2017. *Working the Phones: Control and Resistance in Call Centres.* London: Pluto.

2019. *Marx at the Arcade: Consoles, Controllers, and Class Struggle.* Chicago: Haymarket.

Woodcock, J. & Graham, M. 2019. *The Gig Economy: A Critical Introduction.* Cambridge: Polity

Wright, S. 2002. *Storming Heaven: Class Composition and Struggle in Italian Autonomist Marxism.* London: Pluto Press.

7 Digital Nomads

A New Form of Leisure Class?

CLAUDINE BONNEAU AND JEREMY AROLES

Introduction

Digital nomadism refers to a mobile lifestyle through which individuals can combine work with continuous travel, as they are not tied to a fixed place of residence. It comprises a wide array of professional endeavours, ranging from corporate remote workers to freelancers and digital entrepreneurs. This work modality is distinctive, in that it is also a lifestyle, i.e. a 'distinctive and recognisable mode of living' (Sobel 1981) that encompasses shared patterns of everyday behaviour (Cohen, Duncan & Thulemark 2015). Digital nomads frequently change destination and can, for instance, work in a coffee shop in Chiang Mai (Thailand) in April and then in a co-working space in Amsterdam the following month. Images of success, in the context of digital nomadism, are performed through various promotional discourses, which primarily gravitate around the promise of an emancipatory lifestyle, an image of apparent ease and an ethos of conviviality, to name a few. This chapter investigates the development of this promotional discourse, conveyed through the social media platforms of 'high-profile' digital nomads as well as their coverage by the general and specialised press.

We first examined sixty high-profile digital nomads. They clearly articulate their status as digital nomad on their public social media profiles, blogs and websites. Social media is essential to their work, even in some cases the foundation on which their business model is based. Indeed, many seek to generate income by maintaining a blog and social media accounts where they share their experiences and provide advice to aspiring nomads, establish product placement and advertising partnerships with brands, or sell products and services related to nomadism (e.g. books, podcasts, mentoring, training, conferences, organised retreats, etc.). Hence, they use social media not only to build their professional identity and reputation (see Sergi &

Bonneau 2016), but also to actively 'promote' this lifestyle. Importantly, what distinguishes these nomads from other entrepreneurs (who use social media for self-presentation) is the commodification of their life experiences. The purpose, value and uniqueness of these digital nomads' commercial proposition rely on the promises carried through their storytelling: what they can sell and to whom depend on the story they tell. In order to do so, they must not only convince others of the value of this lifestyle, but also convey their own legitimacy as experienced digital nomads. Through the public display of their success stories on social media – as well as the coverage they receive in the general and specialised press – they contribute to the development of a 'mainstream promotional discourse' around digital nomadism. As Thompson (2019) showed, this discourse does not necessarily reflect the actual lived experience of all digital nomads, who also face a world of precarious employment without benefits. Yet, it exerts a steadily growing appeal on those who aspire to escape the banality of their nine-to-five jobs, work less, earn more and enjoy life.

As we were unpacking the rhetoric underlying these digital nomads' success stories, it became apparent that leisure, along with the freedom required to fully benefit from its hedonistic enjoyment, are the central pillars supporting their narratives. Indeed, digital nomads prioritise their leisure considerations over employment-based location (see Thompson 2019). Aside from a low cost of living, digital nomads select destinations based on their potential for tourism-related activities (e.g. sightseeing, independent exploration of the destination, local culture), self-development activities (e.g. arts, sports, yoga, meditation) and entertainment-related activities (e.g. partying, drinking). Hence, they present digital nomadism as a way to get the freedom necessary to escape the traditional working structures that leave little time for leisure. We found the ways digital nomads articulate the centrality of leisure in their way of living reminiscent of the leisure class described by the American sociologist and economist Thorstein Veblen in 1899. For Veblen, every society has one or more elites. The social nature of the elites persists; only their historical characteristics change. In his first and most famous book, *The Theory of the Leisure Class* (1899/2009), Veblen offers an analysis of the elites of the American society, as well as the power structures of the capitalist society, which were being forged before his eyes. He acutely describes a leisure class composed of the members of business circles who monopolise and accumulate the wealth produced by the greatest number of individuals. In fact, the United States of his time was characterised by the transfer of economic power from handicraft workers to the owners of the means of production and other financiers, as well as the predominance of financial property over other forms of property. For Veblen (2009, p. 33), the term 'leisure' does not connote indolence or quiescence, but rather 'non-productive consumption of time'. Belonging to the leisure class involves showing that one does not need to work, at least not in a common or laborious way, and that one has leisure time at one's disposal.

Most digital nomads are privileged Westerners who can afford to travel benefiting from their passport strength as well as the gap between their Western income and the cost of living in developing countries. Such privileges and inequalities reproduce the traditional imbalance between tourists and locals (Thompson 2019). However, the power structures found at the core of digital nomadism are premised on very different canons than those benefiting the businessmen or the aristocracy studied by Veblen at the end of the nineteenth century. While the mainstream discourse of digital nomadism carries the promises of an easy life, many struggle to generate enough income to sustain this lifestyle. Hence, our purpose here is not to compare the behaviours of today's digital nomads with those of the high-status members of the American society of the late nineteenth century. Instead, we are interested in how Veblen's work can be mobilised as an analytical lens (see Brown 1999; Rojek 2000) through which we can delve deeper into digital nomadism, both as a new work manifestation and as a lifestyle. As such, our chapter sets out to explore the following question: to what extent can digital nomadism be assimilated to a new leisure class *sensu* Veblen? Considering that digital nomads might constitute the 'new faces of success' in our new world of work, we argue that Veblen's work can provide illuminating concepts in our analysis of the mainstream promotional discourse underlying digital nomadism.

The chapter is structured as follows. First, we briefly review the literature around digital nomadism in order to identify the place of leisure in this lifestyle. Second, we explain why Veblen's work is still relevant for the analysis of contemporary social issues. We then examine specific aspects of his *Theory of the Leisure Class* and show how they allowed him to propose a detailed portrait of this specific class of activities. This brief overview of Veblen's work allows us to identify four key dimensions structuring his analysis, namely Differentiation, Emulation, Visibility and Institutionalisation. After briefly presenting the methodology underlying this chapter, we use each of these four dimensions as new points of departure to extend and refine our understanding of digital nomadism. This does not lead to the identification of a new 'leisure class' *per se*, as digital nomadism is blooming in very different economic circumstances from those in which the nineteenth century's leisure class emerged. However, we conclude this chapter by discussing how this 'Veblen-inspired' analysis can act as a generative source of questions, not only for examining digital nomadism but also to look at under-studied aspects of the new world of work.

Digital Nomadism: The Promises of a Leisure-Driven Lifestyle

In 2007, Tim Ferriss published a book entitled *The 4-Hour Workweek: Escape 9-5, Live Anywhere, and Join the New Rich*. In this book, the American entrepreneur and author proposes the principle of 'geoarbitrage', which involves relocating oneself in a country where living costs are lower in order to enjoy 'the benefits of first-world income and developing-world cost of living' (Elgan 2017) while working remotely. Ten years later, Chiang Mai (the largest city in northern Thailand) was named 'the digital nomad capital of the world', following the massive influx of digital nomads who seem to put Ferriss' geoarbitrage principle in practice. This book, together with a series of similar endeavours, played a significant role in popularising the digital nomad's lifestyle. Importantly, while the term was coined more than twenty years ago (Makimoto & Manners 1997), it is only in the past few years that digital nomadism has enjoyed a higher visibility both on social media and in the general press. Importantly, it recently experienced a somehow exponential growth in the light of various technological innovations and developments, with an estimated 4.8 million digital nomads in the United States in 2018 (MBO Partners 2018), thus placing digital nomadism at the centre of discussions on the future of work and new ways of working.

Nested within an 'ecology of work practices' transformed through the emergence of the sharing economy, collaborative entrepreneurship, flexibilisation of work and a multitude of technological innovations (see Aroles, Granter & de Vaujany 2020), digital nomadism covers a wide array of professional endeavours. In particular, digital nomadism encompasses remote freelancers, digital entrepreneurs, employees working for companies that allow them to work from anywhere, as well as individuals engaged in a mix of these activities. Typically, digital nomads are engaged in computer programming, marketing activities, various forms of online consulting and teaching, writing and translation work, graphic designing, customer service and so on. Digital technologies afford flexibility to digital nomads with regards to where, when and how work is conducted. They also allow for the materialisation of new forms of autonomy with regards to business opportunities based on the use of these technologies. 'On-demand' freelancing work platforms such as Upwork, TaskRabbit and RemoteOK – the latter created by Pieter Levels, himself a digital nomad of some renown – offer independent workers new possibilities to find online work that can be carried out from anywhere. Clearly, this also creates problems in terms of the casualisation of work, a lack of stability, prospects and benefits as well as diminishing workers' protection (see Aroles, Mitev & de Vaujany 2019; Bergvall-Kåreborn & Howcroft 2014; Cant 2019; Moisander, Groß & Eräranta 2018).

While working from home or in a shared space (e.g. in a co-working space) has become relatively commonplace (see Bouncken & Reuschl 2018; Spinuzzi 2012), digital nomadism distinguishes itself in that it can be seen to constitute an extreme form of remote work. More precisely, for digital nomads, mobility and remoteness are voluntary and continuous, and not solely related to the contingencies/practicalities of their work. While mobile workers usually travel for work, digital nomads select their location based on aesthetics and leisure considerations (Müller 2016). Since their business model is based on their storytelling, exotic settings and experiences are valued. For digital nomads, tourism-related activities (e.g. sightseeing, independent exploration of the destination and the local culture), self-development activities (e.g. arts, sports, yoga, meditation), but also entertainment-related activities (e.g. partying, drinking) constitute the main forms of leisure. But work and leisure – as well as professional and personal freedom – are more tightly connected for digital nomads than for any other types of workers, as in the case of digital nomadism, 'one provides the means for, is impacted by, and created based upon the other and vice versa' (Reichenberger 2018, p. 377). While tourists travel on specific holiday dates, digital nomads work while travelling

(Nash, Jarrahi, Sutherland & Phillips 2018) in a way that blends together leisure and professional commitments. Both professional and personal arrangements must give them the resources and flexibility required to afford endless travel. Some digital nomads even go beyond the idea of owning/having a fixed place to live (e.g. a permanent home address) and engage in minimalist travelling.

Digital nomadism is also characterised by temporal independence, i.e. the autonomy to choose when they want to work and for how long. For example, they often choose to work long hours on successive days to be able to take days off after, or split their days between work and leisure. Digital nomads seek to incorporate work into a whole 'lifestyle mobility' (Cohen et al. 2015), in which private life is an integral part of their work, and vice versa. In sum, a 'successful' digital nomad is not only an individual who has achieved location independence, but also professional, technological and temporal independence (see Prester, Cecez-Kecmanovic & Schlagwein 2019). This entanglement between leisure and work (or private and professional lives), together with the infatuation for digital nomadism, led to the portrayal of digital nomadism as a lifestyle in itself, with digital nomads tentatively emerging as a new class.

An Overview of Veblen's Approach and Proposition

In 1899, Thorstein Veblen wrote a seminal monograph describing an emerging class in the American society in the late nineteenth century. The strength and precision of Veblen's description of the power structures characterising those times still has the ability to enlighten readers today. As noted by Martha Banta in her introduction of *The Theory of the Leisure Class*' re-edition within Oxford World's Classics collection (Veblen 2009), Veblen reshaped 'economics as a cultural history of material life' (ibid, p. x). For Veblen, the economic studies (of his time) seemed to isolate the market from society. In order to take a critical look at the 'gentlemen of leisure', Veblen not only examined their business practices – and the institutions that make them possible – but also paid attention to their social habits and everyday behaviours. The leisure class described by Veblen (2009) is made up of conservative people who directly hinder change and evolution through their own inertia. For Veblen (2009), today's social relations will form the institutions of tomorrow, and will continue until new circumstances force people to change them. Hence, his analysis of the evolution of society considers features of social life that 'are not commonly classed as economic' (2009, p. 3).

His approach is marked by constant scepticism, allowing him to stay alert to 'new evidence that raised new questions' (Veblen 2009, p. xv), which were left under-studied by his contemporaries at the time. Veblen's methods of scientific inquiry involved the use of data 'drawn from everyday life, by direct observation or through common notoriety' (ibid, p. 3). He often anchors his descriptions in figures or even characters (e.g. the financier, the craftsman, etc.). As these methods were unusual at the time, he was accused of illustrating rather than demonstrating. But his sharp verve and argumentative strategies are powerful and serve his three main objectives well, namely to depict the general structures of a given society, to identify the social relationships and behaviours they generate and to show their impact on consumption. In line with others (see for example Brown 1999; Hillman 2009; Rojek 2000; Scott 2010), we argue that the principles that guided Veblen's analysis of the leisure class remain relevant to understanding the economic and cultural foundations of contemporary socio-economic phenomena. More specifically, we contend that four key dimensions, which are central in his work, might inform our own analysis of work-related practices: (i) Differentiation, (ii) Emulation, (iii) Visibility and (iv) Institutionalisation.

1. **Differentiation.** For Veblen, the rise of the leisure class is a direct consequence of the ancient distinction between honourable activities that were once classified as exploits (e.g. priestly activities, government, warfare and sport), and productive work, in which 'impecunious members of the community habitually put forth their efforts' (2009, p. 218). Hence, one line of demarcation between the leisure class and the general body of the working classes is based on the nature of their respective occupations. For the gentlemen of leisure, to be seen carrying out productive work – referred to as industrial work – is to be lowered in terms of social esteem. Hence, the members of the leisure class sought to be exempted from industrial employment, as this exemption was the economic expression of their superior rank. Veblen (2009) also described the types of leisure behaviours attributable to these elites in contrast to those associated with traditional and mass culture. The leisure activities of the upper

bourgeoisie of the time were based on the culture of aesthetic qualities, the acquisition of which was intended only as an honorary distinction. The sumptuousness of the celebrations it holds and the sophistication of their entertainment activities essentially serve the purpose of distinguishing itself advantageously as part of the economic elite.

2. **Emulation.** At the core of Veblen's theory lies the conceptualisation of consumption as a form of status seeking. The gentleman of leisure compares himself with others and seeks to outperform them in the acquisition of wealth and to display this in various socially approved activities. Hence, the behaviours of the members of the leisure class were motivated by a desire to do better than those with whom they classify themselves. The members of the leisure class of the late nineteenth century rated and graded themselves and others in respect of their relative opulence. Veblen's second chapter, 'Pecuniary Emulation', delves deeper into the consequences of the aspiration to emulate the status held by others. Emulation creates needs that will never be fully met since they are measured by the wealth and honour of others. Hence, the end of effort became the achievement of a favourable comparison with other men. These efforts were guided by various canons of reputability that should be observed. For example, what was considered beautiful was what served no industrial end, for example, domestic animals that had no useful purpose, or expensive goods that had no direct utility, served the emulative end of consumption. For the leisure class to serve as a reference model for others, their behaviours, wealth and power needed to be visible to others (Veblen 2009).

3. **Visibility.** Leisure (i.e. non-productive consumption of time) is evidence of the economic surplus value of rich families. However, leisure is not always performed in public and does not always leave a material trace. Hence, other means must be found to put leisure in evidence. The leisure class' members portrayed by Veblen (2009) cultivated good manners, habits of decorum and aesthetic faculty, which were ostensible signs of their wealth (and described by Veblen as 'conspicuous leisure'). They also consumed valuable goods for appearance. They spent money in valuable presents, expensive feats and entertainments and other noble goods as an evidence of their wealth (what Veblen referred to as 'conspicuous consumption'): 'he becomes a connoisseur in creditable viands of

various degrees of merit, in manly beverages and trinkets, in seemly apparel and architecture, in weapons, games dancers and the narcotics' (Veblen 2009, p. 53). This competition through visible consumption generates an endless demand and therefore constitutes the most powerful driver of economic life itself. Learning how to live a life of ostensible leisure also has effects on consumption.

4. **Institutionalisation.** Developing the 'right' habits of thought and cultivating the aesthetic faculty characterising the leisure class required time and application. These learning efforts, as well as the teaching endeavour that it involved, were required to ensure the transition of the leisure class to its next 'stage of culture' (Veblen 2009, p. 30). As time goes by, a large proportion of the leisure class has been consistently exempt from work for a generation or more, and has obtained a 'social confirmation' within the class itself. This 'select class' 'is large enough to form and sustain an opinion in matters of taste' (ibid, p. 91) and to prescribe its manner of life and its standards of worth. These standards constituted the 'point of departure for a new move in advance in the same direction' (ibid, p. 63), and their observance does not only happen within the leisure class itself, but also 'carries the force of prescription for all classes below it' (ibid, p. 71). Poorer people also wanted to emulate the rich by reproducing their consumption behaviours.

Even though the mainstream discourse about digital nomadism promotes very different values and ideals from those pertaining to the nineteenth century leisure class, there are a number of aspects that can be investigated using these four key dimensions. The following section briefly describes our methods.

Methodological Approach

Our research adopted a qualitative approach to content analysis and drew from several types of online sources. The data collection was conducted in two phases. First, the exploration of popular nomad-orientated forums and groups and the systematic search for related media coverage in the general press allowed us to identified sixty high-profile digital nomads. In order to be included in our study, each individual had to meet the following criteria: (i) be a self-identified 'digital nomad'; (ii) monetise their nomad status in some way; and

(iii) publicly share their experiences online. Hence, we focus on digital nomads who make themselves visible on social media, as well as those who are frequently featured in media stories (and not necessarily on the more successful ones, in terms of revenue or longevity). Second, we closely examined these selected nomads' 'visibility ecosystems', namely their publicly available social media accounts (Instagram, Twitter, Facebook, YouTube and blogs). We documented several aspects such as gender, age range, career field, number of years into the digital nomad lifestyle, education, professional experience, lifestyle, frequency and duration of travel, their pitch, and so on. In addition, we collected photos posted by each digital nomad, thus mirroring the increasingly visual culture on social media (Hand 2012), where images are as much a part of human communication as text or speech (Miller & Sinanan 2017).

Our data analysis process also involved two main phases. First, we performed a manual thematic coding of the data collected in an open and inductive manner (Miles, Huberman & Saldana 2013). This not only involved examining closely the professional journey of these digital nomads but also unpacking the narratives upon which digital nomads craft their digital selves as well as the aesthetics carried by the images. Therefore, our analysis considered both the visual and textual elements of posts, using the descriptions, hashtags and comments to contextualise the pictures (Latzko-Toth, Bonneay & Millette 2017). This first round of coding allowed us to formulate a series of first-order codes that captured the essence of our data, including: the activities through which digital nomads can monetise and professionalise their experience (teaching, conferences, influencing, community building, etc.), the values and aesthetics conveyed by their discourse (freedom, autonomy, wellness, adventure, meaningfulness, self-development, work-life balance, etc.) and the components on which rely their story-line relies (a 'younger generation-specific' vision, the refusal to make compromise, the 'do-it-yourself ethos, etc.). We then crafted our second-order constructs by examining our first-order codes with the lens provided by the four dimensions we have extracted from Veblen's work. This process allowed us to draw connections between our emerging analytical paths. Altogether, this enabled us to better understand the specificities of digital nomadism, to characterise the digital nomads' 'canons of reputability' and to show how they somehow regulate their scheme of life and those of aspiring digital nomads.

Analysing the Mainstream Discourse on Digital Nomadism

Differentiation. Contrary to the leisure class described by Veblen (2009), digital nomads do not differentiate themselves from other classes of workers on the basis of their professional occupations. Indeed, the mainstream discourse of digital nomadism features, we argue, two other forms of differentiations, one from corporate workers and the other from previous generations. Digital nomads want to be exempted from what they characterise as the 'soul-less corporate 9 to 5 life', which in their view is not honourable. Time spent on a regular job in a cubicle with 'only 10 days vacation a year' is not only unworthy, but also comes with obstacles to freedom and autonomy. Traditional work settings, where employees work for others, are presented as incompatible with self-development. Hence, digital nomads see themselves as non-conformist digital workers who diverge from the path followed by the majority. They refuse to make compromises and to accept imposed choices:

We 9-to-5 escape artists choose to defy the status quo because it doesn't work for us. Something in our very nature fights against mediocrity and working our asses off so someone else can achieve their goals. We have our own goals in mind. We wake up every day with the intention of creating our best lives because we have only one life, and it's with a pre-set amount of days.

This differentiation clearly appears in the ideological and aesthetic underpinnings of emancipation and non-conformism found in the mainstream narrative surrounding digital nomadism. For digital nomads, it is not so much 'doing work' that is the problem, but 'doing work that is meaningless'. Hence, they are not rejecting work per se, but they seek to contrast their experience with traditional employment. Elements associated with entrepreneurial values – such as breaking the rules, opposing authority, going for full autonomy, do-it-yourself ethos – are put forward in their discourses.

Furthermore, digital nomads are also aiming for technological, geographical, and temporal independence (Prester et al. 2019). The combination of these different forms of independence provides them with more freedom to pursue leisure activities and self-development. In the narrative of their experience, they put forward a different way of enacting the interplay of work and leisure, which is said to be driven by an underlying intrinsic motivation to find a balance and live a more fulfilling and purposeful life. Their lifestyle is presented as a form of reaction to ideals and imperatives that are dominant in the corporate world: 'After some years working in the corporate world, I realized that I found intolerable just everything about it, and in particular having to attend interminable soul-crushing meetings and to work on other people's silly project'.

This narrative contributes to the creation of a demarcation between insiders (digital nomads), who are passionate about 'living their dreams' and outsiders (corporate workers), who are 'trapped by their comfort and safe in their mediocrity'. Hence, leisure is seen as a way to live life to the fullest. But digital nomads are not only differentiating themselves from other types of workers, but also from previous generations. They no longer tolerate habits of thought formed in the past and therefore consider their lifestyle as an evolution in comparison to the path taken by their parents. Indeed, the conversion to nomadic lifestyle does not only involve the adoption of a new way of working, but often entails embracing new life choices. Their stories convey a 'younger-generation-specific' view on work-life balance, which relies on the excitement, adventures and inherent challenges that come with travel and prioritises well-being in all aspects of life; '. . . our generation is sick of being treated like unidimensional beings that are expected to show up to an office from nine to five, five days a week, 365 days a year . . . There is no work/life balance. There is life and there is life'.

Emulation. Veblen (2009) indicates that the habit of making comparison acts as an incentive for others to (re)direct their energy in a way that would allow them to live up to that ideal. For digital nomads, the value is derived from neither ownership or possession, but rather from individual, self-centred fulfilment and happiness. These characteristics result from their behaviours, preferences and goals. It is the manifestations of moral, physical and aesthetic values related to this ideal that form the 'standard of life' on which comparison can be based (ibid, p. 67). The high-profile digital nomad success stories are efficient means of emulation. They gratify their authors' sense of legitimacy, while informing other nomads (and people aspiring to this lifestyle) about the necessary conditions of reputability defining success within digital nomads' scheme of life. As also noted by Hillman (2009) in his study of the backpacker subculture, which shares many similarities with digital nomadism, this shows a contradiction between conformity (the desire to copy successful nomads to build one's standing) and independence (the glorification of autonomy as a symbol of success). Like backpackers, digital nomads may believe that they are free from the emulation process, but many 'appear to be almost clones of the others' (Hillman 2009, p. 167).

Sustaining a life of travel while working online is the goal to achieve. With digital nomads, favourable comparison is achieved through the degree of freedom, location independence, flexibility and wellness obtained in comparison to others. As Veblen (2009) explains, the standard that guide our efforts is not the average lifestyle achieved, but an 'ideal that lies just beyond our reach' (ibid, p. 71). In the same manner, the digital nomad's lifestyle does not seem considerably in advance or unattainable, but reachable by anyone with the right mind. This idea is reinforced by the promotional discourse of high-profile digital nomads that gravitates around empowerment and self-discovery: 'Anyone can live a freedom lifestyle if they want it badly enough. They just need the guidance and support from others who have "been there and done that".'

They set out to motivate others to become nomads by showing the actions needed to emulate their success and by convincing them that this is not only a sustainable mode of life, but that it is accessible to anyone with the right mind: 'Follow my journey and be inspired. I am truly passionate about helping people learn how to become digital nomads. There is always a way to make it happen so send me an e-mail and an excuse and I will give you a solution'.

Visibility. For digital nomads, leisure is 'the motor that sustains modern life' (Blackshaw 2018, p. 79), and therefore is not performed with the unique goal of providing visible manifestations of wealth. However, in order to gain the esteem of others, high-profile digital nomads must make their freedom and success visible to others. In their case, it is not so much about the public display of their accumulated wealth, but about the public display of specific markers of their lifestyle on social media: 'This is what we had dreamed of doing – and we were actually pulling it off! From country to country we have lived a luxurious lifestyle while working mere hours a day (on the days we decided to work at all) and we did so while sipping cocktails poolside.'

Continuous connectivity and hypermobility inevitably lead to the consumption of ever-new products, gadgets and services, and those are registered as 'markers' of a digital nomad's lifestyle. But it is more the embeddedness of their leisure activities as a crucial part of their lifestyle that is displayed as proof of the level of freedom they have achieved. Through their social media traces, they communicate their accomplishments. They narrate their personal and professional stories, the reasons that led them to become nomads, how they transformed their lives to reach this goal, and how they achieved success. As explained by Humphreys (2018, p. 12), these practices of 'media accounting' provide evidence for and explanation of their presence, existence and action as digital nomads. The narratives of high-profile digital nomads are built around proofs of their achievements (e.g. by sharing detailed monthly income reports). Observers have no other means of judging their reputability and legitimacy as digital nomads than through this display of their lifestyle on social media.

The images that accompany their discourse must not be seen as mere illustrations, but as true anchors serving to materialise and give life to this lifestyle. It is enacted on social media through the documentation of the numerous locations visited, which are not only presented in a 'I was here' fashion, but also in ways that clearly show that travelling is performed on a long-term or permanent basis, and not bracketed off from their 'regular' life. Photos of the work settings – usually set in places generally considered unusual for work that is conducted on a computer – are also used as tangible evidence to convince others that they have truly achieved location-independent work. Taken together, these photos and stories contribute to the popularisation of a certain aesthetic of digital nomadism that is necessary to convey the associated values of freedom, wellness and adventure. They also largely contribute to the 'romantisation' of digital nomadism, since these digital accounts often convey what is desirable about the digital nomad's lifestyle. They orientate on a more symbolic level how aspiring digital nomads should conceive this lifestyle and how they should embody it: 'I will take you through stories that I learned through my experiences and frames that I froze, for you to get a better picture of your next endeavour.'

Institutionalisation. While digital nomadism is portrayed as an alternative to mainstream forms of work, it has become increasingly institutionalised, in part due to the business activities of some of the high-profile digital nomads who realised that they could monetise their experience by focusing on the material and professional needs of less experienced individuals (see Aroles, Granter & de Vaujany 2020).

Some high-profile digital nomads help others achieve their own goals through coaching sessions, online courses, training programmes, mentoring sessions and 'how-to' guides. Through their 'educational' stance, these digital nomads seek to highlight how digital nomadism can be learnt/taught, just like any other profession: 'We want to share with you all we have gleaned. We have helped hundreds of people customize and live out their own freedom lifestyles. We also offer online courses for people looking to grow a profitable online business they can easily and successfully run from anywhere in the world'.

They monetise their vast experience as digital nomads into practical methods and resources in the form of books, podcasts, YouTube channels and public speaking. In particular, this can, for instance, involve organising various events aimed specifically at the digital nomad community (e.g. conferences, workshops, cruises, camps, retreats, festivals and summits), such as DNX, the first digital nomad conference now held annually in English, Spanish and German). The founders – a vegan couple who escaped the corporate world of Düsseldorf and Berlin to become nomadic entrepreneurs – draw from their own previous experience as confirmed nomads to advise and encourage others to become digital nomads like themselves.

Other high-profile digital nomads also provide access to certain networks of highly successful individuals and constructed communities where like-minded individuals can transform their life together, as illustrated in the following quote describing thirty-day international co-working retreats: 'We realized we were building an open and creative community where people could dive into their life in an unstructured way. We wanted to shift people's outlook towards space and time and their routine.'

Some present themselves as the gatekeepers of exclusive experiences that are not necessarily open to anyone interested; a thorough selection process is often involved to make sure that the participants match precise criteria or correspond to a pre-defined profile. For example, a nomad limits the access to his 'gastronomad' experiences to only ten 'adventurous foodies'. Other organisers clearly define their targeted attendees in the description of their events, as shown in the following quote: '[Our retreat] is for the unconventional misfit, the graduated backpacker, the passionately curious. It is a home for those that prioritize the acceleration of their potential.'

Usually held in breath-taking locations, these events come at a price. For instance, the different access packages for a major digital nomad annual conference range from 197 to 997 euros per person. The languages and prices of these events also inform about the intended audience. They create a comfortable bubble where privileged Westerners pay to gather with people of similar demographics and recreate the conditions of a 'Western environment' in developing nations (Thompson 2019). As illustrated by the following quote describing a 'workation' all-inclusive package, turnkey solutions are available for those who are willing to invest in the 'acquisition' of this curated lifestyle: 'Traveling with us is the best way to immerse yourself in new cultures without losing sight of your career, business, or personal project. When you travel with us, you live a life you don't need a vacation from.'

While the values and ideals promoted by high-profile digital nomads substantially diverge from those of the leisure class described by Veblen (2009), they share some similarities with regards to cultural aspects. In a similar fashion to the leisure class, these successful individuals have been enacting the digital nomad's lifestyle long enough to obtain a 'social confirmation' within the digital nomad tribe itself. These normative networks, preferred places, special events and constructed communities are positioned as quasi-mandatory passage points in the process of becoming a fully-fledged digital nomad (Aroles et al. 2020). The strategies that are shared by their organisers and participants (e.g. how to make money online and sustain long-term travel) determine exemplar patterns of behaviour for aspiring nomads, and therefore contribute to the institutionalisation of digital nomadism.

Discussion and Conclusions

Digital nomadism is not only a new technology-enabled form of work, it is also an economic activity and a socio-cultural phenomenon in itself. The mainstream discourse surrounding digital nomadism goes hand in hand with the profound changes taking place in contemporary capitalism, including the pervasive relevance of enterprise culture (Du Gay 1996; Vallas & Cummins 2015), as well as the 'myth of glamorized millennial labor', where the Internet provides access to boundless opportunities (Rosenblat 2018).

In this chapter, we argued that some observations can be made about the character of emulation and conspicuous leisure practice encountered in digital nomadism today. Although Veblen (2009) recognised emulation is practised across all socio-economic levels, he acknowledged that the attitudes and behaviours deemed respectable may vary through time. For digital nomads, the basis of esteem does not revolve around the accumulation of goods or the possession of wealth, as in the pecuniary culture described by Veblen. Indeed, most of them cannot be considered as high-status travellers and are actually proud of themselves when it comes to their ability to obtain 'best value for money' travel arrangements (Hillman 2009). Their reputability is based on their self-made character and their capacity to show increased autonomy and control over their life, as compared to corporate workers and previous generations. High-profile digital nomads have to demonstrate tangible evidence that they are exempt from nine-to-five forms of employment. By publicly displaying their mobile lifestyle, they distance themselves from traditional workers whose lives are deemed undesirable. Their 'badges of honour' are materialised in the form of lists of destinations, aesthetic pictures and online diaries. Their constant movements between countries can be used to impress others and prove their legitimacy. By making these visible on social media, they also propagate particular standards of living and contribute to the popularisation of certain places, events and communities.

While each period brings its fair share of novelty, difference and innovation, various periods can be premised on similar logics that are repeated over time and simply presented in a different manner. For that reason, we contend that seminal theories, such as Veblen's, can act as a generative source of questions to examine contemporary phenomena, including digital nomadism. Veblen showed that the study of economic phenomena cannot be carried out without an understanding of cultural structures and social values. His portrait of the leisure class suggests ways to distinguish different forms of work-related activities and situate them in a broader framework of analysis. In line with others (see for example Brown 1999; Hillman 2009; Rojek 2000; Scott 2010), we argue that Veblen's work is still highly relevant in the exploration of various facets of modern work, economic sociology and work-leisure phenomena.

Through his analysis, Veblen (2009) detects the presence of economic grounds in the leisure class's accepted canons of taste and shows their impact on consumption behaviours. Drawing from our own analysis of the manifestations of digital nomadism, we showed that there is currently a whole set of economic activities based on the 'selling of a dreamed work/lifestyle' by one section of the digital nomads' group who show their dominance over others. Therefore, aspiring digital nomads can achieve their desired status via high-profile digital nomads who have already achieved the status they seek. Carefully curated images of 'work that doesn't seem like work' allow them to construct the digital nomad lifestyle as a commodity that can simply be 'purchased from them'. This offering of goods and services targeting aspiring digital nomads meets their 'demand for the honorific element' (Veblen 2009, p. 104), but are also pivotal in sustaining the sellers' own dream. As Thompson (2019, p. 38) notes, these commercial activities 'becomes almost like a pyramid scheme of selling the dream to the next group of aspirants in order to fund another's lifestyle'. As Veblen observed, standards for emulation are ever-changing, meaning that current goods and services currently considered reputable will be challenged as new standards arise (Scott 2010). Indeed, maintaining an enviable position in a community requires constant effort. Hence, the emulation of desirable work profiles and lifestyle generates other drivers of economic life itself. Further research could look into how the ideals shaping the new world of work fluctuate over time and create an endless demand from individuals who have not yet had access to it.

The mainstream discourse on the digital nomad's lifestyle contributes to the creation of a new symbol of the future of work: aspiring digital nomads accept as their ideal the digital nomads' scheme of life, and endeavour to live up to that ideal. However, achieving and sustaining constant mobility is a challenge and not everyone carries equal changes of 'making it'. At some point, even the most convinced nomads realise that their quest for a leisure-driven lifestyle actually means that they are always working while travelling. Some might switch to a slower travel speed or even decide to return into a more 'traditional lifestyle' after facing too many difficulties (e.g. lack of resources) or feeling the need for a more stable lifestyle (e.g. when children become part of the equation). Additionally, growing environmental awareness might lead to a more direct questioning of the sustainability of such a lifestyle, especially considering the carbon emission associated with air travel. This raises the question of whether digital nomadism is not simply a transitional 'leisure-based' phase rather than an enduring transformation that can be sustained over the whole course of one's life. Future work could use a longitudinal and processual approach to study the various stages shaping the new trajectories of extreme mobile work.

Alongside the mainstream discourse presented in this chapter, we must note that there are also several digital nomads who criticise these narratives and try to present a more nuanced view of this lifestyle, by sharing their difficulties and warning others of the scams and traps they will find on their path. They also uncover different motivations for adopting the 'geoarbitrage' principle as an 'economic coping strategy' (Thompson 2019, p. 28) for young people crushed by massive student loan debt, no local job opportunities and high rent. Yet, these voices describing a world of precarious employment without benefits are, more often than not, eclipsed by the optimistic 'mainstream narratives' depicting digital nomadism as an empowering and fulfilling life. As such, it becomes even more important to study digital nomadism 'in practice' in order to explore what is not accounted for or reported in the 'mainstream narratives' that depict and frame digital nomadism. Researchers could investigate the challenges that other digital nomads face as they seek to distance themselves from the image propagated by the mainstream narratives. This would involve exploring, for instance, the following questions: To what extent do digital nomads recognise themselves in these mainstream narratives? How does their own experience of digital nomadism differ from these stories? Do they consider that these narratives contribute to the stigmatisation of their lifestyle and harm their own image as nomads? These questions remain to be explored in order to continue the reflection opened in this chapter.

References

Aroles, J., Granter, E. & de Vaujany, F. X. 2020. Becoming mainstream: The professionalization and corporatization of digital nomadism. *New Technology, Work and Employment*, 35(1): 114–129.

Aroles, J., Mitev, N. & de Vaujany, F. X. 2019. Mapping themes in the study of new work practices. *New Technology, Work and Employment*, 34 (3): 285–299.

Bergvall-Kåreborn, B. & Howcroft, D. 2014. Amazon Mechanical Turk and the commodification of labour. *New Technology, Work and Employment*, 29(3): 213–223.

Blackshaw, T. 2018. The two rival concepts of devotional leisure: Towards an understanding of twenty-first century human creativity and the possibility of freedom. *International Journal of the Sociology of Leisure*, 1(1): 75–97.

Bouncken, R. B. & Reuschl, A. J. 2018. Coworking-spaces: How a phenomenon of the sharing economy builds a novel trend for the workplace and for entrepreneurship. *Review of Managerial Science*, 12(1): 317–334.

Brown, W. S. 1999. Thorstein Veblen in the twenty-first century. *Journal of Economic Issues*, 33(4): 1035–1037.

Cant, C. 2019. *Riding for Deliveroo: Resistance in the New Economy*. Cambridge: Polity Press.

Cohen, S. A., Duncan, T. & Thulemark, M. 2015. Lifestyle mobilities: The crossroads of travel, leisure and migration. *Mobilities*, 10(1): 155–172.

Du Gay, P. 1996. *Consumption and Identity at Work*. Milton Keynes: Sage.

Elgan, M. 2017. *The Digital Nomad's Guide to Working from Anywhere On Earth*. Retrieved from www.fastcompany.com/3068312/the-digital-nomads-guide-to-working-from-anywhere-on-e

Ferriss, T. 2007. *The 4-Hour Workweek: Escape 9-5, Live Anywhere, and Join the New Rich*. New York: Harmony.

Hand, M. 2012. *Ubiquitous Photography*. Cambridge: Polity.

Hillman, W. 2009. Veblen and the theory of the backpacker leisure class: Status seeking and emulation in the Australian contemporary tourist economy. *Tourism Review International*, 13: 157–171.

Humphreys, L. 2018. *The Qualified Self: Social Media and the Accounting of Everyday Life*. Cambridge, MA: MIT Press.

Latzko-Toth, G., Bonneau, C. & Millette, M. 2017. Small Data, Thick Data: Thickening Strategies for Trace-based Social Media Research. In A. Quan-Haase & L. Sloan (eds.) *The SAGE Handbook of Social Media Research Methods*. London: Sage, 199–214.

Makimoto, T. & Manners, D. 1997. *Digital Nomad*. Chichester: Wiley.

MBO Partners. 2018. *A state of independence in American research brief. Digital Nomadism: A rising trend*. Retrieved from https://s29814.pcdn .co/wp-content/uploads/2019/02/StateofIndependence-ResearchBrief-DigitalNomads.pdf

Miles, M. B., Huberman, A. M. & Saldana, J. 2013. *Qualitative Data Analysis: A Methods Sourcebook*. Thousand Oaks, CA: Sage Publications.

Miller, D. & Sinanan, J. 2017. *Visualising Facebook*. London: UCL Press.

Moisander, J., Groß, C. & Eräranta, K. 2018. Mechanisms of biopower and neoliberal governmentality in precarious work: Mobilising the dependent self-employed as independent business owners. *Human Relations*, 71(3): 375–398.

Müller, A. 2016. The digital nomad: Buzzword or research category? *Transnational Social Review*, 6(3): 344–348.

Nash, C., Jarrahi, M. H., Sutherland, W. & Phillips, G. 2018. Digital nomads beyond the buzzword: Defining digital nomadic work and use of digital technologies. *Lecture Notes in Computer Science IConference 2018*, (April).

Prester, J., Cecez-Kecmanovic, D. & Schlagwein, D. 2019. Becoming a Digital Nomad: Identity Emergence in the Flow of Practice. In *International Conference on Information Systems*, Munich, pp. 1–9.

Reichenberger, I. 2018. Digital nomads – a quest for holistic freedom in work and leisure. *Annals of Leisure Research*, 21(3): 364–380.

Rojek, C. 2000. Leisure and the rich today: Veblen's thesis after a century. *Leisure Studies*, 19(1): 1–15.

Rosenblat, A. 2018. *Uberland: How Algorithms Are Rewriting the Rules of Work*. Oakland: University of California Press.

Scott, D. 2010. What would Veblen say? *Leisure Sciences*, 32(3): 288–294.

Sergi, V. & Bonneau, C. 2016. Making mundane work visible on social media: A CCO investigation of working out loud on Twitter. *Communication Research and Practice*, 2(3): 378–406.

Sobel, M. 1981. *Lifestyle and Social Structure: Concepts, Definitions and Analyses*. New York: Academic Press.

Spinuzzi, C. 2012. Working alone together: Coworking as emergent collaborative activity. *Journal of Business and Technical Communication*, 26 (4): 399–441.

Thompson, B. Y. 2019. The digital nomad lifestyle: (Remote) work/leisure balance, privilege, and constructed community. *International Journal of the Sociology of Leisure*, 2(1–2): 27–42.

Vallas, S. P. & Cummins, E. R. 2015. Personal branding and identity norms in the popular business press: Enterprise culture in an age of precarity. *Organization Studies*, 36(3): 293–319.

Veblen, T. 2009. *The Theory of the Leisure Class*, Oxford: Oxford University Press.

PART III

Politics, Imaginaries and *Others* in the New World of Work

8 Bypassing the Stage of Copper Wire?
New Work Practices amongst the Peasantry

GIBSON BURRELL

Introduction

This chapter is about changes in work practices amongst the 'peas-antry' still working upon the land in twenty-first century India. Herein, 'the peasant is not treated as a remnant of the past, but as an integral part of our time and societies' (Van Der Ploeg 2008, p. xvi). The population in this place may sound very far from conventional under-standing of shifts in technology that regularly affect how work is done in the 'West' but, in fact, the rise of ICTs, especially the smart phone, has the potential at least to shift practices upon lands that have remained unchanged for centuries. Without falling into the trap of material determinism, it might be argued that much of what Western humans called 'work' between the Napoleonic and Second World Wars (1800–1950) had some reliance on the acquisition of copper ore, its smelting into metal and its use in the form of copper boilers, sheets and wire in domestic, military and communication technologies. Large infrastructural requirements accompanied the triumph of copper, so that in some senses a whole material civilisation developed around the electrical and conductive properties of this metal. However, this mode of organising has itself become threatened by a digital revolution. New forms of working are allowed by the post-copper technologies and materials of the twenty-first century, but we must ask how widespread and how deep does this 'rematerialising of organ-isation' actually go?

Now, one could argue that the peasantry was never implicated in the age of copper for they were excluded – deliberately – from the commu-nicative advantages that such wire-based technologies allowed elites. In 1948, after Indian independence, a population of perhaps half a billion people had only 80,000 telephones between them. These devices were for those who managed the economy, not those living upon the land in a subsistence-agricultural mode. But copper wire brings with it not just access to telephones and telegraphs but also a whole infrastructure of centralised control. This control can take the form of a strong socialist, metropolitan-based state apparatus or corporate-based capitalism. It is almost always based on the political and financial centre of the nation state, but real power and control may lie, of course, in other regions. It is this copper-based infrastructure that is being bypassed by the possibilities offered by wireless technologies. But this is not to suggest that mobile devices allow escape from management structures. Bypassing copper wire is to open the peasant up to *more* management rather than less. Peretti (2017, p. 29) argues: 'In 2007, with the invention of the iPhone, a device was created for the passing of trust from the banks to ... tech giants. They are now the new custodians of money'. As 'new' economies become more monetised, the distant banks are circumvented by Vodaphone, Google and Facebook, which appear much closer, since they are carried, structure-like, upon your person. And also, what is being bypassed is the long-standing cloak of invisibility possessed by the peasant in the face of the state and the corporate world. The smart phone renders up the user to numericalisation, identification, location and surveillance. Unlike their quietly hidden existence with copper-based technologies, the peasantry become persons of interest in a digital age. They are a huge, untapped market for the management of their activities. They are literally the bearers of a new financial and commercial structure.

This chapter explores whether new technological modes of working are changing activities within the category of 'peasant' to such an extent that this is giving way to the category of 'employee' – because it is the latter, not the former, who are persons of particular interest to the industrial and industrialising state (and, it might be argued, to Western academics too). The consequences of this enormous binary shift for work practices, and how they are understood by those facing such transformations, could be huge. But, and it is a large but, the concept of 'employee' itself may be in retreat. In the West we know that the rise of the gig economy and zero-hours contracts, along with the difficulty for trade unions in organising such groups of allegedly 'self-employed' staff, creates a world in which the notion of the 'employee' being a person with rights as well as responsibilities, protected under law and capable of collective action, is newly contested (Crouch 2019). In India, these problems in creating the 'employee' as a concept are well understood- but in the other direction. Bhatt (2006, p. 17) tells us the following example is a common one:

A small farmer works on her own farm. In tough times, she also works on other farms as a labourer. When the agriculture season is over, she goes to the forest to collect gum and other forest produce. Year round, she produces embroidered items either at a piece rate for a contractor or for sale to a trader who comes to her village to buy goods. Now how should her work be categorized? Does she belong to the agricultural sector, the factory sector or the home-based sector? Should she be categorized as farmer or a farm worker. Is she self employed or is she a piece rate worker?

Bhatt argues that because this person's situation cannot be easily defined, she has no work status, is denied access to training or financial services and has no 'identity' within the economy. The peasant, even if they wanted to, cannot move easily to the status of employee if they have to travel through this 'intermediate' set of stages of being *in* the economy but not accepted as being *of* the economy. And, if one believed this to be a straightforward linear move from peasant to employee, the gig economy pushes work relations backwards in capitalist time to some 'intermediate' position of pluriactivity (Van Der Ploeg 2008, pp. 32–33). Peasant property is almost always family property, so 'individual' roles are subsumed by collective familial ones. The residual function of the family is upon survival, not monetary returns, and pluriactivity is a partial solution for survival. There is European evidence (Franklin 1969) for the existence of a transitional class, the worker–peasant, who engages with capitalist penetration of the local area and who moves between local forms of employment that still remain predominantly tied to the land. There is not an abandonment of farming but diversification into other modes of working. It is an 'intermediate', or 'transitional', position of working, between that of employee and peasant, outside the conventional binary.

The Peasantry?

The deferred neglect of one side of the conventional binary – the peasant – is foreshadowed across much of social science, including within Marx and Weber, to name but two. Just as the term in common parlance is associated with stupidity and idiocy, the peasantry has been 'soiled' by much of Western social science. Max Weber's writings show a clear call for depeasantrisation, because the peasantry represent a very deep pool of non-rationality. They are 'most lacking in culture' (Gerth & Mills 1948, p. 368), engage in 'primal, naturalistic and unsublimated sexuality' (ibid, p. 349) and are 'inclined towards magic' since 'they are bound to nature and depend on elemental forces' (ibid, p. 283). Most tellingly, they 'have not been trained in order to gain profit' (ibid, p. 365). It is clear that, for Weber, rationality has escaped the European peasantry for the last 2,000 years and they are beyond hope.

For Marx (1987, p. 10), the French peasantry in the mid-1850s were beyond redemption and were characterised thus: 'Their field of production, the small holding, admits of no division of labour in its cultivation, no application of science and, therefore, no diversity of development, no variety of talent, no wealth of social relationships'. Marx's notion that feudalism would come to be replaced by capitalism everywhere led to the so-called *agrarian question* within socialist thought (Lerche 2013). Mitrany (1951) argued that communism had ridden to victory on the back of discontented peasantries, and it has been maintained that, in the 1920s, agrarian populism across Central Europe installed elements of the peasantry into power. Certainly, it is true that Lenin had originally envisaged the Soviet flag to consist of hammer and sword representing the roles of the proletariat and the military in the Revolution. The sickle was only added (replacing the sword) in the early 1920s to show the importance of peasant uprisings in the march of socialism. The peasantry's quietism and political irrelevance was beginning to be questioned (McMichael 2008).

This notwithstanding, it appears that much of Western thought has abandoned the 'peasantry' both as a concept and as a social grouping (Kearney 1996), so on what basis can we place them and theirs back in the centre of thinking – or at least as somewhere on the stage as actors of some note? There is also the question of whether the term 'peasant' is so steeped in Western thought that it has no real utility outside Europe (especially the East) and certainly not in India. It is a term of abuse for many, and so its abandonment is seen as a radical political act of escape from colonial language. These are epistemo-political questions that we must seek to address in some persuasive way as we move towards very intrusive definitional issues. Of whom do we speak?

Our focus in this chapter is upon both the agricultural proletariat who own no land of their own *and* semi-proletarian peasants who work on their own land to provide subsistence for their family yet also work at particular times of the year as farm labourers for local land lords. Non-market considerations will predominate their social and economic relationships (Van Der Ploeg 2008). For each of these groups, there are very different conditions of possibility that we need to recognise and explore, although they do share some common sorts of experience (Harrison 1989, p. 27). For me then, *the peasantry are rural cultivators who produce for subsistence and the market using family labour with very little capital and for whom non-market considerations are crucial.*

Accepting this, what might we seek to make of the 'numbers' here? Across Planet Earth today, how many peasants are to be found? Where are they? Are their numbers decreasing or increasing? What is the scale of the issue of their neglect, if (according to one's definition) between 1.5 and 3 billion people may be defined as the 'peasantry' in 2019? There are vested interests, of course, in manipulating these figures. The World Bank, for example, has long insisted that this category of humanity is in decline and will inevitably disappear (Edelman & James 2011). In this, it is following not only the views of the political Right, but also the Left, for there is a consensus that the peasantry will disappear, not least for structural reasons emanating from the economy, both within the nation state and within the world system. Yet, the numbers do not back up this conjecture. Even the World Bank concedes that 1.5 billion people today are a part of the social class that we might term 'landless labourer' yet are fully imbricated within agriculture. The peasantry is still with us and is reproducing itself at a rate which outstrips the economic processes which seek deliberately to eradicate it (Akram-Lodhi & Kay 2010, p. 280).

Using such a definition allows one to make progress. De Janvry et al. (1989) reviewed the period 1960–1980 to assess the size of the peasantry across the globe. Numerically, the peasantry had *increased*, both in absolute terms and in relation to their share of the economically active population engaged in agriculture. This trend has continued. Whereas in 1970 there were 2 billion peasants upon the planet, by 2010 it was estimated by Van Der Ploeg (2008) to have reached 2.8 billion. Put another way, agriculture actively supports the livelihoods of 3 billion people today. Saragih (2009), a key figure in the

Via Campesina (The Peasant's Way), maintained in 2006 that half the world's population were peasants. By 2010 he stated that more than 2.2 billion people were peasants. As noted above, the World Bank concluded that 1.5 billion people were peasants in the contemporary world.

Employees?

This side of the binary notwithstanding, the assumption today may well be made that the majority of the world's adult population are employees, offering their services for use by, and to be attached to, another human being or company for payment. But Jacques (1996) showed that the notion of the 'employee' was a remarkably recent one and required huge amounts of persuasive work to be undertaken by owners to create a 'discourse' of and about the employee, which would develop a powerful impetus. There are elements in his book *Manufacturing the Employee* that are germane more widely than the United States. He argues that 'where farmland can be had for the taking, a worker need not enter into permanent wage slavery' (Jacques 1996, p. 23). In the United States, as late as 1850, work was organised through interactions between the self-employed. There was little interaction beyond the local community. Face-to-face inter-actions were far and away the most common form of human activity, where 'one' knew the 'other' personally from many meetings, some-times daily, over a long period of time. This was a society of relatively equal (male) individuals. Members were omnicompetent in a relatively closed and fixed universe. There was no split between producer and consumer. Women were seen in this discourse as offering limited competence, primarily in the domestic sphere. As we shall see, there are elements within this picture of a rural lifestyle that resonates with twenty-first-century India. Yet, it may well be that a very different notion – the discourse of the 'employee' – is on the rise across that society (Fisher, Mahajan & Singha 1997, pp. 3–4) in similar ways to those foreshadowed in the West.

For Jacques, the image of a self-employed rural workforce comes under threat from the rise of a corporate world of heavy industry in which enormous mills and factories are being built. The emergence of industrial organisation and big business profoundly remaps the eco-nomic landscape and the boundaries of social life. Separations occur within communities, some boundaries blur and others become deeply entrenched. New categories of 'job', 'wages' and 'employee' become developed within personnel departments and then subject to a developmental discourse within psychology and 'Human Relations'. This is not a 'natural' development, but one that is hard fought against by skilled trade unions and many of those using craft concepts in small-scale manufacturing. Eventually, the notion of the 'employee' becomes discursively predominant in the twentieth century. Although, as pointed out earlier, perhaps today in the West the rise of the gig economy has reintroduced into popular discourse the powerful idea of the self-employed 'entrepreneur' engaged in 'pluriactivity' rather than the collectively organised, fully paid employee (Crouch 2019).

Methodological Issues

Carrying out research on cultures with which one is unfamiliar is fraught with crises. With what justification can we claim to have any insight into the world of others? How can a white male from the United Kingdom (with its woeful past record in Imperial interference) ever hope to understand the Indian subcontinent in the twenty-first century? What terms of contact would be allowable and what lexicon of definitions and concepts is sophisticated enough not to leave an Indian reader holding their head in their hands at the arrogance of a complete stranger commenting upon a different world? My justification here is a very limited one. It is based upon the need to understand – not for purposes of pragmatic interventions of any kind – but to wonder at the lives of other human beings, and thereby to see the inadequacies of one's own life and one's own society. If education means *e-ducere* (to lead out) then many of us need to be led out from our own blinkered confines. But this is never to claim that by visiting a place one has escaped these blinkers. It just implies that one's conceptual framework stands a better chance of being confronted and challenged within the place itself, rather than in the library. And on that heavy empiricist line, let me explain the background to this chapter.

There are about 1.3 billion people living in India today and whilst estimates vary, the majority relies upon agrarian practices. This is a huge nation state, involving many different cultures and at least twenty-seven major languages, and it is blessed with histories that go back perhaps 10,000 years. So, it is little wonder that in India there is concern if the outside analyst uses terms apparently derived from European sources, for as is all too obvious, history, religion, economics and politics are very different in different parts of the world. And our concepts can be just as much part of a history of exploitation as economic relationships are.

The research upon which this chapter is based took place on a field trip to parts of India in 2016. Funded by the Leverhulme Trust by way of a Fellowship to assess 'W(h)ither the peasantry in the study of business and management?', I visited eight agricultural villages in both Gujarat and around Hyderabad. With the help of NGOs and their translators, I was able to visit villages and talk to elders (all male, of course) about the nature of their lives and the changes that are well under way in the working lives of 'the peasantry'. Access to these villages had been negotiated with local NGOs with whom I had been put in contact by doctoral colleagues in the United Kingdom. Everything worked very smoothly and the organisation of meetings with villagers was excellent. We would sit in the shade since the ambient temperature was about 45°C during my stay and I would attempt to work my way through an interview schedule of sorts. Of course, I was not able to speak the local languages, so all my contact at the language level was through a translator. This proved to be most problematic, and in a village about 100 miles north of Hyderabad, an important manager for the NGO acted as translator. I always ended my interviews by asking 'and what do you think about the advice coming from the NGO you've been working with?' Without asking the villagers, my NGO contact said 'They think we are excellent'. I said I was sure that was the case but would he mind asking my respondents the question please. It took two more requests from me for him to put the question to the twelve or so men sitting on the floor in someone's yard around me. With some apparent reluctance, at last he did so and a vigorous debate ensued. It became very heated and lots of people made points. It lasted for about seven or eight minutes, and then the manager said 'They think we are excellent'. At that moment the methodological problems of using translators who have a vested interest in what is being said became crystal clear.

A second methodological problem is that most NGOs working in India see 'development' of the country's rural economy and polity as the *sine qua non* of their existence. Thus, it is to be expected that visitors will be taken to places in which the 'most successful' projects have been undertaken. If one is from the West, one is most likely to be shown villages and projects wherein a 'Western style' of development is ongoing or has taken place. After my Indian visit, I was amazed (and shamed) to discover how famous and sociologically unusual the location of one of my research sites in Gujarat was. The town of Anand is seen within India as a hugely successful area, based upon milk production and associated industry. Since it is at the heart of a 'white revolution', it is by no means in any way typical, although for months I assumed it was. Thus, empirical work of this type is beset from the outset with problems. One is not at all sure whether typical village life is being shown or where very atypical projects are being paraded as success stories. So, the primary evidence presented here about bypassing the stage of copper wire within Indian villages has to be seen in this rural context of very unusual economic 'progress'.

Traditional Work Patterns on the Land in the Age of Copper

I made a home visit to meet a remarkable figure, Ela Bhatt, who lived in Ahmedabad. She was a person of fame and a key figure in SEWA, the self-employed women's association, representing a group for whom 'survival is a struggle' (Bhatt & Jhabvala 2012, p. 1). Bhatt and Jhabvala (2012, pp. 1–2) argue that:

Indian labour laws view work as a relationship between an employer and an employee. In this model of industrial relations, the worker is considered 'an industrial man', a worker with one formal contract, regular working hours and a living wage. In the Indian context this leaves out 90% of our workers, who have no fixed employer-employee relationship, no fixed place of work, and who do many kinds of work, often in the same day, or season to season.

This is, of course, a classic expression of pluriactivity as discussed earlier. And it demonstrates that the state appears to insist upon fixed (possibly Western) categories for its statistics. Numbers that leave out 90 per cent of the workforce because they do not easily fit within an 'industrial model' may have limited utility. The authors go to argue that the concept of work and attitudes towards it are seen very differently through the lenses of European and Indian philosophies. These differences often clash on the ground in people's daily lives. In Hinduism, the work of an individual has to be seen in relation to the cosmos through sacrifice (Yagna). Whatever we consume from nature has to be put back into it. The need to conserve and replenish is seen as part of an unselfishness that is at considerable odds with Western concepts of consumption. Under Islam, dignity and honour are ascribed to labour and no work is too menial or beneath one's dignity. It is the spoken word and the oral tradition that survive in large measure, especially in the countryside and outside the cities, despite the wish of the British for the written word to become the norm. Within the caste system, it is usual to describe four castes, but according to Bhatt and Jhabvala (2012, p. 25) 'in practice there are thousands – all identified with particular kinds of work'. When they describe agricultural labour undertaken by women (ibid, p. 31) we are told the following,

Filling water from the well becomes a communal activity, as does gathering food or firewood. Protecting fields from birds and monkeys is also a communal activity in which encouragement must be given to staying awake ... They have to collect cattle feed, milk the cattle and clean out the cattle shed. They have to rise very early in the morning to tend the cattle and yet, to most women, looking after her cow is a duty of love. Often she worries more about her cow than about her children.

In the village of Bedwa, where I spent some time (and will discuss below), this commitment by women to the family cow and looking after it – or them – was very clear indeed. The authors go on to point to twenty-first-century climatic change and its effects on human life in the village. They say, 'although most families still earn their living working on their own fields or as agricultural workers on other's fields, the climate is increasingly arid, leaving most fields unproductive' (ibid, p. 36). We are told:

Puriben Ahir is a woman who lives in the dry desert village of Madhutra, and has done many types of hard manual labour, from agricultural labour to breaking stones, digging mud and looking after cattle. She says 'my whole life has been a search for getting enough to eat for my family, having enough water, sending my children to school and just be able to have a decent life. I have never been afraid of work, in fact for us work is life. (ibid p. 63)

The socio-economic changes that are underway in Gujarat and elsewhere have introduced the *intermediate trader* into villages. One of the respondents with SEWA, talked to by Bhatt and Jhabvala (2012,

p. 54), says 'I am happy that my skills can bring money into the house. I feel proud. But sometimes I feel exploited ... now I also work for the trader, the market. The trader would cheat us but we did not know that earlier'.

SEWA is a women's co-operative grouping now found in many parts of India, though based in Gujarat, and Ela Bhatt's role as a Founder ties the group back to the writings and teachings of Gandhi, who had an ashram in Ahmedabad (where SEWA is based) at the time of the Champaran agitations in 1915. Thereafter, Gandhi believed in a *sarvodaya* economic model, which literally means 'welfare, upliftment of all' and was decidedly non-capitalist. Whilst it was Nehru's vision of a 'socialist'-inspired India that triumphed, Gandhi's ideas of anti-materialism, vegetarianism, craft production on a small scale, the denouncement of rapid industrialisation, localised production of staple goods and foods and a rejection of class analysis all had a strong influence for decades. His vision of a village-dominated economy was often described as 'rural romanticism', and his call for a national ethos of personal austerity and non-violence has not sat well with the development of industrialisation. Today, however, many environmentalists see in 'Gandhism' a way forward, for not only India but for the globe.

India has many serious political issues that it faces now, but the emphasis here is very narrowly upon the rise of the concept of the 'employee'. Not only do state statistics emphasise the notion of the employee as a major category. It has been estimated that India is seeking to move 100,000 people from the land into the more urban, industrial areas in very short time frames, although these are unpublicised targets derived from Chinese experience (Skype interview with Vijay Mahajan). Yet the land provides a living for well over half a billion people. There are many who would argue, with some justification, that rural practices of production and consumption have been little changed for centuries, if not millennia. But there are signs that practices are being shifted, noticeably by demographic and technological change. In production patterns that have lasted a thousand years – and were unaffected by telegraph and telephone services that required wires and telegraph posts – new wireless telephony appears to have enabled social change to come about in quite rapid ways.

Emplacing the Peasant upon the Grid of Capitalism

As already indicated, in 1948, India had a maximum stock of 80,000 telephones, or adequate coverage for about one hundredth of 1 percent of the population. The history of Imperialism almost everywhere is about denial of modern technology to the peoples of a colonial territory and to use such technologies to control them through the forces of Empire. Thus, in the Indian subcontinent, apart from the machinery of the Raj, copper wire was known to few. Copper wiring provided the communication arteries of the civil service, the Indian army (Burrell 2018) and the railway system but outside of the telegraph poles running alongside the railway tracks, the countryside was devoid of any sign of copper wire and what it could provide. However, the new telecommunications systems that are wireless have been developed and utilised in India, which changes the world of work in significant ways. My focus will be upon the peasantry and how mobile technology has opened up many possibilities for a heavily rural population, but ownership patterns concerning the telecommunications systems remain significant by offering constraints as well as openings to new worlds of work in the fields of South Asia.

In the age of copper, work patterns from 1850 were originally dependent upon an Imperial world in which Cable and Wireless Ltd.'s technologies constrained social change in work, politics and economic development. In a post-copper world, these have been altered into work forms dependent upon a context provided *inter alia* by Vodaphone Ltd. In 1896, twenty-four of the thirty cable-laying ships in the world were owned by British companies, which allowed them to operate two-thirds of the world's cables. Copper cables were an artery of Imperialism. In India, all the major cities and towns in the country were linked with telephones but, as we have seen, there was a tiny number of them, given the size of the country. After 1948, growth remained slow because the telephone was seen more as a status symbol than a useful item of organisational or domestic life. The number of telephones grew to 980,000 in 1971, 2.15 million in 1981 and reached 5.07 million in 1991 when economic reforms were initiated in the country.

By May 2019, India's telecommunications sector was the second largest in the world in terms of number of telephone users (both fixed and mobile phone) with 1.183 billion subscribers. Because of market size and competition between providers, it has one of the lowest sets of tariffs in the world. Today, there are four main providers, including Vodafone, whose merger with Idea Cellular was completed at the end of August 2018. This merger created the largest telecom company in India in terms of subscribers and revenue, and the world's second largest mobile network in terms of number of subscribers. Vodafone's strategy in India is of major importance to new modes of working in that country (BBC 2017; Peretti 2017). Internet usage is also the second largest globally, with 460.24 million broadband internet subscribers in the country. Currently, India has a population of 1.3 billion, with 1.23 billion digital biometric identity cards, 1.21 billion mobile phones, 446 million smartphones and 560 million internet users. It has embraced the world of ICT at a very fast pace indeed. Also important is the fact that telecommunication in India has been greatly supported by the INSAT system of space satellites. This is one of the largest domestic satellite systems in the world, linking most of the country by telephone, radio, television and the Internet. Due to the rapid growth of the cellular phone industry in India, the original copper wire landlines faced stiff competition from cellular operators and the number of wireline subscribers fell to just 22 million customers in 2018, from nearly 38 million in December 2008.

Smartphones, in a population such as India's, bypass all the constraints provided by the absence of copper infrastructures. Communications need no longer be face-to-face. It has become easier to talk with members of one's own family, other villages, other regions of the same country and with burgeoning collective organisations such as co-ops. They allow the transfer of money without the need for a near-by banking presence in the 'real' world, as opposed to the virtual. Therefore, they help shift the emphasis away from rural bartering to monetary exchange, because they emplace the peasant upon the grid of capitalism, rendering them open to electronic advertising, seeking loans, investment opportunities and all that finance capitalism has to offer. Not to be underestimated are the ways in which the smartphone offers instant access to the correct time (Thompson 1967). It is possible to arrange 'appointments' rather than interactions where both parties are in the same space at precisely the same time; it pressurises people to turn up 'on time' and it makes the temporal dimension much more exploitable. The smartphone, primarily in the hands of Vodaphone

(BBC 2017), renders up millions of people to changes in their work practices upon the land.

So, it appears from these numbers that India has embraced a post-copper telecommunications world in which wireless electronics has largely replaced a system based upon centralised control through telegraph poles following railway lines. This is a significant shift, with many consequences for those living a rural lifestyle. Now clearly this assertion is a simplification, suggesting some form of technological determinism or dependence on shifts in capitalism and ignoring the role of Gandhi, Partition, nationalistic governments, mobilisation of the peasantry, Hindu nationalism, NGO and United Nations involvement and many other features of past and contemporary India (Sanyal 2014; Thorner 1982). But our aim is much more limited and our focus much more concentrated. It is solely upon agricultural work practices.

Work Practices within Agricultural Villages

The first thing of note in all of the villages I visited was the circumstances in 2016 of prolonged drought and the daily temperatures of 45°C. Reservoirs were empty – totally – the soil was bone dry and the groundwater had dropped to a very low level. One farm I was taken to, 120 miles north of Hyderabad, had plenty of running water for a very green and lush set of fields. It turned out that the farmer had possessed a well that had been dug out by hand by his family to a depth of 100 feet but that all the wells in the area at that depth for the normal water table had run dry. This particular establishment had 'invested' in mechanical digging to a depth of 100 metres, where water was abundant. The farmer had used modern technology to solve an age-old problem for his land. Its greenness in a harsh, brown landscape was very obvious. And that is why I was shown *this* farm especially.

In these green fields, and in a noontime temperature of 44°C, there were many women working, picking a crop. There was one young man in the field, not working but sitting under some movable shade. I was told he was the gang master. I asked how many women was the farmer employing. My interpreter asked the farmer this question and he answered 'about 100 rupees worth'. In other words, he subcontracted his agricultural work of this kind to a gang master, who was paid the cash and then paid the women from that sum. It also meant apparently, that the farmer had no idea of whom and of what his labour force consisted, apart from their monetary cost. They were, to him, somewhat disembodied 'hands'. There is little evidence here of ancient face-to-face interaction and the absence of abstract relationships in favour of communal ones. These women field workers were, in our world anyway, dematerialised from the farmer's immediate concerns by an intermediary gang master. They were someone else's 'employees'.

This gender dimension was obvious in all the villages I visited. In Gujarat, in the village of Bedwa, there was a milk co-operative in which cow and buffalo milk was collected and sorted early every day by women in the villages surrounding the processing plant. The co-operative had been founded in 1957 and, according to records from 2015, had 1,649 members producing on average about 9,000 litres of milk from their animals. There were 492 landless farmers, 1,064 members had up to two hectares of land and 77 members had more than 2 hectares. There were 420 women members of the co-operative and 1,229 men. During my early morning visit, it was these women who were bringing in tiny amounts of milk for collection and payment, but all was weighed by male employees of the co-op. These women walked with their children and their pails of milk to the collection site. On the other hand, men on motorbikes brought into the weighing facility many gallons of milk from larger farms, strapped to their bikes in all sorts of precarious ways. All was assessed for fat content and volume and a price offered and taken for it. Somewhat later in the morning, the husbands and brothers of the women arrived to collect the cash for that morning's volume and quality of milk. I was told that the women had gone back home and were most likely making break-fast for the family, afterwards having the role of taking the children to local schools before returning home. By this time of day, the men were becoming less sedentary and had joined the queue for payment. The milk was mainly sold to the Amul diary in the local town of Anand and was made into all sorts of dairy products for sale across India, and even for export. The villagers were thus implicated in a very large industrial enterprise within the food industry.

So, what represents *new work practices* within these descriptions? Well, first, we are talking milk here. Within societies where cows are venerated, commercial milking was not common. Amul's own docu-mentation (2015, p. 5) states that the nation 'till 1970s was struggling with milk scarcity and heavy dependence on import of dairy products'.

Then there was a 'White Revolution', in which the dairy industry 'took off'. There has been a big shift within the life of these villagers in the twenty-first century to embrace cow milk as having both food value and economic value. Whilst Bedwa had a steady population over the years and numbered 6,500 in 2015, membership of the milk co-operative had virtually doubled between 1977 and 2007. Second, as we have seen, the collecting point for this milk is owned by a farming co-operative. These are by no means unusual but their development has been encouraged as a form of reducing both the costs of produc-tion and of marketing. The village's admixture of cow and buffalo milk was part of Amul's great success in marketing milk products to the Indian population. The capitalist market is being felt both in terms of demand for the village's products but also in what it has to offer to those whose lives have been so constrained by rural locality. Third, the collectivisation of milk consolidation by the co-operative has allowed some resources to go back into the village, conceived of as a community. Education, particularly in the building of schools and kindergartens, has been the primary beneficiary of the collectivisation since 1957. But so too has irrigation and its 'other', flood defences. The discourse is now of 'investment' of communal 'funds', which opens up Bedwa to a plethora of economically driven assessments, both quanti-tative and qualitative. The village may well have been held up as a great example of community activism, but there was a feeling that 'progress' was seen in a particular collectivist yet economics-driven way. Yet, at the same time, hardship stalked the land. My mentor (Kumar 2015), in setting up this visit and telling me much about rural India, wrote to me before my visit saying:

[T]here has been a rather fierce and early summer here, with unusually high temperatures in March, and rising thereafter. As a result of the El Nino and failed monsoon last year, there is a drought in large parts of the country, which has affected farmers in all sorts of ways ... There is an on-going agrarian distress in central, western and northern India.

Thus, what I witnessed in the villages may well have been the result of climatic weather changes evident in 2016, rather than the ongoing social situation. Crucial here is the notion of space and its links to work practices. Space measures out what can be produced when. It speaks of possibilities and threats to livelihood. It is based on very detailed knowledge of local conditions of rainfall, wind direction and available seed stocks. New work practices via the mobile phone, utilising regional weather stations, novel seeds and market intelligence have upset this localised sense of spatial and temporal balance. As detailed local knowledge becomes less salient, it allows movement away from the immediate neighbourhood. More is known of further away on screens in one's pocket.

Fourth, and most noteworthy perhaps, is that the payment made to each (male) supplier of milk every day was via their smart phones. Whilst there was cash exchanged in the milking reception area, the emphasis was now on electronic payments. It has been claimed that telecommunication has not only supported the socio-economic development of India but has played a significant role in narrowing the 'rural–urban divide' wherein town and country face many different levels of access to resources. The very important features of geographical distance and what it allows and constrains may well be overcome by electronic devices sending signals travelling at the speed of light. If the phone user cannot get to market, the market can come to the user. And the opening up of the market for goods, services and *labour* within hitherto tight locales has been a crucial element of the digital shifts. By dealing digitally with their savings of daily incomes for milk supply, the account holder allows access to the telecoms company, the bank, marketing companies, goods manufacturers, the state apparatus and other people in similar situations yet hundreds of miles distant. As I have argued above, the peasant farmer becomes emplaced in the grid of capitalism, from which few seek to escape. This has revolutionised the nature of the relationship into one based upon (quasi) capitalist forms of control rather than traditional modes of domination.

Traditionally, the absence in the landscape of large amounts of copper wire hanging from posts or laid underground, except to support the workings of the Imperial government, may be thought of as representing a *limiting* colonial approach to communication. What could connectivity produce but popular discontent as word spread of Imperial malediction?

But wireless technology, having no need of huge amounts of copper to produce connectivity, produces a system that is intrinsically 'post-imperial' and pro-capitalist. It is sometimes said to be *enabling*. Indeed, wireless technology requires such a post-imperial system to make its successes possible. Costs are reduced dramatically if there are huge markets for wireless products. Instead of one or two state bureaucratic enterprises having sole need for telephonic and telegraphic capability, if every citizen requires a device, produced under a large-scale industrial manufacturing regime, we are quickly in the stages of 'late capitalism'. With large markets, advertising of other products is much easier, and it is possible to create new perceived needs within an audience. Post-imperialism has very different enabling logics from what has gone before. Primarily, newly independent governments desire enhanced control of what happens upon their soil and 'development' of the economy previously proscribed by the Imperial forces, in which goods and services are more widely available. And the telecommunications revolution comes along with this new promise of delivering the goods. The evidence seemed to indicate that there were linkages between telephony and rural development, so that mobile telephony was a cause rather than a consequence of development. Kumar and Thomas (2006, p. 307) reveal not only the importance of mobile telephony but also the unusual 'advanced' nature of my fieldwork sites when they say:

Cheap and easy access to mobile phones can certainly make a positive contribution to the welfare of the urban and rural poor. Farmers can bypass brokers and keep abreast of market prices of their crops, and sell directly to retailers and even customers. However, subsistence farmers—who make up the majority in India—cannot afford to access phones. Milk producers as in Anand, Gujarat, who have brought about a white revolution in western India, could perhaps be able to own a mobile, but most poor dairy workers in India do not possess the wherewithal to do so.

But this was written ten years before my visit and we might reasonably expect a greater spread of mobile phone ownership in the intervening decade. Undoubtedly, the area of mobile telephony is also a battle ground for control of propaganda and fake news, access into the homes of the populace, and generally the diminution of political risk by the powerful.

New Forms of Work from Ownership Changes

In my visit to Hyderabad, in part I was the guest of a large private foundation, which had been set up by the owner of a hugely successful pharmaceutical company (Reddy 2005). On one occasion I made a trip to two villages that were presented as good examples of the Foundation's work and were clearly seen as success stories. But the image I received from talking (albeit through translators) to the men in these villages was of villages in population decline. Local land owner-ship patterns are not based on primogeniture but upon the sharing of resources equally within each generation. Improved public health means there are many more surviving (male) siblings to contend with as time progresses. Thus, an eighty-acre farm in 1948 that might have comfortably supported a whole extended family becomes reduced by 2018 and by the death of two generations of the family into many fractured landholdings of just a few acres. And if these become too small to be sustainable and, as a result, several brothers leave for the factories of Hyderabad or similar places across the subcontinent, the remaining brother is not allowed by cultural norm to farm his absent brothers' land. For they may come back at any time and have the right to find it as they left it. Land ownership is thus a crucial factor, alongside climate change, in seeing how work practices develop from digital technologies in twenty-first century India.

The dynamics of the social shifts within the peasantry could be seen to suggest that processes are at work thst have wide implications, even though the conditions of possibility for each of these groups may be *very* different. The argument is that most peasants have few posses-sions, own little and are increasingly burdened by large-scale debt imposed upon them by rentiers and landowners. The market enters the lives of the peasantry via new telecommunications in the form of the smart phone. There is encouragement of this communication device by the state and by private telecommunications providers such as Vodaphone. Once the market is involved, local banks start to play a role in the manufacture and maintenance of debt through the devices on sale. This thesis then argues that such 'forced commerce' produces a level of indebtedness, which in turn creates more and more unfree agricultural labourers and semi-proletarian farmers where once there had been a degree of independence. Status considerations that are well understood in such peasant communities give way to relationships based on impersonal contract. Literacy becomes more central in order to understand these contracts rather than the 'character' of a neigh-bourhood, and of a neighbour who will help in cases of hardship. Expert knowledge based on peasant experience with local soils and local weather conditions gives way to knowledge generated by algo-rithms gleaned from experts via the Internet – often based in the West. They appear to be able to predict the unknown. Under these sorts of condition, large landowners tend to prosper. Peasants in some places have become much more like employees subject to external control and influence, now encouraged by possession of cheap mobile devices. Pressure from creditors, newly accessed, creates the loss of ownership. In one village of 2,000 families outside Hyderabad where I visited, 200 families had moved into the city since they could neither access bank loans, because of the drought, nor afford the interest rates money lenders would charge. This sometimes leads to impoverishment and even to abandonment by the extended family. After this, in a universal thesis of peasant impoverishment, comes penury, then beggary and then moves into prostitution (Gerber 2014). Eventually, so the argument goes, comes suicide. The suicide rate in Indian farmers has reached very high levels in the last decade.

It will be noticed that this particular set of societal processes is *not* predicated upon the end of the age of copper in a technological sense. Shrinking farm sizes are not connected to the telecommunications revolution via the work practices on the land itself, but they do impact work upon much smaller sized farms, making it much more difficult for those remaining to make a living. However, the absence of owners from the land and their flight to the city, and the inability of those left behind to utilise that same land *is* fuelled to some extent by the lure of urban bright lights. And where does this lure burn brightest? Upon television screens and upon the smart phone.

Moreover, it is possible to question the long-term viability of such shrinking arrangements of ownership (Kearney 1996, pp. 110–111). Tiny land holdings raise the question of whether they can produce enough surplus agricultural product for the market, or even if they can produce enough for simple subsistence! In places, perhaps, we can witness the evolution of surplus producing peasant communities into villages of 'infrasubsistence' peasants. Here a plurality of work *has to be* undertaken to maintain one's living. Ongoing expansion through growth in scale is impossible for such villagers. Whether this is a blessing or not, they are removed from financial and industrial capital and have less access – if indeed any – to credit and new technologies (Van Der Ploeg 2008, p. 1). These places may produce less than they consume, forcing new work practices upon the peasant, such as seeking an employer on a permanent basis or moving location. Changes such as these may come about through untenable land holdings of such small size that even subsistence is impossible. Eventually, marginalisation in some places, at some times, becomes irresistible. And enforced 'employment' results. Of course, this move from the status of peasant to the status of employee has long been predicted by the Economist, the World Bank and the IMF (Handy 2009)! Yet we must recall that these social categories are too crude. For by no means does this relate to the way of all social processes affecting the peasantry. It is what was glimpsed in the areas around an economically active Hyderabad. In Gujarat, things were different. In other words, social change has to be seen as contextualised. It depends upon so many factors, particularly in a nation the size of a subcontinent.

Conclusion

My argument has been that the 'peasantry' is a social category of some salience and that there are forces at work that seek to emplace the peasant, some would say 'eventually', upon the grid of capitalism. In so doing, these processes would have the effect of changing the work practices of these labourers, which may have remained stable for centuries. Implicated in these changes are the new mobile technologies, which open up the hidden lives of the peasantry to the glare of commercial interests. Within their prior *terra incognita*, they now become revealed as putative consumers and as locatable upon the grid. They may embrace 'employment' willingly or not, but at the moment, pluriactivity (Van Der Ploeg 2008, pp. 32–33) seems to be much more common, in which the shifts in labour and work practices to *accommodate local conditions* that might take place are possibly more of emphasis rather than of substance. The employee–peasant binary is not enough to help us understand but perhaps relatedly, neither, in our world, is the employee–entrepreneur one. When 'we' look at changes in the West, from an introverted occidental perspective, 'we' tend to make massive assumptions about the similarity of starting points to social and economic change, assumptions about the cause of developments and about the trajectory of such change. It is a useful reminder to consider the non-occidental globe of perhaps 5 billion people and suspect, as one has here, that deterministic unidirectionality is not necessarily useful in looking backwards or forwards in time. Cultural difference interprets technology through its own 'orientation' (sic) and this may be the ultimate downfall of the tech giants that currently appear to control so much of the new world of work.

References

Akram-Lodhi, A. H. & Kay, C. 2010. Surveying the agrarian question (part 1): Unearthing foundations, exploring diversity. *The Journal of Peasant Studies*, 37(1): 177–202.

Amul Company 2015. *41st Annual Report*. Anand, Gujarat.

BBC 2 2017. Episode 2 of Three Part Documentary, *'Billion Dollar Deals'* presented by J. Peretti.

Bhatt, E. R. 2006. *We Are Poor But so Many: The Story of Self-Employed Women in India*. Oxford University Press.

Bhatt, E. R. & Jhabvala, R. 2012. *A History of SEWA*. Ahmedabad: Navaji de Publishing.

Burrell, G. 2018. Imperialism and the Military-Peasantry Complex. In J. Grady & C. Grocott (Eds.) *The Continuing Imperialism of Free Trade: Developments, Trends, and the Role of Supranational Agencies*. Cheltenham: Edward Elgar, 59–71.

Crouch, C. 2019. *Will the Gig Economy Prevail?* Cambridge: Polity.

De Janvry, A., Sadoulet, E. & Young, L. W. (1989). Land and labour in Latin American agriculture from the 1950s to the 1980s. *The Journal of Peasant Studies*, 16(3), 396–424.

Edelman, M. & James, C. 2011. Peasants' rights and the UN system: Quixotic struggle? Or emancipatory idea whose time has come? *Journal of Peasant Studies* 38(1): 1–32.

Fisher, T., Mahajan, V. & Singha, A. 1997. *The Forgotten Sector: Non-Farm Employment and Enterprises in Rural India*. London: Intermediate Technology Publications.

Franklin, S. H. 1969. *The European Peasantry: The Final Phase*. London: Methuen.

Gerber, J. F. 2014. The role of rural indebtedness in the evolution of capitalism. *Journal of Peasant Studies*, 41(5): 729–747.

Gerth, H. H. & Wright Mills C. (eds.) 1948. *For Max Weber*. London: Routledge and Kegan Paul.

Handy, J. 2009. 'Almost idiotic wretchedness': A long history of blaming peasants. *Journal of Peasant Studies*, 36(2): 325–344.

Harrison, J. E. C. 1989. *The Common People: A History from the Norman Conquest to the Present*. Roermond: Fontana.

Jacques, R. 1996. *Manufacturing the Employee: Management Knowledge from the 19th to 21st Century*. London: Sage.

Kearney, M. 1996. *Reconceptualizing the Peasantry: Anthropology in Global Perspective*. Boulder, CO: Westview.

Kumar, A. 2015. *Organizing Tataland, The Modern Nation: A History of Development in Post/Colonial India*. PhD Thesis: Lancaster University.

Kumar, K. J. & Thomas, A. O. 2006. Telecommunications and development: The cellular mobile 'revolution' in India and China. *Journal of Creative Communications*, 1(3): 297–309.

Lerche, J. 2013. The agrarian question in neoliberal India: Agrarian transition bypassed? *Journal of Agrarian Change*, 13(3): 382–404.

Marx, K. 1987. The Peasantry as a Class. In T. Shanin (ed.) *Peasants and Peasant Society*. London: Basil Blackwell.

McMichael, P. 2008. Peasants make their own history, but not just as they please. *Journal of Agrarian Change*, 8(2–3): 205–228.

Mitrany, D. 1951. *Marx against the Peasant*. London: George Weidenfeld and Nicholson.

Peretti, J. 2017. *Done: The Billion Dollar Deals and How They're Changing Our World*. London: BBC Publications.

Reddy, K. A. 2005. *An Unfinished Agenda: My Life in the Pharmaceutical Industry*. Haryana: Portfolio.

Sanyal, K. 2014. *Rethinking Capitalist Development: Primitive Accumulation, Governmentality and Post-colonial Capitalism*. London: Routledge.

Saragih, H. 2009. *Statement by Mr. Henry Saragih, General Coordinator of La Via Campesina at the United Nations General Assembly*. New York: UNO

Thompson, E. P. 1967. Time, work-discipline, and industrial capitalism. *Past & Present*, 38: 56–97.

Thorner, A. 1982. Semi-feudalism or capitalism? Contemporary debate on classes and modes of production in India. *Economic and Political Weekly*, 17(49): 1961–1968.

Van Der Ploeg, J. D. 2008. *The New Peasantries: Struggles for Autonomy and Sustainability in an Era of Empire and Globalisation*. Abingdon: Earthscan.

9 Critical Theory and the Post-work Imaginary

EDWARD GRANTER

Introduction

Critical Theory is a practice of analysing society dialectically. In so doing, we seek to highlight the irrationalities of contemporary capitalism (Granter 2014), that is, to reveal the ideological status of various concepts, understandings and experiences. This is known specifically as *negative dialectics* (Clegg & Pina e Cunha 2019, p. 12; Neimark & Tinker 1987). Language, politics, the media, everyday life – all contain traces and echoes of the dominant ideologies that sustain and legitimise the capitalist system of domination. These traces represent the 'universal in the particular' (Granter 2019, p. 233) and serve as evidence of the formatting of life as an after-image of capital. Everything exists as part of a totality and so culture, society and ideology must be seen as mutually reinforcing the domination of capital – until such time as people become conscious of its hidden hand in all aspects of life. This would constitute a revolutionary breakthrough – the end of capitalism – and this is what Critical Theory works towards.

Later the Critical Theor*ists* will be introduced but, as a statement of purpose, the overall aim of this chapter is to explore the idea that the end of work can form, amongst others, an important conceptual lens through which to conduct Critical Theory. The end of work as an idea contains many of the concepts that are central to Critical Theory: freedom, authenticity, reason and, importantly, contradiction. Perhaps the greatest contradiction of all is that the technical, social and organisational means to transform the way we work, to end work as toil and compulsion, to use our time autonomously and to make society fairer and more decent, already exist. It is capitalism that has created this possibility, and yet it is capitalism itself that seems to prevent it being realised. What can account for this, if not a coalescence of ideological, cultural, political and social factors that work against the possibility of freedom from work? Critical Theory attempts to reveal how these elements of the totality fit together to obscure the possibility of freedom, and this process of revealing carries the utopian impulse of liberation. Critical Theory need not be the preserve of one group of writers; it is a way of thinking, a method (Horkheimer 2002) that can be employed by others who share an interest in a fairer society.

In the first part of this chapter, the early cultural and intellectual trajectory of the end of work is traced, since it is important to understand it as an idea that has developed in relation to other social and cultural developments. Marx – Critical Theorist *avant la lettre* – is introduced as the key figure in modern understandings of the end of work, and from here we introduce the Frankfurt School Critical Theorists, focusing on Herbert Marcuse. An account of André Gorz's contribution to the Critical Theory of work is then given, including his notion of 'living dead capitalism'. Following ideas of the end of work to the present day, the chapter sketches some outlines of the current 'wave' of post-industrial utopianism, alongside a discussion of *why* the end of work seems to emerge in the intellectual and public consciousness at certain historical junctures. In conclusion, Critical Theories of the end of work are positioned as a form of utopian thinking that is useful and relevant to a critique of contemporary work and society.

A Brief History of (the End of) Work

Work in pre-industrial or 'pretechnological' (McLean & Hurd 2015, p. 50) societies was radically different from work as it is understood under late capitalism (Sahlins 1972). If contemporary work is compulsory – regulated and disciplined through economic, temporal, social and ideological frameworks – work in pre-capitalism was characterised by compulsion only in the sense that survival necessitated the provision of the community's more-or-less immediate needs (Granter 2009, p. 13). Hunting, gathering, cooking, repairing, etc. for twenty-one to thirty-five hours a week (Sahlins 1972, pp. 34–35) is hardly fully automated luxury (Bastani 2019); however, work remained an activity, and a concept, without the ontological and ideological dominance with which it is imbued today.

In the more socially stratified context of the ancient civilisations, fantasies of a world without work were in some ways unnecessary if one belonged to the slaveholding elite. If one reverses Weiner's

argument that 'the automatic machine … is the precise economic
equivalent of slave labour' (Weiner 1950, cited in Rifkin 1995, p. 78)
then one could characterise classical Greece as the prototypical fully
automated economy. For the intellectual elite, the ideal was a life of
'music and contemplation … philosophy' (Applebaum 1992, p. 64),
an existence free from the compulsion to work. Exempt from toil,
Greek citizens could take an active part in political life, own land
and manage its cultivation, and wage war on neighbouring proto-
states. In a sense then, a highly polarised version of the end of work,
has already existed. Even so, the notion of a scarcity and toil-free life
did make an appearance in the popular culture of the time. The
Deipnosophistae of Athenaeus provides an insight into the comic
poets' utopian take on work: 'The central idea in them all, carried to
heights of hyperbole typical of Old Comedy, is to portray circumstances in which things happen of their own accord, *without* involving
human toil' (Baldry 1953, p. 50); self-opening gates, self-frying fish,
self-kneading dough, etc. (Baldry 1953). Baldry's parting word on
these accounts conjures up the notion that writing on the end of work
has been part of a critique of wider society all along: 'Whether the
comic poets described the remote past or conjured up a fantastic
future, the faults and foibles of their fellow-citizens were their main
concern' (ibid, p. 60).

Turning to mediaeval Europe, it is interesting to note that scholars
have drawn parallels between contemporary end-of-work debates, and
those taking place at the University of Paris in the 1250s; Robertson
and Uebel argue that work was one of the 'determinant factors of
social identity in late mediaeval Europe' (2016, p. 3), indicating that
the rise of work to the social centrality associated with the industrial
revolution, did not occur *ex nihilo*. Schor, in her popular book *The
Overworked American*, citing a number of sources (Schor 1993,
p. 45), argued that some peasant families in fourteenth-century
England may have worked only 1,620 hours per year, over 150 days –
although she concedes that these figures relate to a period of 'unusually
high wages' (Schor 1993, p. 47). A characterisation of mediaeval life as
one of carnivalesque leisure (Clark & Van Der Werf 1998, p. 830) is
open to dispute and indeed, one of Schor's sources observes elsewhere
that 'even before 1750 some [rural] workers were putting in work
years of nearly 300 days' and that these days were 'long and hard'
(ibid, p. 836). By these calculations, workers 'seemingly did as much

per day in mediaeval England as in England at the end of the Industrial Revolution' (ibid, p. 836).

Whatever the specifics of working life in the West before industrialism, Sir Thomas More (1478–1535) felt that it was enough of an issue to make a six-hour day an element of his *Utopia* (Mavor 2016). Although at the same time, idleness was not to be countenanced; life beyond work was to be purposeful and worthwhile. With More we see a connection established between work and consumption, in that more durable goods and houses would mean less work invested in replacement and repair. As industrialisation took hold, other 'utopian' writers such as Charles Fourier (1772–1837) began to place work and production at the centre of their critiques of nascent industrial modernity. Fourier was a notably eccentric figure and his proposal of using 'Vestals – female virgins age[d] between fifteen and a half and twenty' (Granter 2009, p. 37) as, arguably, some sort of 'bait' for industrial armies' (Spiers n.d., p. 7) appear inappropriate from today's perspective. He does hold an important place in the history of the end of work, however, as one of the first writers to place the notion within a critique of work under industrialism: '[T]he systems of industrialism … serve to enrich finance, big business and the great property owners, and leave the people nothing but hunger and nakedness as the wages of slave labour which is often performed in workshops where men are locked up for eighteen hours a day' (Fourier 1972, p. 122).

Despite the fact that by the nineteenth century the cultural and ideological cachet of work was well established, it was rejected by Fourier, who described work for the majority as 'profitless boredom' (1972, p. 148). Fourier's solution was a thoroughgoing reorganisation of society based on the 'laws of Attraction'. Work is to be allocated according to individuals' 'passions' and made varied and pleasurable. Work, for Fourier, is to be transformed into something 'akin to play' (the phrase is taken from Bastani 2019, p. 55).

Capitalist Modernity and the End of Work

As with much of modern social theory, when it comes to the end of work, we can credit Marx with producing the conceptual frameworks that are of most enduring resonance. Drawing on an array of influences, from Aristotle, to German philosophers such as Schiller and Novalis, to Fourier and beyond, Marx established the ideal of work as an autonomously chosen activity associated with experiential plurality and creativity (Marx 1975). Productive activity is an important part, perhaps *the* most important part, of what makes us truly human and so for humankind to realise its full potential, it should produce according to this ideal.

Almost by definition, this ideal represents, 'as in a *camera obscura*' (Marx 1845), the inverse of what work under capitalism seemed to Marx to be like. Marx provides a critique of work under capitalism that emphasises its brutal compulsion, its physical costs, its ontological costs, its tendency to be experienced as something external, imposed, *alien* (Marx 1975, p. 329). Marx was no technological determinist but he did highlight the role played by technology, under specific relations of production, in shaping the experience, and the potentialities, of work. Mechanised factory production reduced the worker to a 'mere appendage' of the machine (Marx 1974, p. 451), yes, but at the same time, this nascent form of automation held the possibility of two more positive, interconnected corollaries. First, Marx highlighted the potential of technology and advanced production systems to reduce the burden of necessary work (Marx 1977, p. 820). Second, he pointed to the tendency for work under capitalism to become a truly social, interconnected, co-operative process, where people play a mediated, rather than a direct, role in production (1993, p. 705; 1977, p. 820). Under such circumstances, it should be possible to reduce working time for all who desire it, and to move to a new definition of worth or wealth based more on individual freedom to use one's time autonomously, rather than on the 'theft of alien labour time' (Marx 1993, p. 705). For Marx, work as we know it – that is, work as a matter of necessity – was not something to be idealised for its own sake; rather, it was something that could be, and should be, transformed into a truly human practice and reduced in temporal terms, in order to expand the 'realm of freedom' (Booth 1991, p. 9) in which people can define their own destinies and that of the social collective.

Critical Theorists and the End of Work

The Critical Theorists were a group of Marxist academics who became known also as the Frankfurt School (for an intellectual biography of the group see Jay 1996), for an introduction to their work see Kellner

1989 and for an outline of their relevance to the sociology of work and organisation see Granter 2014, 2019). At its centre were: Theodor Adorno (1903–1969); Max Horkheimer (1895–1973) and Herbert Marcuse (1898–1979) who, as Jewish Marxists, were forced to escape fascism and leave Germany in the 1930s to continue their work from the United States. Adorno and Horkheimer returned to academic posts in Frankfurt in the 1950s. They developed Critical Theory as an adaptive current of Marxism, carrying forward the understanding of productive activity as central to human beings. Although Adorno is also relevant to the end of work debate (Gunderson 2018), it is in the writings of Marcuse that we find the end of work advocated and explored in the most significant way.

Marx is the most important influence on Marcuse and, like his predecessor, he placed work at the centre of what it means to be human (1973, p. 29). Once again following Marx, he argued that work under capitalism tended to be toilsome and alienating – a matter of compulsion rather than autonomy. By the time Marcuse had published *Eros and Civilization* in 1955, the potential of automated systems to reduce the burden of work was even clearer than Marx 100 years previously. These systems should be used, according to Marcuse, to reduce work in the 'realm of necessity' (Marcuse 1987, p. 105) to a minimum. In an ironic rhetorical use of the concept of alienation, he suggests that: 'The more complete the alienation of labour, the greater potential of freedom: total automation would be the optimum' (Marcuse 1987, p. 156). In fact, alienation as a *state of experience for the worker* was to be all but eliminated in Marcuse's vision of an automated utopia. The notion that automation could *reduce* alienation is in keeping with Marx's conception of workers as, increasingly, co-ordinators of complex systems, and indeed, Blauner's work on alienation seemed to bear out the potential for high levels of automation, under certain conditions, to lead to lower levels of alienation (Blauner 1964).

If automation could reduce necessary work to a minimum, or facilitate the transformation of work into something 'akin to play' – positions Marcuse appeared to hold at various points, why did toil and heteronomous work persist? Why did work continue to take up so much time? First, the Marcuse of *Eros and Civilization* pointed to 'surplus repression' (Marcuse 1987, p. 35), a concept developed as part of a Freudian-influenced exploration of the more instinctual elements of work and social control. Whilst the pre-automation age demanded a repression of people's sexual and playful instincts so that they could muster the discipline and self-denial necessary to wrestle a means of survival from nature, modern advanced technological systems made this repression unnecessary; they made possible 'the abolition of labour and the affirmation of the libido and play in social relations' (Musto 2010, p. 84). In short, contemporary workers were operating advanced production systems under the aegis of a work ethic more suited to early industrial society. Second, Marcuse draws attention to the role of consumption, or more accurately, consumerism, in perpetuating work, needlessly. The concept of 'false needs' is operationalised; 'Most of the prevailing needs to relax, to have fun, to behave and consume in accordance with the advertisements, to love and hate what others love and hate, belong to this category of false needs' (Marcuse 1986, p. 5). Along with the planned obsolescence of consumer goods, this system of false needs keeps people trapped in a destructive dialectic of work/consume. What should they be doing instead? Developing their 'human faculties', deploying their 'individual and collective desires', rebuilding 'the natural and built environment' (Rachlis 1978, p. 81), 'creative experimentation with the productive forces' (Marcuse 1970, p. 66).

The shift to a society based on creative experimentation and the desires of the collective would be revolutionary – this would be a socialist society (Zilbersheid 2008, p. 405). Since the 'end of work' (Marcuse 2005, p. 111) would require a revolution, it would also require a revolutionary consciousness or a 'new sensibility.' The events of May–June 1968 in France, and the counterculture more generally, gave Marcuse hope that a new sensibility was emerging, but ultimately this 'exhilarating, joyous festival' (Poster 1975, p. 373) failed to lead to truly revolutionary change. The problem for Marcuse and other post-work utopians is that in order for a new sensibility to emerge, the current ideology of production, consumption and capitalist system-atisation must be transcended, but in order for it to be transcended, a new sensibility must first emerge (Marcuse 1970, p. 80). From the perspective of the current system of domination, in Marcuse's work, as elsewhere, there is a sense that the system of work and consumption must be maintained, even artificially, in order to keep such revolutionary possibilities in check.

André Gorz: Living Dead Capitalism

This artificial maintenance of alienated labour in the face of utopian possibilities was something that André Gorz; a 'French Marcuseite' (Anonymous 1969, p. 10) and 'well grounded in Critical Theory' (Brown 1991) characterised as 'living dead capitalism' (Gorz 1985, pp. 37–39). If one subscribes to Gorz's theory, and indeed those of later writers, it is the period in which we now live. This central contradiction, and the way it is sustained and structured through politics and ideology, continues to represent one of the most theoretically fertile areas in terms of using post-work imaginaries to critique the present organisation of society. It is a concept that lends itself particularly well to analysis using Critical Theory, since it highlights the ideological nature of capitalism – in contrast to the more rational ways of being that lie beyond it.

Gorz is a highly significant figure in the intellectual history of the end of work, although in the latest wave of the debate, he tends to be under-acknowledged, if he is mentioned at all (with some exceptions, see for example Frayne 2015; Mason 2016). It is hard to say when this recent wave began, but Frayne's 2015 book *The Refusal of Work* did much to bring the post-work imaginary into the academic and public consciousness). Rising to what passes for prominence in European neo-Marxist terms, in the 1980s with his book *Farewell to the Working Class* (1980, English translation 1982), Gorz's analysis mirrors that of Marcuse in that it is a totalising critique of capitalism. He makes clear that the end of work is a key element in the transition to communism, and one that can only succeed if capitalism is overcome (Gorz 1967, p. 10). In the discussion which follows, Gorz's work is situated in historical and intellectual context; in particular, we examine the possible social formations related to the end of work, the possibilities for a positive post-work future, and the reasons why these possibilities remain unfulfilled – even as capitalism takes on increasingly irrational features.

The 1980s was a period of economic restructuring along neoliberal lines and, in many Western societies, rising unemployment. At the same time, computerisation began to mature as a central part of productive life and represented another dimension in the conceptual career of automation. Little wonder, perhaps, that this period produced an outpouring of anxiety over the future of work, much of it centred on the concern that there already was not, and in the future certainly would not, be enough of it to go around. This is in contrast to the period in which Marcuse was writing, in that the 1960s was for many a more optimistic time where automation was still often seen as signifying the possibility of increased leisure, rather than leading to socially disruptive levels of unemployment. And so the period witnessed a slew of books on the future of work or the end of work which extended, in the United States in particular, into the 1990s (Aronowitz & DiFazio 1994; Bleakley 1985; Handy 1984; Jenkins & Sherman 1979; Rifkin 1996; Robertson 1985).

What is particularly interesting in the work of Gorz and this wider discourse is the way visions of the future of work tended to posit 'imaginaries', which are both positive and negative in characterisation (Westwood 2000). As Aroles, Mitev & de Vaujany (2019, pp. 293–294) point out, there is a long-term and continuing tendency in future-of-work literature to posit both utopian and dystopian futures. In one conceptualisation, automation allows for increased leisure and free time, whilst promoting a generalised increase in skill and education levels. Society is able to overcome the problem of technological unemployment by radically re-engineering its material, social, cultural and political systems. One element of this might be a guaranteed income that is separated from the need to work. People are able to pursue their interests and self-development in an era of post-scarcity – a utopian future. In the other, automation leads to widespread unemployment and social dislocation. Although some benefit from new ways of working with advanced technology, automation renders many people surplus to requirements. Unless perhaps one belongs to the capitalist superclass (Rothkopf 2008), this is a dystopia.

This summary skates over a variety of differentiation, thematically and politically. Looking at the future of work is not the same as envisioning, and prescribing a post-work utopia, as Gorz does. For Gorz, there were various possible scenarios, and these are interwoven with accounts of the artificial perpetuation of the work-based economy, and its abolition. In one scenario, permanently employed workers become a 'narrow stratum, alongside vast numbers of unemployed' (Gorz 1985, p. 31). This polarisation thesis is reminiscent of Beck's 'Brazilianization of the West' idea (2000) and sees the privileged elite co-exist substantively, if not experientially, alongside 'a dispossessed social majority: slum dwellers in the shadow of skyscrapers precariously existing on crime and the underground economy' (Gorz 1985, p. 31).

Something that is noted more or less in passing in much critical writing on the end of work is the often racialised character of marginalisation. One exception to this is Rifkin's analysis of the African American experience (1996, pp. 69–80). He shows how black Americans were 'caught between technologies' (Rifkin 1996, p. 73); having been de jure liberated from slavery (which has its own significance in the conceptual history of the end of work, as we have seen) many African Americans remained in the Southern states, working in agriculture. When cotton picking was mechanised in the 1940s, black Americans found themselves 'invented out of a job' (Bix 2000) – victims of technological unemployment. This, amongst other developments, played a part in the great migration of Southern black workers to the industrial cities of the north – Chicago, Detroit, Cleveland, Philadelphia. Steered (in part by limitations imposed by structural racism) into significant concentrations in unskilled manufacturing jobs, African Americans were then hit harder than most when *these* jobs were in turn automated from the 1950s on (Rifkin 1996). This line of analysis brings Rifkin on to considering automation's role in the creation of the urban underclass (1996, p. 77). If one accepts that such a concept can in fact be operationalised, Black Americans make up a significant part of this group and find it harder to escape from it, since they have been denied the educational opportunities needed in order to become part of the rising knowledge class. The concept of 'structural violence' (Ralph 2014, p. 199) captures both the causes of black Americans' marginalisation, and its consequences. Eliminated from the world of work, the most marginalised 'turn to the ruthless business of drug trafficking, thereby mimicking the entrepreneurial spirit of capitalism. Like their legal counterparts, they kill, maim and destroy people's lives in the process of making a profit' (Ransby 1996, p. 6) Others such as Venkatesh (2008), Bourgois (1995), Farber (2019) and others have pursued this line of analysis, the former two in ethnographic detail. The drug economy is seen as a (perhaps *the*) only viable career option in socially, racially and economically segregated areas where de-industrialisation has seen decently paid work, perhaps any work, 'disappear' (Wilson 2011). One corollary of this growth of an alternative narco-economy has been the high levels of criminalisation and incarceration of African American men (Rifkin 1996, p. 77).

Through this system of mass incarceration, these workless, 'surplus' people can be (more or less) safely contained. In a sense then, there are many communities in which work *as conventionally known* has already ended, although it is notable that this fact is rarely mentioned in mainstream accounts of the 'possible' social costs of automation and the end of work. Although space precludes a detailed discussion of this issue here, the same could be said for worklessness (or wagelessness) in the global South (Denning 2010). More generally, the point has been made that research on the future of work has tended to be 'Western-centric' (Aroles et al. 2019 – they also note exceptions such as Graham, Hjorth & Lehdonvirta 2017, and Wood, Graham & Lehdonvirta 2018).

Some of those denied access to the privileges of full-time labour *do* still work in the 'legitimate' economy, as part of a servant class (Meagher 2003, p. 146), some of whom 'are forced into desperate, frenetic competition to sell domestic or sexual services to the narrow stratum of well-paid workers and employers' (Gorz 1985, p. 31) Elsewhere, Gorz points to young people, members of the new class of *précaires* (Gorz 2003, p. 98) 'who deliver their hot croissants, newspapers and pizzas' and do 'odd jobs' as another element of this servant class, a social category that was thought to have been made obsolete during the early twentieth century (Gorz 1989, p. 6). This scenario is certainly familiar to scholars who have charted the rise of non-standard or precarious work, and more recently the gig-economy (Edgell & Granter 2019, pp. 193–224). As economic rationality (Gorz 1989) spreads ever more deeply into everyday life, those who are cash-rich but time-poor rely on these contingent workers to put up their furniture, walk their dogs, and organise the contents of their refrigerators (Rodrigues 2020).

This set-up is functional for the perpetuation of the society of work. It is the organisation of capitalism in *'ways which hide its reality'* (Gorz 1985, p. 34). The core of relatively privileged, full-time workers remain committed to the ideology of work, which for them continues to deliver the goods, and the precariat have no choice but to cling to the notion of work, *any work*, or be cast into a stigmatised, marginalised underclass of the full-time unemployed. This further notion of work as intertwined with social control is perhaps under-theorised in Gorz and beyond, but offers a potentially interesting dimension of the end-of-work concept. Frayne highlights the disciplinary potential of splitting the population into a binary relation of working/not working (2015, p. 99). In this moral economy, the non-working are demonised (see also Graeber 2018, p. 243). Even in areas where there simply are not enough jobs for the unemployed to do, they are constructed as failed individuals; condemned to a life of poverty, yes, but undeserving of help since this is a problem of their own making (Frayne 2015, p. 100). This view of unemployment remains a politically legitimised cultural trope and if a moment of levity can be permitted, is summed up as follows:

The idea they're trying to get across is that unemployment is caused by the unemployed not wanting to work. Maybe this is true. In which case, in the 1920s everyone was full of beans, but in around 1931 three million people decided they couldn't be bothered for a few years, though they perked up again around 1938 which was handy as it was just in time for the war. (Steel 2012)

This ideological and cultural formation is similar to other forms of control, in that it appears to exist in a self-reinforcing pattern; it operationalises elements of precisely *its own ideological and cultural formation* as signifiers, in a way in which possibilities of alternatives are obfuscated. It is, to use the term in the Marcusean sense, *one dimensional*.

Work as a form of social control can operate in a number of ways. As Gorz would have it, and echoing Marcuse's analysis, work and consumption exist primarily as 'instruments of control in the hands of a ruling class whose power no longer rests on property but on controlling the system of control' (1985, p. 39). Work is perpetuated '"to keep people occupied"' (Gorz 1982, p. 72). Graeber (2018, p. 284), in a similar vein, implies that work plays a role in occupying people's time so that they have little of it left in which to politically organise and actively change the status quo: 'As Orwell noted, a population busy working, even at the most useless occupations, doesn't have time to do much else. At the very least, this is further incentive not to do anything about the situation'. The role of work in maintaining social control, or discipline, in the Foucauldian sense is explored by Macherey. Through a combinatory reading of Marx and Foucault, he highlights the centrality of production relations in establishing a society of norms. Once capitalist control over the labour process (work) is established, this form of discipline becomes generative of a more generalised system:

In a society of norms everything is programmed or can be programmed. The behavior of each individual compelled to take his place in a process that is molded in such a way loses the character of individual actions possessing an intrinsic value. It is listed, catalogued, formatted according to functional criteria that are not up for discussion and impose themselves by claiming to be self-evident. (Macherey 2015)

In an analysis that also draws on the work of Foucault, Guizzo and Stronge (2018) make a similar point, noting that work 'performs a larger social role: not only does it determine the provision of food, shelter and other needs, but also influences the ways individuals think and act'. The end of work, by these accounts, would threaten the system of domination as it presently exists. Put even more simply, to end work would involve, as discussed previously, a revolutionary transformation of politics, culture and society.

We do find in the work of Gorz a set of more positive post-work scenarios. For example, he raises the possibility of a new social subject, a 'non class of non-workers' (1982: 67). These are the precarious workers encountered above, for whom work has become increasingly meaningless, who drift 'from one temporary 'McJob' to another, always retaining enough time as possible to follow the favoured activities of their tribe' (Gorz 1999, p. 61). It is not entirely clear at present that precarious, gig-economy workers (the group perhaps most accurately matching Gorz's neoproletariat) have truly developed a new sensibility that favours a wholesale re-evaluation of work, or in fact seek an escape from temporary work by re-entering the traditional model of full-time, secure work through a process of regularisation (Edgell & Granter 2019, p. 205) Given the ideological and cultural persistence of work as a source of economic and personal value (not to mention as the means to survive), it seems that for many, '[u]nder capitalism, the only thing worse than being exploited is not being exploited' (Denning 2010, p. 79). From the perspective of capital, the reserve army of the precariously employed serves its own disciplinary functions. In a society where secure, well-paid jobs are in short supply, work 'put[s] on airs, as rare goods do' (Basso 2003, p. 197).

Supposing that an escape from the work-based society *was* achieved, in a way in which social catastrophe could be avoided, what would people do with their time? Gorz, in a section of *Paths to Paradise* entitled 'the politics of time', envisions an era defined by 'the pleasure of creating, giving, learning, establishing with others non-market, non-hierarchic, practical and effective relationships' (1985, p. 107). In practical terms, Gorz, like many other post-work utopians, advocates a form of universal basic income. Even more practically, he calls for the establishment of collective facilities that can provide people with a space for autonomous work. Community centres with facilities for reading, music, Do It Yourself (DIY) and so on (Gorz 1985, p. 103). In addition, a collective, co-operative sector of non-market service and exchange should be established. In the sphere of necessary work that still exists, activity and relationships should be redefined through negotiation over elements such as technological change, nature of jobs and staffing levels, and work-time (Gorz 1985, p. 104). Others have sketched out a similar meaningful future 'beyond employment' (Pym 1990, pp. 137–155), in some cases literally, with books featuring drawings depicting collectivised gardens and community media centres (Harper & Ward 1990, pp. 149–154). Lang, nearly forty years later, finds the DIY ethic alive and well in post-industrial Cheetham Hill, a significantly deprived, multicultural area of Greater Manchester in the United Kingdom. Lang found that at the Welcome [community] Centre, people marginalised by the mainstream economy of work found fulfilment in affective labour; teaching and learning English, creating hair salons, 'a beauty parlour, a clothes exchange point, a bike repair container, a furniture repair space, and a circuit of translators on request' (Lang 2020, pp. 163–164). Although Lang observes that work retained its social and cultural value for the community centring on the Welcome Centre, she also notes that the participants were operating on an 'alternative logic' of 'trust and reciprocity' (Lang 2020, p. 160).

The End of Work 4.0

The end of work is once again a 'hot topic' in academia and the public sphere, with a plethora of books appearing in recent years (Bastani 2019; Brynjolfsson & McAfee 2014; Fleming 2015; Frayne 2015; Graeber 2018; Mason 2016; Srnicek & Williams 2015; Susskind 2020, *inter alia*). Clearly this is the latest in a number of iterations of the end-of-work thesis and we have seen in this chapter that visions of a post-work world are nothing new. It should, however, be noted that it is possible to *imagine* a world without work, independently of whether one accurately predicts that this will actually come to pass.

It is not entirely clear why this (or any other) surge of interest in the end of work appear in the collective consciousness, but some patterns are discernible.

In the 1950s and 1960s, relatively low levels of unemployment and high levels of consumer spending created the conditions for a so-called revolt against work, or at least the perception of one (Reeve 1976). This was coupled with the development of a counterculture that (temporarily) appeared to reject conventional notions of work and career. At the same time, automated technology continued to develop in manufacturing and, increasingly, in corporate administration. In the 1980s, as already noted, economic restructuring and rising unemployment played a role, and in the 1990s, corporate restructuring and, once again, automation, this time facilitated by advances in computing is relevant.

Automation is a recurrent theme and the most recent set of debates comes at a time of new developments around not only roboticisation, but artificial intelligence (AI) and artificial neural networks are argued to threaten to eliminate potentially catastrophic numbers of jobs. Frey and Osborne's article on the susceptibility of jobs to automation is particularly influential, with their prediction of 47 per cent of American jobs at risk of elimination (2013, p. 47). Notably, there is a sense that this time around, service and 'white collar' professional jobs are at significant risk of automation (Frey & Osborne 2013). Since a very large proportion of the population are now employed in these sectors, interest in the threat of technological unemployment has risen, just as it did in previous eras when manufacturing workers, then a key occupational group, were threatened by automation and the economic restructuring. Management consultancies and think-tanks have seized the moment (Sturdy & Morgan 2018) suggesting the possibility that a 'cultural circuit of capital' (Thrift 2001) has emerged to shape the 'future work' agenda. Groups of scholars have coalesced around ideas of a crisis of work, and the liberatory politics necessary for overcoming it. See for example https://autonomy.work/ and https://futuresofwork.co.uk/. A number of researchers associated with the latter grouping have been critical of many of the assumptions underlying dreams of a workless world (Pitts & Dinerstein 2017), whilst not abandoning the possibilities for radical change in and beyond a society dominated by capitalism models of work and production.

Scepticism aside, attention now turns to sketching the content of the current crop of post-work imaginaries. Bell (1973, p. 456) noted that the 'elimination of scarcity, as the condition for abolishing all competitiveness and strife, has been the axial principal of all utopian thinking' and whilst technology can eliminate jobs, it is seen by some as having the potential to lead to 'new vistas of abundance' (Bastani 2019, p. 11). In an account that shares many thematic similarities with the (much) earlier work of Etzler (1842), Bastani (2019, pp. 94–116) highlights the significance of renewable energy in facilitating 'fully automated luxury communism'. Tending also to foresee a world beyond scarcity (or at least its technical possibility), most of the contemporary visionaries of the end of work (Bastani, Frayne, Srnicek and Williams, Mason, Graeber, Susskind), as Gorz and many others have done, posit that some form of decoupling of income from work will be needed in order to move beyond the wage-based economy. This would allow, for instance, the expansion of freely chosen, autonomous activity along the lines of Marx's vision of hunting in the morning, fishing in the afternoon, criticising after dinner (Srnicek & Williams 2015, p. 121). And once again echoing Gorz, a more co-operative form of economic exchange, beyond the wage and the market, is suggested (Bastani 2019, p. 210; Mason 2016, pp. 275–277). Dystopic visions linger, however, just as they always have done. Even accounts that do not appear to advocate a revolutionary supersession of capitalism, point to the tendency for automation to increase social inequalities (Brynjolfsson & McAfee 2014; Susskind 2020). Others echo the dystopic visions of the 1980s, witness some of Srnicek and Williams' predictions of automation's effects, *should it proceed subject to the current tendencies of capitalism* (2015, p. 104): 'Slum populations will continue to grow due to the automation of low-skilled service work ... Urban marginality in the developed economies will grow in size as low-skilled, low wage jobs are automated ... The challenges to workfare, immigration controls and mass incarceration will deepen as those without jobs are increasingly subjected to coercive controls and survival economies'.

Many of the defining features of the post-work imaginary then, remain surprisingly consistent. Or perhaps not so surprisingly, since many of them, particularly the most radical (Bastani 2019; Frayne 2015; Mason 2016; Srnicek & Williams 2015) function as a critique

of capitalism, as did those of Marx, Marcuse and Gorz. There is a new
world of work where the pathologies, injustices and irrationalities of
capitalism continue, even in the face of potential freedom and material
abundance, and there is a new world beyond work where these potentials are fully realised; a future beyond capitalism.

Conclusion: The End of Work as Critical Social Theory

The most radical post-work imaginaries function as a form of critical
social theory because they situate work as part of a 'pathological
organization of society' (Granter 2009, p. 2). They show how this rests
on an irrationality that can only be explained, in turn, through an
analysis of prevailing systems of domination. The central irrationality
is the fact that the means exist to eliminate poverty, toil, needless
consumption and alienation, but that these means are not utilised. To
enact this elimination would entail a re-evaluation or, more accurately,
revolution in the understanding of the role of work. Though much
critical social theory of the end of work owes a great debt to Marx, it
also tends to follow the established school of Critical Theory (the
Frankfurt School) in prioritising the need for theoretical and analytical
adaptation, and so each iteration offers new avenues of critique.

Work at present is defined in ontological, political and ideological
terms as a mediating function between the system of capitalism and the
experience and consciousness of the majority of the population. Since
the domination of capital depends on the continued centrality of
capitalist relations of work and production in this mediating function,
these relations must be sustained through an array of measures. These
measures continually evolve, albeit sometimes as 'variations on a
theme'. They range from the promotion of the ideological and cultural
centrality of work, the ramping-up of consumerism, to the structuring
of work in ways that polarise the working population into masters and
servants, to the marginalisation and repression of groups who are
considered surplus to the requirements of the productivist society.
One of the central functions of the post-work imaginary lies less in
its vision of the future, and more in its analysis of why this future has
failed to materialise – or has been prevented from so doing.

At the same time, like Marx (though he may not have agreed with
this characterisation) the Critical Theorists and many later advocates
of a workless future carry the impulse of utopianism. Weeks

characterises the vision of a life 'no longer subordinate to work' as one that can open up 'new theoretical vistas and terrains of struggle. The point is that these utopian demands can serve to generate political effects that exceed the specific reform' (2011, p. 221). As Segal argues, 'to be effective as social criticism, a utopian vision should be concrete enough to be applicable to the real world; and it should be detached enough to be truly critical (1985, p. 157). Radical theories of the end of work fit with this notion of a utopian demand because they are based on analyses of social reality, of 'actually existing tendencies' (Weeks 2011, p. 211). If utopian demands are based on social reality, their descriptions of what life in a world without work would be like, posit an alternative, possible reality, one based on co-operation, community, autonomy and freedom – truly new ways of working, beyond the conventions within which society currently operates.

Astra Taylor (2018) recalls Sylvia Federici proclaiming: 'Don't let them make you think that you are disposable'. Taylor's point is that the work of social reproduction is often excluded from mainstream predictions of technological unemployment; given the fact that this is the work done predominantly by women, perhaps this is no accident. Broadening the concept of social reproduction somewhat, this leads to the possibility that paradoxically, one possible utopia might in fact be based on a continuation of work, rather than its abolition. Whilst automation, computerisation, robotisation and AI can render the production worker, the service worker, even the legal or architectural professional redundant, what of the work that is required to create a more just, fair, peaceful society? We have seen the role of 'affective labour' in the interstices of a decaying post-industrial capitalism in Lang's recent research (Lang 2020), but what if this form of labour could become the new defining model of 'work' beyond capitalism? Any transition to a more socially just world would entail remedying the problems beset the society of capitalist work. The psychological and cultural costs of generations of poverty and social dysfunction, crime and deprivation, inequalities in education, racial, gender and other forms of discrimination, poor healthcare, environmental degradation ... For Rifkin, the 'postmarket era is handing us an opportunity to rebuild communities, schools, public infrastructure, broken families, and displaced lives' (Leicht 1998, p. 40). In short, fixing the damage done by the structural violence of capitalism may require a great deal of work, although in a scenario where work is as fulfilling as it is useful, there is no reason for it to resemble the alienated, heteronomous, often unnecessary activity that work represents for many at present. Of course, in a future round of debate over the end of work – and there will surely be many – the question of whether artificially intelligent robots are capable of this re-engineering of society may arise. But seen from the perspective of today, such a revolution is unlikely to be automated.

References

Anonymous 1969. *FRANCE: May 1968, WORKERS REBEL!* Available at: www.marxists.org/history/erol/1960-1970/francemay68.pdf (Accessed: 30 January 2020).

Applebaum, H. 1992. *The Concept of Work.* New York: SUNY Press.

Aroles, J., Mitev, N. & de Vaujany, F. X. 2019. Mapping themes in the study of new work practices. *New Technology, Work and Employment*, 34 (3): 285–299.

Aronowitz, S. & DiFazio, W. 1994. *The Jobless Future.* Minneapolis: University of Minnesota Press.

Baldry, H. C. 1953. The idler's paradise in Attic comedy. *Greece and Rome*, 22(65): 49–60.

Basso, P. 2003. *Modern Times, Ancient Hours*, trans. G. Donis. London: Verso.

Bastani, A. 2019. *Fully Automated Luxury Communism.* London: Verso.

Beck, U. 2000. *The Brave New World of Work.* Cambridge: Polity Press.

Bell, D. 1973. *The Coming of Post-Industrial Society.* New York: Basic Books.

Bix, A. 2000. *Inventing Ourselves out of Jobs?* London: Johns Hopkins University Press.

Blauner, R. 1964. *Alienation and Freedom.* London: University of Chicago Press.

Bleakley, D. 1985. *Beyond Work – Free to Be.* London: SCM Press.

Booth, W. 1991. Economies of time: On the idea of time in Marx's political economy. *Political Theory*, 19(1): 205–222.

Bourgeois, P. 1995. Workaday world, crack economy. *The Nation*, 4 December: 706–711.

Brown, D. 1991. Review critique of economic reason by Andre Gorz, Gillian Handyside and Chris Turner. *Journal of Economic Issues*, 25(3): 866–870.

Brynjolfsson, E. & McAfee, A. 2014. *The Second Machine Age.* London: W. W. Norton.

Clark, G. & Van Der Werf, Y. 1998. Work in progress? The industrious revolution. *The Journal of Economic History*, 58(3): 830–843.

Clegg, S. & Pina e Cunha, M. 2019. *Management, Organizations and Contemporary Social Theory*. Abingdon: Routledge.

Denning, M. 2010. Wageless life. *New Left Review*, 66: 79–97.

Edgell, S. & Granter, E. 2019. *The Sociology of Work*. London: Sage.

Etzler, J. A. 1842. *The Paradise within the Reach of All Men...* London: J. Cleave.

Farber, D. 2019. *Crack: Rock Cocaine, Street Capitalism, and the Decade of Greed*. Cambridge: Cambridge University Press.

Fleming, P. 2015. *The Mythology of Work*. Chicago: University of Chicago Press.

Fourier, C. 1972. *The Utopian Vision of Charles Fourier*, trans. J. Beecher, and R. Bienvenu. London: Jonathan Cape.

Frankel, B. 1987. *The Post-industrial Utopians*. Cambridge: Polity.

Frayne, D. 2015. *The Refusal of Work*. London: Zed Books.

Frey, C. B. & Osborne, M. A. 2013. *The Future of Employment: How Susceptible Are Jobs to Computerisation?* (Working Paper). Oxford Martin School: University of Oxford. Available at: www.oxfordmartin .ox.ac.uk/publications/the-future-of-employment/ (Accessed 30 January 2020).

Gorz, A. 1967. *Strategy for Labor*, trans. M. A. Nicolaus and V. Ortiz. Boston: Beacon Press.

1980. *Adieux au proletariat: au–dela du socialisme* Paris: Galilée.

1982. *Farewell to the Working Class*, trans. M. Sonenscher. London: Pluto.

1985. *Paths to Paradise*, trans. M. Imrie. London: Pluto.

1989. *Critique of Economic Reason*, trans. G. Handyside and C. Turner. London: Verso.

1999. *Reclaiming Work*, trans. C. Turner. Cambridge: Polity.

2003. *L'immatériel. Connaissance, valeur et capital*. Paris: Galilée.

Graeber, D. 2018. *Bullshit Jobs*. London: Penguin.

Graham, M., Hjorth, I. & Lehdonvirta, V. 2017. Digital labour and development: Impacts of global digital labour platforms and the gig economy on worker livelihoods. *Transfer: European Review of Labour and Research*, 23(2): 135–162.

Granter, E. 2009. *Critical Social Theory and the End of Work*. Farnham: Ashgate.

2014. Critical Theory and Organization Studies. In P. Adler, P. DuGay & G. Morgan (eds.) *The Oxford Handbook of Sociology, Social Theory and Organization Studies*. Oxford: Oxford University Press, pp. 534–560.

2019. The Frankfurt School and Critical Theory. In S. R. Clegg & M. Pina e Cunha (eds.) *Management, Organizations and Contemporary Social Theory*. Abingdon: Routledge, pp. 223–244.

Guizzo, D. & Stronge, W. 2018. Keynes, Foucault and the 'disciplinary complex': A contribution to the analysis of work. *Autonomy*, 2.

Gunderson, R. 2018. Degrowth and other quiescent futures. *Journal of Cleaner Production*, 198: 1574–1582.

Handy, C. 1984. *The Future of Work*. Oxford: Blackwell.

Harper, C. & Ward, C. 1990 [1974–1975]. Visions. In V. Richards (ed.) *Why Work*. London: Freedom Press, pp. 149–154.

Horkheimer, M. 2002 [1937]. Traditional and Critical Theory. In M. Horkheimer (ed.) *Critical Theory; Selected Essays*. New York: Continuum, pp. 188–243.

Jay, M. 1996 [1973]. *The Dialectical Imagination 1923–1950*. London: University of California Press.

Jenkins, C. & Sherman, B. 1979. *The Collapse of Work*. London: Methuen.

Kellner, D. 1989. *Critical Theory, Marxism and Modernity*. Baltimore: Johns Hopkins.

Lang, L. 2020. You Make Do with what You've Got. In G. Evans (ed.) *Post-industrial Precarity*. Wilmington, NC: Vernon Press, pp.151–171.

Leicht, K. T. 1998. Work (if you can get it) and occupations (if there are any)? What social scientists can learn from predictions of the end of work and radical workplace change. *Work and Occupations*, 25(1): 36–48.

Macherey, P. 2015. The Productive Subject. *Viewpoint Magazine*, 31 October. Available at: www.viewpointmag.com/2015/10/31/the-productive-subject/ (Accessed: 30 January 2020).

Marcuse, H. 1970. The End of Utopia. In H. Marcuse *Five Lectures*. Boston: Beacon, pp. 62–82.

1973 [1933]. On the philosophical foundation of the concept of labor in economics (trans. D. Kellner). *Telos*, 16: 9–37.

1986 [1964]. *One Dimensional Man: Studies in the Ideology of Advanced Industrial Society*. London: Ark.

1987 [1955]. *Eros and Civilization*. London: Ark.

2005 [1968]. A Conversation with Herbert Marcuse. In D. Kellner (ed.) *Herbert Marcuse, the New Left and the 1960s*. London: Routledge, pp. 154–164.

Marx, K. 1845. *The German Ideology*. Available at: www.marxists.org/archive/marx/works/1845/german-ideology/ch01a.htm (Accessed: 30 January 2020).

Marx, K. 1974 [1867]. *Capital*. London: Dent.

1975 [1844]. Economic and Philosophical Manuscripts. In L. Coletti (ed.) *Early Writings*. London: Penguin, pp. 279–400.

1977 [1894]. *Capital Vol. III*. London: Lawrence and Wishart.

1993 [1857-8]. *Grundrisse*. London: Penguin.

Mason, P. 2016. *Postcapitalism*. London: Penguin Books.

Mavor, C. 2016. The Closed Cosmogony of Utopia. 8 September 2016. *Frieze*. Available at: https://frieze.com/article/closed-cosmogony-utopia (Accessed: 30 January 2020).

McLean, D. D. & Hurd, A. R. 2015. *Kraus' Recreation and Leisure in Modern Society*. Burlington, MA: Jones and Bartlett Learning.

Meagher, G. 2003. *Friend or Flunkey?* Sydney: UNSW Press.

Musto, M. 2010. Revisiting Marx's concept of alienation. *Socialism and Democracy*, 24(3): 79–101.

Neimark, M. & Tinker, T. 1987. Identity and non identity thinking: A dialectical critique of the transaction cost theory of the modern corporation. *Journal of Management*, 13(4): 661–673.

Pitts, F. H. & Dinerstein, A. C. 2017. *Postcapitalism, Basic Income and the End of Work: A Critique and Alternative*. Bath Papers in International Development and Wellbeing, No. 55, University of Bath, Centre for Development Studies (CDS), Bath.

Poster, M. 1975. *Existential Marxism in Post-War France*. Princeton, NJ.: Princeton University Press.

Pym, D. 1990 [1981]. The Other Economy as a Social System. In V. Richards (ed.) *Why Work*. London: Freedom Press, pp. 137–149.

Rachlis, C. 1978. Marcuse and the problem of happiness. *Canadian Journal of Political and Social Theory*, 2(1): 63–89.

Ralph, L. 2014. *Renegade Dreams*. London: University of Chicago Press.

Ransby, B. 1996. US: the Black Poor and the Politics of Expendability. *Race and Class*, 38(2): 1–12.

Reeve, C. 1976. The "revolt against work", or fight for the right to be lazy. *Fifth Estate*. Available at: www.fifthestate.org/archive/279-december-1976/the-revolt-against-work-or-fight-for-the-right-to-be-lazy/ (Accessed: 30 January 2020).

Rifkin J. 1996 [1995]. *The End of Work*. New York: G.P. Putnam.

Robertson, J. 1985. *Future Work*. London: Gower/Maurice Temple Smith.

Robertson, K. & Uebel, M. 2016. *The Middle Ages at Work*. New York: Palgrave Macmillan.

Rodrigues, A. 2020. Gig economy now making workers organize groceries in rich people's fridge. *VICE*, Jan 09. Available at: www.vice.com/en_us/article/qjd8vq/gig-economy-now-making-workers-organize-grocer ies-in-rich-peoples-fridges (Accessed: 30 January 2020).

Rothkopf, D. 2008. *Superclass: The Global Power Elite and the World They Are Making*. New York: Farrar.

Sahlins, M.D. 1972. *Stone Age Economics*. New York: Aldine de Gruyter.

Segal, H. P. 1985. *Technological Utopianism in American Society*. Chicago: University of Chicago Press.

Schor, J. B. 1993. *The Overworked American*. New York: BasicBooks.

Spiers, S. n.d. Women in Utopia: Charles Fourier's Theory of the Four Movements. Available at: www.academia.edu/32791990/Women_in_Utopia_Charles_Fouriers_Theory_of_the_Four_Movements (Accessed: 30 January 2020).

Srnicek, N. & Williams, A. 2015. *Inventing the Future*. London: Verso Books.

Steel, M. 2012. When Tories demonise the workless. *Independent*, 28 November.

Sturdy, A. & Morgan, G. 2018. Management consultancies: Inventing the future. *Futures of Work*, Issue 1. Available at: https://futuresofwork.co.uk/2018/09/05/management-consultancies-inventing-the-future-2/ (Accessed: 30 January 2020).

Susskind, D. 2020. *A World without Work*. London: Allen Lane.

Taylor, A. 2018. The automation charade. *Logic Magazine*. Available at: https://logicmag.io/failure/the-automation-charade/ (Accessed: 30 January 2020).

Thrift, N. 2001. "It's the romance, not the finance, that makes the business worth pursuing": disclosing a new market culture. *Economy and Society*, 30(4): 412–432.

Venkatesh, S. A. 2008. *Gang Leader for a Day: A Rogue Sociologist Takes to the Streets*. London: Penguin.

Weeks, K. 2011. *The Problem with Work*. Duke University Press.

Weiner, N. 1950. *The Human Use of Human Beings: Cybernetics and Human Beings*. Boston: Houghton Mifflin.

Westwood, S. 2000. Re-branding Britain: Sociology, futures and futurology. *Sociology*, 34(1): 185–202.

Wilson, W. J. 2011. *When Work Disappears: The World of the New Urban Poor*. New York: Alfred A. Knopf.

Wood, A. J., Graham, M. & Lehdonvirta, V. 2018. Good gig, bad big: Autonomy and algorithmic control in the global gig economy. *Work, Employment and Society*, 33(1): 56–75.

Zilbersheid, U. 2008. The utopia of Herbert Marcuse part 1. *Critique*, 36(3): 403–419.

10 | *Exploring the New in Politics at Work*

A Temporal Approach of Managerial Agencies

FRANÇOIS-XAVIER DE VAUJANY AND
AURÉLIE LECLERCQ-VANDELANNOITTE

Introduction: Everyday Managerial Agency as Producing New Public Policies

In the context of ongoing work transformations (e.g. generalisation of entrepreneurship, end of traditional frontiers between work and private practices or consumer and producer practices, increasing mobility digital transformation of work practices), it seems that, more than ever, 'managerial agency' transforms society and our way of life (Aroles, Mitev & de Vaujany 2019; Barley 2010; Daskalaki, Hjorth & Mair 2015; Farias, Fernandez, Hjorth & Holt 2019; Pennel 2013). By managerial agency, we do not mean the usual sense of managers' ability to get things done. Agency refers to the 'transformative capacity' to induce movement, both symbolically and materially (see Schatzki 2010 for the difference between agency and action). It relies on a set of activities (teleological set of behaviours) and practices (meaningful patterns of behaviours such as 'introducing oneself', 'giving a phone call', 'asking a question'...), that are articulated in such ways that agency recombines elements of practices through activities to create new practices. Managerial agency is thus mainly about an 'acting together' teleologically, generally conducted in a competitive environment (with a scarcity of resources), including other teleological activities reflexive about their environment.

The political effect of management and organisation is far from new. A long time ago, founding Management and Organization (MOS) scholars (e.g. Burnham 1941; Drucker 1945; Follett 1918, 1919) had already noticed that, in a world increasingly constituted by organisations and management, politics and societal transformations originate more and more from the latter. As recognised by

Hickson et al. (1980, pp. 1–2) in their inaugural *Organization Studies* editorial, organisations are conceived of as 'both the implements of societies and institutions which shape the societies that use them'.

Nowadays, both digital infrastructures and globalisation, coupled with the development of new ways of working (Aroles et al. 2019; Kingma 2019), have taken this trend further, granting managerial agency a highly transformative political power in society. Recently, managers have started to purposefully justify their evolving status in alternative self-descriptions as 'entrepreneurs', 'professionals' and 'project leaders (Brocklehurst, Grey & Sturdy 2009; Locke & Schone 2004), thus emphasising their potential for action and change. In this vein, entrepreneurial agency (as a widespread act of setting up one's job and pushing forward explicitly a business model) (Matlay & Westhead 2005), digital nomads (Makimoto & Manners 1997), everyday users of digital technologies (as feeders and consolidators of global digital infrastructures), and new collaborative communities and movements (as new spaces for social activism sometimes catalysed by the two previous trends) (Garrett, Spreitzer & Bacevice 2017; Hjorth & Holt 2016), increasingly mould their environment (Barley 2010) in ways that deeply transform politics and the experience of politics in Western countries (Cerny 2000; Lallement 2015). Uber, Facebook and Airbnb, for example, offer business models that deeply and globally transform societies. They also change the modalities of deep political processes such as the legitimation of collective activities, the sense of representativeness (which is more and more global) and even the sense of democracy, in increasingly continuous and direct ways (Häkli & Kallio 2014; McGregor 2011). In contrast, usual political agencies (e.g. of governments and national policies) appear weaker and weaker in our global and liquid world, in particular compared to the rise of participative democracy (Bacqué, Rey & Sintomer 2005).

Surprisingly, both the changing nature of work and management and its underlying political dimensions remain largely neglected phenomena in MOS. While Parsons (1965) considered in his seminal book an analysis of the way organisations influence the larger sociocultural context in which they are embedded as one of the most important mandates for organisational theory, MOS scholars have paid little attention to this phenomenon for decades (Barley 2010). On the one hand, with few exceptions (Aroles et al. 2019; Cappelli & Keller 2013; Dale 2005), they deal weakly with ongoing work transformations as part of organisational phenomena and organising processes. They also rarely explore this new relationship between managerial agency and political agency. On the other hand, while political sciences stress numerous new modalities of political agency in society (e.g. new social activism and the role of digital infrastructures in the emergence of radical or more incremental changes in political structures), and explain the role of corporate structures (such as multinational corporations, (MNC)) in this move, they do not fully capture the relationship between managerial and political agencies, nor changes in managerial agency itself (see e.g. Barley 2010; Cerny 2000; Epstein 1969).

We contend in this chapter that managerial agency has the potential to transform society and the sense of togetherness at a scale and depth that used to be that of political agency in the 1930s, 1940s and 1950s (in the golden age of Keynesian and 'stop and go' policies). New digital (the Internet) and physical infrastructures (third-places and an increasing connectivity inside and between cities) favour reflexive managerial agency in ways that continuously reinvent society and our way of life. In a way, public policies (as setting up reflexively an agenda for the future of society and the sense of togetherness) are more and more outsourced to private, managerial agencies. We call this growing isomorphism between managerial and political agencies 'co-politicisation', implying an increasing convergence between those endorsing the roles of manager (e.g. entrepreneurs) and those endorsing the role of politicians (as explicitly elected and with a specific mandate to participate in everyday democracy).

In the analysis of this growing isomorphism between managerial and political agency, we emphasise a deep ontological rupture. While MOS founders called for an exploration of the wide implications of a society constituted by formal organisations seen as 'building blocks' (see Barley 2010; Hunter 1953; Parsons 1965; Selznick 1949), our discourse goes beyond the mere 'managerialisation' of politics. On the one hand, the 'corporatisation of politics' (Epstein 1969) and the 'managerialisation of politics' are more about the intrusion of managerial ideology into political debates and political activities; on the other hand, the 'politicisation of corporations' corresponds to a growing transformation of the political field and public policies (Barley 2010), through lobbying and influencing strategies of governments and political institutions (Epstein 1969). Critical perspectives in MOS research have already drawn attention to the social consequences of corporate power (Clegg 1989; Clegg & Dunkerly 1980; Courpasson 2008; Courpasson & Clegg 2006; Perrow 1972, 2002). However, such an issue, which has received far more interest in Europe than in the United States, largely focuses on the organisation's internal life, thus limiting our understanding of the power and influence of managerial agency on wider society, politics, markets and law (Barley 2010).

In this essay, we defend a more diffuse and pervading view of political dimensions as constitutive of the myriad of managerial agencies constituting emergently the political dimensions of our world (beyond the structures, dispositives, decision processes and instances of medium or large corporations as institutional actors). Our focus is on managerial agency and managerial activities themselves, conceived of as an 'acting together'. Thus, we do not mean that there are no interesting analytical dimensions that could be common for both phenomena (i.e. 'managerialisation of politics' and 'politicisation of corporations'). The collapse of the legitimacy of usual political agencies, which seems sometimes to be compensated by an increasing use of managerial rhetoric and techniques to convince of the rigour and effectiveness of the management of the city, country and administration is probably the other side of the coin. And the decrease of usual political agency in a global world (making national budgets or monetary policies less effective) also requires rethinking the necessary theories and categories to conceptualise political agency (Cerny 2000).

As a result of these evolutions, politics seems, more than ever, to be in crisis. The appropriation of political infrastructures by managerial agencies creates a crisis of politics itself, such that we have never produced so few commons (Dietz et al. 2003; Mattei 2012; Ostrom 2002) and meaningful collectives. If each individual can now express his/her individual voice, collectivity becomes a mere sum aggregated of voices by search engines, algorithms and Artificial Intelligence. Thus, we ask: How can we make sense of this crisis of the politics in the abovementioned context of 'co-politicisation'? In particular, how can we understand the gradual move of democratic infrastructures from the context of institutions (with representative democracy rituals such as votes, and agoras such as parliaments) to management (with more and more communicative infrastructures that produce political protests and political movements or more simply, direct individual expressions)?

To address these questions, we contend that a temporal approach can help in understanding the crisis of politics in the context of new ways of working, where managerial and political agencies increasingly merge[1]. To that end, we introduce Paul Ricoeur (1985)'s temporal and narrative thought on the 'crisis of the present' in which our society could remain stuck. The past, present and future no longer flow. The past is 'museified' (i.e. fossilised, mummified, reified and non-resonant) and the future is linked to a set of utopian thoughts in the present. This results in the manifestation of a strange form of presentism, a temporalisation that appears disconnected from the emotions and affects prone to making temporalities flow in narratives. If the past is dead and the present is filled with utopia, then the present becomes an eternal move towards the future. After describing this temporal and narrative crisis, we explore the temporal breaks at stake in new forms of organising. We conclude by suggesting that new modes of organising may be missing managerial practices likely to produce the extra-temporality needed to recreate meaningful resonance in contemporary ways of working and living.

This essay is organised as follows: after presenting new ways of working as drivers of political transformation and introducing the concept of co-politicisation to refer to the growing isomorphism between managerial and political agencies, we address the issue of 'politics in crisis' through the development of a Ricoeurian temporal approach of the 'crisis of the present' observed in new ways of working.

Co-politicisation and the Transformative Political Power of Managerial Agency

A longue durée *View on Work Transformation: The End of Enclaves and the Shift to a New Semiosis*

How has managerial agency become a key component of contemporary politics? To understand this, we need a *longue durée* perspective. In most Western countries, the Middle Ages has been a time of major closures and enclosures, solidifications, entifications and oppositions

---

[1] And we see in the increasing interweaving of management and politics a major phenomenological aspect of the 'new' in 'new ways of working' – a novelty that makes sense mainly from a *longue durée* perspective.

(de Vaujany 2010a, 2010b; Kieser 1989). This is in the Middle Ages period in which communities, guilds and corporations have taken shape and expanded in Europe. These proto-bureaucracies are constitutive of enclaves. Etymologically, enclave comes from the vulgar mediaeval Latin expression *inclavare*, derived from *clavis*, with 'key' as a prefix and 'in' emphasising a result. An enclave is what is closed with a key, an inside, an individual or communitarian home.[2] Such a place and dispositive of closure (lock, key and walls) could not be widely accessed in the Middle Ages. Monastic organisations, castles and fortified cities were among the first places in Europe to systematise closures at such a massive level in Western countries. With them, territories, everybody's space, gradually open the way to private property, enclosures and a clarification of private ownership.

The monastery (to focus on this important enclave) is surrounded by emptiness or (let us use this paradoxical expression) a particular emptiness: forests. Forests of the Middle Age were immense, non-regulated areas, areas of non-right[3] that robbers and outlaws of all kind, but also more and more, commercial flows, inhabited and crossed. In contrast, inside the enclave and the vast deforested areas depending on it, rules are gradually established, along with new forms of collective rationality. Collective activity constructs simultaneously unique time and spaces, a totality. We are involved in an eschatological time, which will be interrupted at some time by an apocalypse. An outside exists, reified by an enclave. It is first of all a spatial and temporal emptiness. From the eleventh to the eighteenth centuries, universities had gradually become enclaves as well. More generally, after the Middle Ages (or at the end of a long Middle Ages to use Le Goff's (1957) expression), the world has been gradually covered by enclaves. More

---

[2] The notion of conclave appears at the same time (thirteenth century) and is also interesting. It corresponds to a room that can be closed with a key. For the Catholic Church, the conclave is also a strong decisional time: that of the nomination by the collectivity of locked cardinals of the successor of Saint Peter – the new pope. In this strong archetypal setting (for most Western countries and their imagery), the process of decision requires a spatial closure, but not necessarily a spatial closure (there is no deadline for the decision, even if this locked space is not favourable to a very long decision process). It is nonetheless necessary to be in a locked space to decide. Closure and obligation are both internal (the collective, stabilised through the closure, decides alone) and external (the rest of the world, the forest, does not decide).

[3] See, or rather listen to, Serres (2007) on this issue.

generally, with the explosion of the number of bureaucracies from the eighteenth to the twentieth century, the world has been gradually covered by enclaves, which are more and more enclaved into each other materially, socially (legally) and temporally (sharing the same temporalities locally and more and more globally). Forests, on their side, have kept decreasing and disappearing.

But at the turn of WWII (with the rise of a new semiosis, see de Vaujany & Mitev 2017) and in an accelerated manner since the late 1980s, the tendency seems to reverse itself. We are, again, surrounded by large forests, but they are, this time, invisible (Serres 2007). The web, its infrastructures and different layers, are an area of non-right for traditional enclaves, which do not manage to 'enclave' and regulate these new areas. The vast liberalisation of our world (described namely by Fukuyama's 2006 provocative thesis about the end of history), the emergence of a market and a time both deeply (globally) integrated, make regulations more and more (and obviously) heterogeneous and difficult. As a result, work is depicted as increasingly novel, flexible, disembodied, autonomous, collaborative, entrepreneurial, platform- and project- based (Aroles et al. 2019), as recognised by managers themselves in self-descriptions of their status, who prefer to identify themselves to the alternative mentality of the entrepreneur, which is positively contrasted with the 'back-covering, 'jobsworth' mentality of the bureaucratic manager' (Brocklehurst et al. 2009, p. 9).

Furthermore, in this context, the number of independent workers and entrepreneurs (Locke & Schone 2004) is exploding. It had been predicted that in 2020 there would be more independent workers than waged employees in the United States (MBO 2014[4]). As a tendency, crossed evolutions of waged employment and entrepreneurship and all kinds of independent activities are largely in favour of independent work (see e.g. Pennel 2013). In most Western countries, economies have created between three and ten times more independent workers

---

[4] www.union-auto-entrepreneurs.com/wp-content/uploads/2016/01/2014-MBO_ Partners_State_of_Independence_Report.pdf This strong statement and the general move towards a self-employed society has been the subject of numerous discussions (see e.g. this great critical HBR post by Justin Fox https://hbr.org/ 2014/02/where-are-all-the-self-employed-workers/). What remains is a clear increase of self-employment in most Western countries, with a stronger increase for some categories (i.e. artists, creative works, communication, IT and digital jobs).

since the mid-2000s. Work increasingly takes the form of an external-ised, independent activity, organised by and through platforms. Work and organising processes are thus more and more decentred (Introna 2019), in that the crowd, the market and the complex agency of digital infrastructures, instead of visible dominant stakeholders (i.e. organisa-tions), are at the heart of these modern forms of productive value creation.

In this context, it seems that individuals become, or rebecome, more of a simple working force (intellectual or physical) that vast numerical, juridical and capitalistic assemblers assemble and disassemble (more and more from afar and by involving situations of mobility), depending on the needs of products and financial markets (largely performed by digital infrastructures themselves) (de Vaujany, Leclercq & Holt 2020). All this is done of course far beyond usual frontiers and boundaries of collective activity ('firms' and 'organisa-tions'), the states surrounding it and the legislations applying to it. Again, new spaces (at the heart of assemblage and its adjustments) make it possible to host entrepreneurial activities; for example, employees from more traditional structures may be 'excubated' into these places, and even people in precarious situations may find there a position of social reinsertion (in particular for collaborative spaces subsidised by public structures). These new modes of value production and innovation are increasingly conducted in the context of collabora-tive and third-places (fab labs, makerspaces, hackerspaces) (Lallement 2015). The third-places orchestrate new network-based logics of auto-production (Anderson 2012) that interest classical companies, which try to fight there against a kind of law of the tendency towards decline in the rate of innovation, in particular relevant innovations (i.e. mean-ingful at some points for a customer).

A Key Consequence of Work Transformations around Communities: A Growing Isomorphism between Managerial Agency and Political Agency

In this context marked by the end of enclaves and work transform-ations, we want to emphasise three interrelated trends that lead to a growing isomorphism between managerial agency and political agency. We see three trends at the heart of the growing isomorphism:

a new openness and connectivity (trend 1), a new semiosis (trend 2) and a new political consciousness (trend 3).

The first trend (new openness and connectivity) reflects the end of enclaves and the greater connectivity between managerial agencies. More and more, enclaves disappear, both temporally and spatially. From a temporal perspective, the boundaries between work and home, consumers and producers, collapse, as well as the specific practices corresponding to them. From a spatial perspective, the advent of mobility as a new sociological paradigm (Urry 2007), the development of mobile technologies and of new forms of work (e.g. teleworkers, digital nomads, the generalisation of virtual and distributed modes of collective activities, Bosch-Sijtsema, Ruohomäki & et Vartiainen 2010; Messenger & Gschwind 2016) have paved the way to new, more opened forms of collective activity. In addition, the connectivity of these apparently fragmented activities keeps increasing. The infrastructure of the Internet at large, and the network technologies around it (e.g. Wi-Fi), or the new informational platforms inside it (e.g. Google), make it possible to draw on amazing resources and connecting globally without accumulating the huge capital that would have been necessary forty years ago. New physical forms, such as third-places in general (Oldenburg 1989) and collaborative spaces in particular (e.g. co-working spaces) (Fayard 2019; Garrett et al. 2017; Petriglieri, Ashford & Wrzesniewski 2019 ; de Vaujany & Aroles 2019), but also the new transport infrastructures make it possible to connect and reconnect to a community of employees and/or customers very easily. This trend towards openness and connectivity has dramatically 'desenclaved' managerial agency and the usual perimeter of its effect, which become potentially more global, more public, more tightly bounded into everyday activities of the employee and customers involved in it.

The second trend (new semiosis), which is largely imbricated to the first one, is about the way we give a meaning to what we do (Peirce 1978; de Vaujany & Mitev 2016). Semiosis is about both the meaning and the material conditions of its production and reproduction. A semiosis is historically situated. The process of sensemaking we are involved in (i.e. semiosis) has dramatically changed since the late 1990s. More and more, we outsource information and cognitive routines (Serres 2012; de Vaujany & Mitev 2016). The digital world is much more than a big set of tools and data. It is also a set of routines.

We do not remember precisely a piece of information, but rather the way to find it (e.g. the keywords we typed) on Google. Most of all, part of our routines of socialisation are also changed virtually by these tools. Even when they do not use Facebook, teenagers develop friend-ships in a Facebook-like manner and in the context of parties, think about the fact that 'potentially', pictures can be taken during the event and be put on line on Facebook, WhatsApp or Snapchat. Most of all, the media itself is not expected to be meaningful in the interpretation (in contrast to the Middle Ages, see de Vaujany & Mitev 2016), which means that more than ever, information flows globally, beyond any private or public distinctions, and is likely to be very quickly part of the public or political debates as part of a collective, open expression of individuals (Besley & Burgess 2001). In this context, again, managerial agency is likely to blur the line and enter into public and political debates, liking the 'acting together' with the 'living together'.

Lastly, the third trend (new political consciousness) is about an increasing political reflexivity, in particular of the young generation, and beyond usual political categories such as class or professions. Class and access (or not) to private properties do not seem to be a boundary anymore, in particular with the emergence of the so-called sharing economy (Botsman & Rogers 2011) (which seems to be very compat-ible with the capitalist system, de Vaujany et al. 2019). And the political discourse is not the prerogative of politicians themselves or a political class anymore, as it seems that more and more activities 'hack' political debates[5] (Häkli & Kallio 2014; McGregor 2011). Interestingly, individuals reflexively discuss political topics, often in the context of more or less stabilised communities, which meet virtu-ally and/or physically. Each individual feels s/he has something to say, and it is legitimate to do it. This political consciousness is probably less theorised and ideological than in the 1960s, but it is political in the sense that it relates to society at large and the sense of togetherness mainly based on connectivity. Contemporary managerial agency both relies on and favours this political context: It relies on it in the sense that it increasingly sells products and services taking into account this new political consciousness and sense (or need) of community. It favours it in the sense that it creates new vocabularies, buzzwords

---

[5] See the very interesting case of Audrey Tang www.booksandideas.net/Civic-Hacking-and-our-Political-Future.html.

but also ecosystems (with new labels, new cooperatives or new infrastructures inside the infrastructures inside the web) that encourage this
new political consciousness.

As an example, by surfing on the three aforementioned trends, Uber
is clearly transforming society, favouring a move from contract- to
revenue-based capitalism, breaking the privileges of some corporations, changing the nature of society and the sense of togetherness
inside the city. Has anybody voted for or against it? No. This political
transformation is there. Ford also had a political agency in the 1920s
and 1930s: Mass production was more than a managerial choice, it
was a new society based on mass consumption, and this is particularly
obvious from a Marxist perspective. However, today's connectivity,
new semiosis and new political consciousness have radically changed
the scale and nature of the relationship between managerial and political agency. Political consequences of managerial agency are more
unforeseeable, pervading and brutal than in the 1920s and 1930s.
They are maybe closer to temporality from the Leninist view of events
and revolutions, i.e. his approach of the revolutionary crisis, spontan-
eity of the crowd and of the revolutionary movement (Coombs 2013).

More invisibly, thousands of smaller entrepreneurial projects and structures in Paris, London, New York, Shanghai, Delhi and elsewhere in the
world do the same in a much more emergent manner. The web and
numerous physical forums or mobilities inside the city give an amazing
infrastructure to do it. Digitality provides new routines to do it. The
dynamics of emergent communities structure a collective envy as well.

'Co-politicisation' as a Recognition of the Political Power of Managerial Agency

Our thesis is also not about the influence strategies (e.g. lobbying
activities) of (large) companies in the context of legislative processes.
It is neither to insist on the social responsibility (in relationship with
business ethics or corporate social responsibility). *The thesis defended
here is more radical than that of other discourses (more strategic than
political): We contend that managerial actions (in particular entrepreneurial ones) have the potential to become more and more political by
themselves.*

By 'political', we mean the convergence of three political dimensions
of managerial actions:

- Communication towards citizens and society at large (more than immediate customers)
- Modes of representativeness of a collective, a discourse or an action, as incorporated in communicative infrastructures
- Systems of legitimacy

Communication towards citizens corresponds to a specific phenomenon. Big companies have for a long time started to address an audience that goes far beyond their effective customers base (e.g. Coca-Cola in the United States). Since the 1990s, companies have more and more 'talked' to citizens (as potential consumers or influencers) and society at large. They endeavour to be actors in and of the city, talking inside the agora to everybody, as other citizens. Facebook, Google, Amazon but also numerous start-ups are now in this grey area that goes far beyond usual categories, such as 'prospective' or 'potential' customers. In the context of their extended value co-creation processes, today they address citizens and citizen consciousness as much as our instincts for consumptions. And this is probably in the worlds of the city and the citizenship today where the highest fences and barriers to their development exist.

The modes of representativeness of a collectivity, a discourse or an action correspond to the issue on which the rupture is particularly radical. The legitimate processes through which an actor or a technology can 'talk' for a totality (a nation, an occupational community, an industry...) are largely institutionalised and legalised in most Western countries. Institutions and institutional procedures make it possible to identify legitimate spokespersons and to open public spaces to movements of protestation. The Internet and, more recently, social networks such as Facebook, have made it possible to gather opinions quickly and massively from an aggregation of heterogeneous opinions, reviews, likes and retweets, which are particularly visible and traceable. Modes of representativeness and existence of reflexive collectivities about their identity (class for themselves) and projects have been disrupted and are not really questioned by old institutions; (the role of Facebook has thus been important in recent social movements and the human quest for freedom and democracy, such as during the Arab Spring, the Yellow Vests movement or the 2019 Hong Kong protests). Everybody's voice can express itself among the noise of the multitude, and can be isolated and valorised very quickly. The representative and the illustrative (as the quantitative versus qualitative divide in terms of data and data treatment) are only a question of degree in the exploration of spokespersons and strategic traces by a collectivity. It was probably not among Facebook, Google or Amazon's ambitions to become true *political infrastructures*, but this is clearly what happened. Facebook is on the verge of minting its own money (Andriotis, Rudegeair & Hoffman 2019), Google is participating in the management of smart cities (sidewalk projects), Airbnb is concerned about collecting tourism taxes, tactics to ensure the right to be forgotten have been delegated to Google, and Facebook is taking the lead on identity issues (Faravelon & Grumbach 2016). Likewise, in the context of more commercial third-places, it was probably not in the objective of WeWork to reinvent socialisations and new ways to gather and aggregate social entities (workplaces and home for numerous entrepreneurs), but this is what they are starting to do. WeWork agencies and others co-working actors' agency are transforming macro-dimensions of political and societal life. The co-living trend and its use in the political sphere epitomise this emergent transformation.[6]

Lastly, it is the whole system of production of legitimate actors and legitimate discourses in and about the city and its management that is disrupted. Through a new focus on digital infrastructures, it is tempting to give a more systemic aspect to the convergence between managerial and political agencies described here. Beyond traditional media and political institutions (their elective and consultative processes), Facebook settles norms, new legitimate channels for political claims (from those of hackers to those of terrorists) and new processes to identify and constitute legitimate entities. The bulk of digital actors, local as well as global, contribute to give an unprecedented visibility to desires, expectations, trends, which are at the heart of our societies. In a way, they *make* more than they constitute the actors and discourses that will be potentially legitimate (as grounded into the crowd itself[7]).

Management thus becomes political in the strongest sense of the term. If the distinction between consumers and producers becomes more and more obsolescent (with the idea of 'co-creation' or 'value

---

[6] See the support given by former mayor of London (Boris Johnson) to the Fish Island Village project: www.huffingtonpost.com/adi-gaskell/londons-leading-role-as-a_b_9367478.html

[7] The Internet itself is nothing more than a technical infrastructure upon which other (compatible) layers will emerge, closer to contents.

co-creation') (Kane & Ransbotham 2016), that between citizens (e.g. citizen entrepreneurs) and politicians (in the sense of people with a 'mandate' to produce a political discourse) also becomes more and more obsolescent. We call this long-term process of blurring and interweaving co-politicisation.

Yet, in this context marked by the prevalence of the 'politics', the latter has simultaneously entered into crisis. The political consequences of management today, in particular those of entrepreneurship and so-called new (collaborative) ways of working foster a deep crisis in our sense of togetherness. Management does not contribute to (or avoid damaging) the emergence of communities in our present, a process we which would like to call here 'communalisation'. This is the issue we would like to explore in our second part.

Politics in Crisis, or a 'Crisis of the Present'

Failures of Managerial Agency: The Communalisation Process Is out of Order

New ways of working, such as entrepreneurship, obviously have a deep transformative political power. Recent research in MOS suggests that that entrepreneurship is inherently political (Daskalaki et al. 2015), and invite scholars to recognise the importance of 'entrepreneurial politics' (Hjorth & Steyaert 2009). As highlighted by Daskalaki et al. (2015, p. 420), the availability of new resources, such as social media, have enabled individuals and their networks to 'enhance their collective capacity by assembling active forces and directing them via new organisation'. Entrepreneurial initiatives thus nurture the emergence of bottom-up social transformations, creating new institutional orders and ultimately new models of citizenship (Daskalaki et al. 2015). Similarly, Farias et al. (2019, p. 555) consider that the process of organisational creation opens new spaces of action and of attention, through which entrepreneurs are able to express their voice and shape the (re)distribution of resources and attention, further 'altering what it is to say and do things meaningfully, legitimately and with authority'.

The joint emergence of a higher connectivity, a new semiosis and a new political consciousness thus deeply transforms the agentic power of management, which has become political, more than merely societal. Thus, while politicians and activists, managers and entrepreneurs have long been considered as distinct categories of actors, the boundaries between their roles have become increasingly blurred and porous as a result of growing co-creation and co-production processes of value, leading to what we call co-politicisation. Co-politicisation implies that our democracies' infrastructures and political discourses can increasingly be produced by entrepreneurs. In particular, as mentioned above, three dimensions of contemporary societies appear as deeply transformed by co-politicisation: public communication, modalities of representativeness and systems of legitimacy.

Yet, beyond such effects, or the potential for such a transformative political power, this prevalent approach remains very 'spatial' and at the surface of the phenomenon. New ways of working, such as entrepreneurship, develop products and services that may constitute as many political opportunities, and that can be appropriated by various stakeholders as such. But they increasingly fail in their core political ambitions and accomplishments, in that they end up missing the point. MOS research has already highlighted, in well-known critiques of the human capital model and neo-liberalism, that the ideal of entrepreneurialism could serve as an 'ideological alibi for the radical responsibilisation of the workforce' (Fleming 2017, p. 702), prompting growing economic insecurity, lower productivity, diminished autonomy and worrying levels of personal debt (ibid p. 691).

In this context, we contend in this chapter that as managers/entrepreneurs/freelancers/intrapreneurs have started to play political, liberal roles, their (artificial) appropriation of political infrastructures has tended to create, in turn, a crisis of politics. For example, we have never expressed so much politics at the level of society, while, paradoxically, producing so few commons (Dietz et al. 2003; Mattei 2012; Ostrom 2002). More than ever, everybody can express their voice, all the more that new mediators (such as the Internet, Facebook and Twitter) exist and can aggregate such voices in new collectives. But such collectives are built in ways that are not meaningful or resonating anymore, as if there were no collective voice to be expressed and heard, and no collective activity in which people, constituted as a community, could regain their bearings.

To illustrate this view, let us take the example of recent social protests: as shown by the Yellow Vests movement in France, each individual, as a citizen, now has the possibility to express their own, autonomous, individual voice, but without building, in turn, any meaningful or resonant collective and community (Rosa 2019). For the first time in French history, a government is unable to listen to its citizens and to each individual voice, and, in turn, each individual voice is unable to be expressed in an audible and clear manner, and thus, to be heard. There is no desire for a collective project. Through Internet mediations, people do not know who they really are (as anonymous subjects), nor to whom they really address (who are their enemies or allies). Latour (2019) sees in this transformation the production of a new form of liberalism, where atomistic elements of a society (including Yellow Vests themselves, considered as neoliberal actors) express a multitude of individualistic, autonomous and selfish opinions, leading to a deeper crisis of politics. Similarly, the recent protests in Hong Kong highlight the contradictory effects of the use of social media on political movements (Friedman 2019). While social networks such as Facebook and Twitter have made it much easier to orchestrate the social revolt, it has also become increasingly difficult for this collective to be heard – as recognised by Friedman (2019), 'when everyone has a digital megaphone, it is much harder for any leader to aggregate enough authority not just to build a coherent set of demands but, more important, *to make compromises* on them, at the right time, to transform street energy into new laws'.

In the same vein, as regards new work practices, network technologies have provided contemporary managers/entrepreneurs/workers with an increasing political transformative power. However, with such technologies, and the information age more broadly (Castells 1996), coupled to new forms of entrepreneurial activities (Matlay & Westhead 2005), work has become more mobile, distributed, untethered, entrepreneurial and autonomous, such that its nature has changed from a collective, shared experience to an increasingly individualised and highly personalised experience. The collective experience of work has been lost in this move (Gregg 2018), leading to the development of more fragmented work relationships, networked constellations, including zero hour contracts and unstable relationships (Fleming 2017) marked by neither long-lasting relation nor emotional attachment, better summarised under the term 'gig' or platform economy (Friedman 2014). We thus contend that new ways of working, and entrepreneurship in particular, can have political effects and a potential political transformative power, but that these effects are less and less obvious because of a 'temporal' crisis that the philosopher Paul Ricoeur (1985) helps us understand.

Back to Ricoeur's Thesis: Temporality Is Community and Togetherness

In his famous triptych *Temps et récit*, Ricoeur (1985) explores the intricate relationship between time, temporality and narratives. In particular, in the conclusion of *Time and Narrative*, volume 3, he develops the idea of a present in crisis in which our society could remain stuck. The past, present and future no longer flow. For Ricoeur, the present is in crisis when the experience of the past in the present is 'museified' (i.e. fossilised, mummified, reified and non-resonant), dead, closed, and when our future (our 'horizon of expect-ations') is too open and grounded on distant utopias that will never materialise. A museified experience of the past thwarts any reminiscence or meaningful engagement with what was. Somehow similarly, utopias detach the future from the lived experience of the present. Anticipations are disconnected from hermeneutic processes that are then outsourced 'out there'. In a way, our main experience of the present is made of eternal futures, i.e. continuously outsourced anticipations of what will happen next, mainly new enthusiastic and promising becomings. We see consultants, management gurus, experts, opinions and trends both aggregated and performed by social media as playing a key role in this process, as the main producers of this futurist narratives, and in that sense, becoming more and more political.

This new managerialist politics results in the manifestation of a strange form of presentism, a temporalisation that appears discon-nected from the emotions and affects prone to make temporalities flow in narratives. At the end, the present is not rooted anymore in the past, and is continuously driven towards 'new', 'innovative', 'disruptive' futures enacted by utopia. Present becomes an eternal future, an ever-reformulated promise, a horizon out of reach and continuously reput at a remote distance. According to Ricoeur (1985, p. 422), we are involved in relations to the world that 'at least situate the present of this action, indivisibly ethical and political, at the point of articulation of the expectation's horizon and the space of experience'. The epoch 'is characterised both by the remoteness of the expectation's horizon and a narrowing of the space of experience' (Ricoeur 1985, p. 422). Indeed, the 'present is entirely in crisis when expectation takes refuge in utopia and when tradition turns into a dead deposit' (Ricoeur 1985, p. 422). The historical present is threatened by the fragmentation through which the space of experience and expectation of horizons results in schisms.

Ricoeur (1985) thus develops an insightful reflection on the crisis of the present, and offers a perspective that sets out to reassemble the past, the present and the future, stretched out in time, emphasising the structural reciprocity between temporality and narrativity (Sarpong, Eyres & Batsakis 2019). Ricoeur's thought is all the more relevant that, without this ontological presence of an open past and a lived future in the present, the very possibilities of becoming a collective, a community, with a transformative political power, simply vanish. Individuals cultivate a place between society and community precisely through a shared lived past and a projected identity nurtured in a fluid narrative. Otherwise, forms of organising become dead, still, closed, and even alienating narratives (see Rosa 2019). In the end, Ricoeur (1985) highlights a very interesting situation in society that we see as key in new ways of working, namely the crisis of the present.

A Crisis of Present in New Ways of Work ng

We link the phenomenon described by Ricoeur (i.e. the crisis of the present) to new ways of working, in particular contemporary entrepreneurship, which is more and more expected to be 'collaborative'. In a managerial world where workers are more and more individualised, where collaborative techniques and practices become central precisely because interindividual relationships have become key. But collaboration simply means following collaborative utopia and applying extra-layers of collectivity, which are removed when the technique or the platform is removed. Collectivity and togetherness are not desired or even felt. They keep vanishing, to be replaced by another utopia or project.

We contend that the generalisation of collaborative entrepreneurship and intrapreneurship, as well as the rise of remote, mobile and digital work and their modes of management, foster and cement the crisis of the present and, consequentially, the crisis of the politics described above. Platform capitalism and the associated new work practices imply the dissolution of traditional organisations and a corrosion of the collective aspect that has long characterised organising. They enact technology in ways that increasingly personalise and individualise work, and even make the long-lasting collective experience of labour impossible. While they enable new forms of flexibility, value creation and productivity, technological developments simultaneously contribute to a loss of the experience of labour as a collective activity (Gregg 2018). In particular, by applying Ricoeur's concept of the crisis of the present to new modes of organising (such as collaborative entrepreneurship), we explain how an overemphasis on the present is grounded on practices and processes linked to new forms of organising that foster individuality and interindividuality, thus preventing any political, transformative power in the end.

How to describe contemporary modes of organising? Let us imagine thousands of people with their eyes closed, practising mindfulness in a big stadium. They are all seated together, next to one another, in a place full of noises and movements that nobody cares about. Each individual feels her/his breath and is deeply connected to present time, the 'moment' passing. As nobody talks, the stadium does not become a public space or an agora. If we imagine at some point that a speaker tells them loudly what will happen next in their lives, the beautiful new things that are waiting for them outside the stadium, we will be close to the 'present in crisis' described by Ricoeur (1985). The present becomes a fragile instant passing or, for those who are still open to the world, an eternal future made of the voice of the speaker. The stadium is not a shared space, a public space, an agora devoted to sharing speech in Arendt (1998)'s sense. It is merely a common space.

The past is not cultivated nor is it narrated. Maybe we can feel that at this moment we have a long history, but it is not really part of the experience. Contemporary forms of organising are more and more stuck in the epoch described by Ricoeur (1985, p. 422) as characterised by 'the remoteness of the expectation's horizon and a narrowing of the space of experience'. This implies a weak communalisation process. New forms of organising, and collaborative entrepreneurship in particular, can be described through the lack of resonances they produce, which tend to be increasingly 'mute', 'repulsive', or even 'alienating' (Rosa 2019), as they are increasingly embedded in a vision of 'present in crisis', in contrast with a vision of 'present that flows'.

While in a 'flowing/resonating present', past, present and future are melted in the narration, the situation of a 'present in crisis' is characterised by the disjunction of past, present and future from/in the narration, as observed in situations marked by excessive presentism, overemphasis on the 'here and now' beyond any memory, reminiscence and anticipation. While in the first situation (flowing/resonating present), the narration describes and co-produces solidarities (temporally and beyond), the 'present in crisis' scenario is characterised by narration as a mirror of individuality and interindividual relationships. Some new work practices are prime examples of this crisis of the present in new forms of organising: mindfulness, the idea of promoting 'well-being' at work, holacracy (Robertson 2015), individual entrepreneurship and collaborative entrepreneurship (Miles, Miles & Snow 2005; Miles, Miles & Snow 2006; Rocha & Miles 2009). They are increasingly characterised by an overemphasis on the present grounded into practices and processes that foster individuality and interindividuality. In contrast, more meaningful and resonating practices (such as co-operative, solidarity, common writing, or co-operative entrepreneurship) could allow us to join past, present and future in the narration in new forms of organising while producing solidarities.

Following Ricoeur, we thus argue that time and temporality are key dimensions of new ways of working and that the latter produce today problematic communalisation, a sense of belonging and ways to relate and respond to each other (Cunliffe & Locke 2019), which can be described as a 'crisis of the present' (Ricoeur 1985). Indeed, new forms of organising produce narrative and temporal ruptures that are dangerous for our sense of belonging and society, that are yet essential to political action. We see in new modes of organising exaggeratedly narcissistic and individualistic experiences of the present of work. Immediate senses are not felt anymore, but connected to a large set of mediations themselves extending and pushing further a perception that becomes decentred at some point (de Vaujany 2019; Introna 2019). Interestingly, all the narratives produced by contemporary managers/entrepreneurs/workers reflecting upon themselves are becoming reversible for themselves. The narcissist force produced by the aggregation of individuals and the contents they produce on line and off line keeps narrating for and about itself in a circular way. The reflection is immediate (no real memory of past reflection, too much energy and attention are caught in the numerous reflections offered in the present) and just 'here'. The past, in particular the remote past, is not really part of the story. And the future is abundantly part of lived experience as what appears now the sphere of digital media and the world of organisations that pervade all aspects of our lives is made of the utopia, scenarios, numbers, indicators, visions of management. Interestingly, we all feel (wrongly) that we are in a way the manager telling the story we read or live about our future that is co-constructed. In a way, the present of work becomes an eternal future made of the numerous innovations, novelties, disruptions, visions we read and live.

Conclusion

To conclude, this essay calls for prudence about the supposed trans-formative political power of managerial agency expressed in new ways of working, and collaborative entrepreneurship in particular. 'Co-pol-iticisation' implies a growing isomorphism between managerial and political agencies, and suggests a transformation of the agentic power of management, which has become, more than ever, political. However, this essay highlights that new ways of working (and entre-preneurship in particular) has undeniably contributed to put the pre-sent in crisis, and by doing so, has fostered the resurgence of a renewed form of liberalism that they paradoxically denounce with the collab-orative utopia.

Thus, in line with recent research that explores ways of relating and responding to others, for example through 'anticipational fluidity' (Cunliffe & Locke 2019), and research that recognises the importance of time in organisations as a force (Holt & Johnsen 2019), this essay invites future research to explore the numerous organisational attempts at producing solidarities and true communalisation processes. In particular, future research could explore how past and future are relocated at the heart of the present experience of community, in ways that enhance our social notion of collective reflection in organisations (Gutzan & Tuckermann 2019), and in society. Other research could explore broader social movements (hackers, co-operativism, third-places, DIT...) and alternative methods of knowledge (co)-production (e.g. citizen sciences), in order to understand how they could contribute to new shared narratives that are essential to the political transform-ation of our society.

References

Anderson, C. 2012. *Makers: The New Industrial Revolution.* New York: Crown Business.

Andriotis, A.M., Rudegeair, P. & Hoffman, L. 2019. Facebook's New Cryptocurrency, Libra, Gets Big Backers. *The Wall Street Journal.* www.wsj.com/articles/facebooks-new-cryptocurrency-gets-big-backers-11560463312

Arendt, H. 1998. *The Human Condition* (2nd ed.). University of Chicago Press.

Aroles, J., Mitev, N. & de Vaujany, F. X. 2019. Mapping themes in the study of new work practices. *New Technology, Work and Employment,* 34 (3): 285–299.

Bacqué, M. H., Rey, H. & Sintomer, Y. 2005. *Gestion de proximité et démocratie participative.* Paris: La Découverte.

Barley, S. R. 2010. Building an institutional field to corral a government: A case to set an agenda for organization studies. *Organization Studies,* 31(6): 777–805.

Besley, T. & Burgess, R. 2001. Political agency, government responsiveness and the role of the media. *European Economic Review,* 45(4): 629–640.

Bosch-Sijtsema, P., Ruohomäki, V. & Vartiainen, M. 2010. Multi-locational knowledge workers in the office: Navigation, disturbances and effectiveness. *New Technology, Employment and Work,* 25(3): 183–195.

Botsman, R. & Rogers, R. 2011. *What's Mine Is Yours: The Rise of Collaborative Consumption.* New York: Harper Business.

Brocklehurst, M., Grey, C. & Sturdy, A. 2009. Management: The work that dares not speak its name. *Management Learning,* 41(1): 7–19.

Burnham, J. 1941. *The Managerial Revolution: What Is Happening in the World.* New York: John Day Company.

Cappelli, P. & Keller, J. R. 2013. Classifying work in the new economy. *Academy of Management Review,* 38(4): 575–596.

Castells, M. 1996. The net and the self: Working notes for a critical theory of the informational society. *Critique of Anthropology,* 16(1), 9–38.

Cerny, P. G. 2000. Political agency in a globalizing world: Toward a structurational approach. *European Journal of International Relations,* 6(4): 435–463.

Clegg, S. R. 1989. *Frameworks of Power.* Newbury Park, CA: Sage.

Clegg, S. R. & Dunkerley, D. 1980. *Organization, Class and Control.* London: Routledge.

Coombs, N. 2013. *Politics of the Event after Hegel.* Ph.D., Faculty of History and Social Sciences.

Courpasson, D. 2008. We Have always Been Oligarchs: Business Elite in Polyarchy. In S. R. Clegg and C. L. Cooper (eds.) *The Sage Handbook of Organizational Behaviour.* Sage, 424–443.

Courpasson, D. & Clegg, S. R. 2006. Dissolving the iron cages? Tocqueville, Michels, bureaucracy and the perpetuation of elite power. *Organization*, 13(3): 319–343.

Cunliffe, A. L. & Locke, K. 2019. Working with differences in everyday interactions through anticipational fluidity: A hermeneutic perspective. *Organization Studies*. DOI: 10.1177/0170840619831035.

Dale, K. 2005. Building a social materiality: Spatial and embodied politics in organizational control. *Organization*, 12(5): 649–678.

Daskalaki, D., Hjorth, D. & Mair, J. 2015. Are entrepreneurship, communities, and social transformation related? *Journal of Management Inquiry*, 24(4): 419-423.

de Vaujany, F. X. 2010a. Activités marchandes, activités administratives, marché et organisation: une approche sur la longue durée via l'Eglise. In: A. Hatchuel, O. Favreau and F. Aggeri (eds.) *L'activité marchande sans le marché*. Paris: Presses de l'Ecole des Mines de Paris.

2010b. A new perspective on the genealogy of collective action through the history of religious organizations. *Management & Organizational History*, 5(1): 65–78.

2019. Legitimation Process in Organizations and Organizing: An Ontological Discussion. In *Materiality in Institutions*. Cham: Palgrave Macmillan, 343–377.

de Vaujany, F. X. & Aroles, J. 2019. Nothing happened, something happened: Silence in a makerspace. *Management Learning*, 50(2): 208–225.

de Vaujany, F. X., Leclercq-Vandelannoitte A. & Holt R. 2020. Communities versus platforms: The paradox in the body of the collaborative economy. *Journal of Management Inquiry*, 29(4): 450–467.

de Vaujany, F. X. & Mitev, N. 2016. Le tournant materiel. In F. X. de Vaujany, A. Hussenot and J. F. Chanlat (eds.) *Les théories des organisations: grandes tournants*. Paris: Economica.

2017. The post-Macy paradox, information management and organizing: good intentions and road to hell? *Culture & Organization*, 23(5): 379–407.

Dietz, T., Ostrom, E. & Stern, P. C. 2003. The struggle to govern the commons. *Science*, 302(5652): 1907–1912.

Drucker, P. 1945, 2017. *Concept of the Corporation*. New York: Routledge.

Epstein, E. M. 1969. *The Corporation in American Politics*. Englewood Cliffs, NJ: Prentice-Hall.

Faravelon, A. & Grumbach, S. 2016. Platforms as Governments. *The Internet, Policy & Politics Conferences*, Oxford Internet Institute.

Farias, C., Fernandez, P., Hjorth, D.,& Holt, R. 2019. Organizational Entrepreneurship, Politics and the Political. *Entrepreneurship & Regional Development*, 31(7–8): 555–566.

Fayard, A. L. 2019. Notes on the Meaning of Work: Labor, Work, and Action in the 21st Century. *Journal of Management Inquiry.* DOI: 1056492619841705.

Fleming, P. 2017. The Human capital coax: Work, debt and insecurity in the era of Uberization. *Organization Studies,* 38(5): 691–709.

Follett, M. P. 1918. *The New State: Group Organization, Solution to Popular Government.* New York: Longmans, Green.

1919. Community as process. *Philosophical Review,* 28: 576–588.

Friedman, G. 2014. Workers without employers: Shadow corporations and the rise of the gig economy. *Review of Keynesian Economics,* 2(2): 171–188.

Friedman, T. 2019. Hong Kong's protests could be another social media revolution that ends in failure. *New York Times.* www.nytimes.com/2019/09/17/opinion/hong-kong-protest.html

Fukuyama, F. 2006. *The End of History and the Last Man.* Simon and Schuster.

Garrett, L. E., Spreitzer, G. M. & Bacevice, P. A. 2017. Co-constructing a sense of community at work: The emergence of community in cow-orking spaces. *Organization Studies,* 38(6): 821–842.

Gregg, M. 2018. *Counterproductive: Time Management in the Knowledge Economy.* Durham, NC: Duke University Press.

Gutzan, S. & Tuckermann, H. 2019. Neat in theory, entangled in praxis: A practice perspective on the social notion of collective reflection in organisations. *Management Learning,* 50(3): 319–336.

Häkli, J. & Kallio, K. P. 2014. Subject, action and polis: Theorizing political agency. *Progress in Human Geography,* 38(2): 181–200.

Hickson, D., Flemming, A., Franco, F., Hofstede, G., Kieser, A., Cornelis, T. & Lammers, J. C. 1980. Editorial. *Organization Studies,* 1(1): 1–2.

Hjorth, D. & Steyaert, C. 2009. *The Politics and Aesthetics of Entrepreneurship.* Cheltenham: Edward Elgar.

Hjorth, D. & Holt, R. 2016. It's entrepreneurship, not enterprise: Ai Weiwei as entrepreneur. *Journal of Business Venturing Insights,* 5: 50–54.

Holt, R., & Johnsen, R. 2019. Time and organization studies. *Organization Studies.* DOI: 10.1177/0170840619844292.

Hunter, F. 1953. *Community Power Structure.* Chapel Hill: University of North Carolina Press.

Introna, L. 2019. On the making of sense in sensemaking: Decentred sensemaking in the meshwork of life. *Organization Studies,* 40(5): 745–764.

Kane, C. & Ransbotham, S. 2016. Content as community regulator: The recursive relationship between consumption and contribution in open collaboration communities. *Organization Science,* 27(5): 1258–1274.

Kieser, A. 1989. Organizational, institutional, and societal evolution: Medieval craft guilds and the genesis of formal organizations. *Administrative Science Quarterly*, 34(4): 540–564.

Kingma, S. 2019. New ways of working (NWW): Work space and cultural change in virtualizing organizations. *Culture and Organization*, 25(5), 383–406.

Lallement, M. 2015. *L'âge du faire*. Paris: Seuil.

Latour, B. 2019. Pour la première fois, on a un gouvernement incapable d'écouter et un peuple incapable de s'exprimer. www.franceinter.fr/emissions/l-invite-de-8h20-le-grand-entretien/l-invite-de-8h20-le-grand-entretien-18-janvier-2019

Le Goff, J. 1957, 2000. *Les intellectuels au Moyen Age*. Paris: Editions du Seuil.

Locke, R. & Schone, K. 2004. *The Entrepreneurial Shift*. Cambridge: Cambridge University Press.

Makimoto, T. & Manners, D. 1997. *Digital Nomad*. Chichester, UK: Wiley.

Matlay, H., & Westhead, P. 2005. Virtual teams and the rise of e-entrepreneurship in Europe. *International Small Business Journal*, 23 (3): 279–302.

Mattei, U. 2012. First thoughts for a phenomenology of the commons. *Socialisation and Commons in Europe*, 75.

McGregor, J. 2011. Contestations and consequences of deportability: Hunger strikes and the political agency of non-citizens. *Citizenship Studies*, 15(5): 597–611.

Messenger, J. C. & Gschwind, L. 2016. Three generations of Telework: New ICTs and the (r)evolution from home office to virtual office. *New Technology, Work and Employment*, 31(3): 195–208.

Miles, R. E., Miles, G. & Snow, C. C. 2005. *Collaborative Entrepreneurship: How Communities of Networked Firms Use Continuous Innovation to Create Economic Wealth*. Stanford University Press.

2006. Collaborative entrepreneurship: A business model for continuous innovation. *Organizational Dynamics*, 35(1): 1–11.

Oldenburg, R. 1989. *The Great Good Place: Cafes, Coffee Shops, Community Centers, Beauty Parlors, General Stores, Bars, Hangouts, and How They Get You through the Day*. New York: Paragon House.

Ostrom, E. 2002. Reformulating the commons. *Ambiente & sociedade*, 10: 5–25.

Parsons, T. 1965. Suggestions for a sociological approach to the theory of organizations. *Administrative Science Quarterly*, 1(1): 63–85.

Peirce, C. S. 1978. *Ecrits sur le signe*. Paris: Editions du Seuil.

Pennel, D. 2013. *Travailler pour soi: quel avenir pour le travail à l'heure de la révolution individualiste?*. Paris: Seuil.

Perrow, C. 1972. *Complex Organizations: A Critical Essay.* Glenview, IL: Scott, Foresman and Company.

2002. *Organizing America: Wealth, Power and the Origins of Corporate Capitalism.* Princeton, NJ: Princeton University Press.

Petriglieri, G., Ashford, S. J. & Wrzesniewski, A. 2019. Agony and ecstasy in the gig economy: Cultivating holding environments for precarious and personalized work identities. *Administrative Science Quarterly,* 64(1): 124–170.

Ricoeur, P. 1985. *Temps et récit* (Volume 3). Paris: Le Seuil.

Robertson, B. 2015. *Holacracy: The new Management System for a Rapidly Changing World.* New York: Henry Holt and Company.

Rocha, H. & Miles, R. 2009. A model of collaborative entrepreneurship for a more humanistic management. *Journal of Business Ethics,* 88(3): 445–462.

Rosa, H. 2019. *Resonance. A Sociology of Our Relationship to the World.* Trans. J. Wagner, Cambridge: Polity.

Sarpong, D., Eyres, E. & Batsakis, G. 2019. Narrating the future: A distentive capability approach to strategic foresight. *Technological Forecasting and Social Change,* 140, 105–114.

Schatzki, T. R. 2010. *The Timespace of Human Activity: On Performance, Society, and History as Indeterminate Teleological Events.* Lexington, KY: Lexington Books.

Selznick, P. 1949. *TVA and the Grass Roots: A Study in the Sociology of Formal Organization.* Berkeley: University of California Press.

Serres, M. 2007. Les nouvelles technologies: révolution culturelle et cognitive. Conférence sur les nouvelles technologies lors du 40è anniversaire de l'INRIA. www.youtube.com/watch?v=ZCBB0QEmT5g

2012. *Petite Poucette.* Paris: Éditions Le Pommier.

Urry, J. 2007. *Mobilities.* Polity Press: Cambridge.

Conclusion

Experiences of Continuity and Change in the New World of Work

JEREMY AROLES, FRANÇOIS-XAVIER DE VAUJANY AND KAREN DALE

This edited volume has endeavoured to link micro-social experiences of work with the wider macro-social context in which these changes operate, so as to provide a rich and detailed account of the most prominent manifestations of the 'new' world of work. As they delved into the minutiae of the new world of work, the chapters of this edited volume have explored some of the continuities and discontinuities in ways of working, as a means of fleshing out the socio-economic context of the micro-social experiences of work. In particular, three aspects of these changes and continuities have recurrently emerged throughout the chapters. These are: (i) creativity and changing skills; (ii) the time and space of work; and (iii) the changing nature of the employment relationship and beyond. In this concluding chapter, we reflect further on these themes.

Creativity and Changing Skills

The first aspect of new ways of working, which is both 'new' and has a longer, richer and more complex history, which we would like to highlight is the focus on creativity and craftwork. Whilst we link these together here, they clearly have distinctive characteristics of their own. Creativity, as a human activity and ability, could of course be said to have always been central to the economy, notably through inventions and innovations (Kaufman & Sternberg 2010). However, in the contemporary economy, it is our contention that it has come to the fore. As expressed by Townley, Roscoe & Searle (2019, p. 1): '[C]reativity is at the vanguard of contemporary capitalism ... the creative economy has changed the nature of work'. Many of the issues discussed within this volume have been influenced by this changing focus, even where they were not linked directly to the creative industries per se.

The greater informalisation and diversity in the time and space of work can be seen as related to different ways of organising, which come from more 'craft forms of production': small scale, valuing autonomy and using discrete forms of working, and thus networked or collaborative in ways that are different from those of large-scale industry. Thus, the maker movement, hackerspaces, open source communities, fab labs, neo-craftsmanship and so on have a kinship to traditions of creative, cultural and craft work, which may or may not have been 'inside' the formal economy (see de Vaujany & Aroles, *this volume*; Peiro, *this volume*). Co-working spaces, both intentional and unintended, informal or marketised (see Brakel-Ahmed, *this volume*) partake in this connection to creativity and craft, with workers who are not formally or contractually connected to each other or to the workplace, and a level of autonomy in spatial and temporal organisation that is not typically associated with employment. A new interest in craftwork and 'maker' approaches to work has also come to the fore (e.g. Anderson 2012; Bell, Mangia, Taylor & Toraldo 2018; Lallement 2018). This indicates a move away from or against mass production and commercialisation, although this has also been appropriated as a strategy by some corporations. Importantly though, it has an emancipatory aspect through an embodied engagement with the material world, which can potentially speak to broader concerns of climate change, waste and sustainability.

Importantly, the skills and forms of labour, which are especially valorised in contemporary forms of work, are also related to these traditions. 'Immaterial labour' is defined by Hardt & Negri (2000, p. 290) as 'the labor that produces an immaterial good, such as a service, a cultural product, knowledge or communication'. These encompass the use of skills such as the manipulation of symbols, intellective and informational transaction and the production of affect, and which, as Lazzarato (2014, p. 77, emphasis added) notes, 'involves a *series of activities that are not normally recognized as "work"*. Although originally integral to occupations and fields such as fashion, advertising, software production, photography and audio-visual production and cultural industries, immaterial labour can now be seen to have become part of many jobs and organisations (see for instance Farrugia 2018).

These aspects pull in two opposite directions. Creative work itself has traditionally frequently been insecure and precarious as a living (Luckman 2014). Its commercialisation into the 'creative industries' has often maintained poor terms and conditions of work (see Morgan & Nelligan 2018). However, characteristics of creativity have become more valorised, and held up as an exemplar of extrinsic satisfaction and pleasure in work, of freedom and authenticity. Thus, it has become linked with an alternative to traditional modes of working and employment. Yet these different dimensions of creative work need to be remembered and the tensions and contradictions within carefully explored. Chapters in this volume both illustrate the imagining of different, alternative ways of working (see Peiro, *this volume*) and also discuss the inequalities that have been organised into some new ways of working (see Howcroft, Mumford & Bergvall-Kåreborn as well as Woodcock, *this volume*).

The Time and Space of Work

The second aspect of contemporary work that has come under scrutiny is how the time and spaces of work have changed (see Aroles, Mitev & de Vaujany 2019). Many writers point to the intensification of workload and the pressures, especially through digitisation, on workers' time, as well as how this increases the potential for control over workers in time and space (Felstead, Gallie, Green & Inanc 2013; Sewell & Taskin 2015). In contrast to this, many new ways of working seek alternatives to the traditional times and spaces of work, and to increase autonomy and life-work balance – whether this actually translates into more autonomy and control is a different matter though (see Veen, Barratt & Goods 2019; Wood, Graham, Lehdonvirta & Hjorth 2019). Within the chapters of this volume, we have seen a diversity of relationships with time and space, and this provides an important reminder that there are different experiences of work relations, and these involve multiple temporalities and spatialities. In her book on the different timescapes of contemporary culture, Sharma (2014) criticises generalising accounts of the 'speed-up' of contemporary society, which do not contextualise the differential experience of people with time and space, and the political nature of this relationship. As she notes: 'Temporalities do not experience a uniform time but rather a time particular to the labor that produces them. Their experience of time depends on where they are positioned within a larger economy of temporal worth.' (Sharma 2014, p. 8).

This perspective undoubtedly resonates with the focus of this volume on the diverse experiences of new ways of working. The different relationships with time can be seen in different ways across the chapters of this book. The 'digital nomads' (see Bonneau & Aroles, *this volume*) seek to escape the synchronisation of their time and place from that connected with the traditional employment relationship through the power relations of the full time contract, which has long been assumed to be the norm of work. This is exemplified in the image of the white, male, able-bodied worker, who worked full time hours throughout his working life, and which has been critiqued in relation to gender and diversity in the workplace, as workers with caring or childcare responsibilities, or disabilities, or who experienced racism and other forms of discrimination could not fit into this norm. Whilst the image of the digital nomad is of one who can escape these temporal and spatial constraints, the worker in the so-called gig economy, one who acquires paid work through a digital platform or is on a zero-hours contract, has a very different experience of time and space in these new ways of working (see Howcroft, Mumford & Bergvall-Kåreborn, *this volume*). In Huws, Spencer, Syrdal & Holts's (2017) study of these new forms of working arrangements across Europe, examples of lived experiences are recounted that bring home just how uneven is the politics of time and space in contemporary work. Although some platform workers have found the temporal flexibility they were looking for, the predominant experience was of a lack of control over time and space, and even therefore over the needs of one's own body. Food delivery cyclists recount how they have no control over how long they have to wait at restaurants and therefore how many paid jobs they can fit in; platform workers found their shifts had been changed 'by the app'. This resonates strongly with the experiences recounted and discussed by Woodcock (*this volume*).

Similarly, the possibilities of digital, information and communication technologies have been seen to create an 'electronic envelope' (Felstead, Jewson & Walters 2005), which has transformed the spatial and temporal possibilities of work. However, Sharma (2014) again points to the potential problems in seeing technology as the causal agent here. As she suggests: '[T]he temporal is political regardless of speed and is present no matter what the dominant technologies of the day are' (2014, p. 11). Thus, we must question 'a uniform technological effect brought on by a particular media' (ibid).

On the aforementioned issues and avenues, we see phenomenological (e.g. hermeneutic phenomenology) and experiential perspectives as particularly promising lenses to explore the processes of embodiment, spacing and temporalisation at stake in new ways of working. Research on new ways of working tends to be rather descriptive and a-theoretical. We believe that authors such as Husserl, Heidegger, Henry, Arendt, Jonas, Girard and Weil could help provide interesting concepts to theorise the temporal and spatial dimensions of new ways of working. They could help us deconstruct the 'new' in new ways of working, make sensible the issue of continuity–discontinuity, conceptualise the temporalisation at stake in some new nomadic, collaborative and distributed work practices, illuminate the emergence of atmospheres and affects in and around new work practices and the broader relation between the so-called novelty of contemporary work and the history of work and management. The pragmatist approaches of Peirce, James, Dewey and Mead could also provide very interesting consequentialist views, along with process approaches such as those of Whitehead and Deleuze, in order to unpack the metaphysics of temporality and events.

The Changing Nature of the Employment Relationship and Beyond

As well as the assumption that it is technology that is driving a different temporal and spatial relationship with work, the same technological determinism is found in many general discussions of the changing nature of the employment relationship itself (see, for instance, debates on automation). However, whilst digital platforms and mobile technologies facilitate changes to the employment relationship, they clearly do not determine it. As mentioned in the introduction, many of the 'new ways of working' that we see at the current time have been seen before in one guise or another, and have a historical development rather than appearing out of the blue, as it were. Thus, it is important to engage with the specific experiences of those working with and through digital technologies and the power relations that they are enmeshed in, including those of historical and cultural development.

This is something that is pursued by both Burrell (*this volume*) and Granter (*this volume*).

Lack of freedom and the power relations of the more 'traditional' employment contract drive the notion that freedom and authenticity can be achieved through ways of working that are not arranged around the traditional contractual relationship. However, with the progress of the so-called gig economy, it has become more apparent that the employment contract can also provide statutory rights and protections that are not available outside the contract (see Woodcock, *this volume*). This has led some groups of gig workers to mobilise around gaining legal recognition as employees (Tassinari & Maccarrone 2017; Wood, Lehdonvirta & Graham 2018).

Debates about new ways of working have predominantly centred around these insecurities that are characteristic of platform workers, and politically we understand this, given the erosion of working conditions that has been experienced. However, this volume seeks to give attention to a range of new ways of working reflecting a diversity of experiences. Yet there are also some key changes that affect both workers who have secure employment contracts and those who work more informally, and that cut across those who experience precarity and constraint, as well as those who feel they have achieved a degree of pleasure or authenticity in their work. In the work of Peter Fleming, this is linked to the changing ideology of work itself, such that work has become a 'way of life' (2015, p. 6), where work has the tendency to become not something that we *do*, but something that we *are* (2015, p. 37). In that context, it is pivotal to reflect on the roles played by bodies and processes of embodiment in new work practices (see Küpers, *this volume*).

In his lectures of 1978–1979, Foucault elucidates the development of ideas and institutions that promulgate the 'generalization of the economic form of the market ... throughout the social body' (Foucault 2008, p. 243). His analysis of Human Capital Theory (e.g. Becker 1964; Schultz 1961) sheds some light on one strand by which this takes work out of the specific factory or office, and into all social relations as well as into our own psyches. The development of Human Capital Theory posited that capital – in the sense the resources to produce a future income – is not situated externally to workers, in the hands of capitalists, but rather labour itself can be seen as capital, with the abilities and skills that workers have being their 'human capital'. From this point of view, then, it is rational for workers to seek to maximise their human capital, their opportunity to achieve a greater return on their own capital. As Foucault comments, this attitude means that 'the worker himself [sic.] appears as a sort of enterprise for himself' and the economy is made up of these individual 'enterprise-units' (2008, p. 225). As Fleming argues, the consequences of this are that: '[H]uman capital(ists) are competitive individualists, preoccupied with investing and enhancing in their own economic value. From this point of view, life itself is a personal and permanent commercial project that requires business ambition to generate future income and avoid losses' (2017, p. 692). Fleming further asserts that this paved the way for 'radical responsibilization: where each individual human capitalist becomes entirely responsible for his or her economic fate' (2017, p. 697). The consequences of this in relation to contemporary work include the increasing individualisation of work; and the creation of work cultures that emphasise 'choice' and autonomy, but encourage intensification and the degradation of conditions of work, as the worker is expected to bear the costs of training, or illness, or uniforms, themselves, as their own mini-enterprise. As such, it is important to engage with the politics of work and to ponder over the increasing political agency of managerial activities (see de Vaujany & Leclercq-Vandelannoitte, *this volume*).

This discussion points to how some contradictions and tensions emerge in relation to new ways of working and the diverse experiences of them. Often alternatives are sought to traditional forms of employment with its controls, its constraints on the time and place of work, and the lack of intrinsic value and authenticity found in paid work. And yet, whilst it is possible for some to shape an alternative to this, there is also the ideology of work and how it has bored its way into our wider social relations, which means that new ways of working can also encompass the worst excesses of economic individualism. These can sometimes be found in the same place, where for example platform work is experienced as flexible and enabling for some workers, and discriminatory and exploitative for others (Huws et al. 2017). Here again, the detour towards philosophical concepts and discussions could help reinvigorating these debates. Marxist as well as post-Marxist views of work and industrial relations could help go beyond simplistic, romanticised and emancipatory views of new ways of working.

How to Explore This New World of Work?

What conceptual tools, empirical settings and methodological sensibilities need to be mobilised in order to unpack this new world of work? This is, we contend, an important question and one to which the chapters of this edited volume provide many different and interesting suggestions. Concerning conceptual tools, one such possibility is to revisit, or remobilise, influential work from the humanities in general in order to unpack the ways in which the world of work is changing and repeating itself. This can involve engaging with prominent philosophical work, such as that of André Gorz (Granter, *this volume*), Thornstein Veblen (Bonneau & Aroles, *this volume*), Hartmut Rosa (Küpers, *this volume*), Maurice Merleau-Ponty (de Vaujany & Aroles, *this volume*) and Paul Ricoeur (de Vaujany & Leclercq-Vandelannoitte, *this volume*). It can also take the form of a serious involvement with the work of influential social scientists, such as Joan Acker (Howcroft, Mumford & Bergvall-Kåreborn, *this volume*). In view of the descriptive and often utopian nature of most discourses and publications about new ways of working, a detour towards experiential, sensible, embodied or affective perspectives could be a way to extend ongoing research to explore in depth the lived experience and becoming of contemporary work. Undoubtedly, this travel could be extended through the work of numerous philosophers such as Nietzsche, Foucault, Deleuze, Levinas and Jonas.

Regarding empirical settings, engaging with the new world of work can entail exploring spaces and places traditionally thought of as outside the 'formal realm of work', including hotel lobbies (Brakel-Ahmed, *this volume*) or new types of space, which are increasingly part of the ecology of new work practices, such as hackerspaces (Peiro, *this volume*) or makerspaces (de Vaujany & Aroles, *this volume*). In parallel, the increasing digitalisation of work also calls for in-depth investigation of online-platform-based work so as to be attuned to the ways in which concerns encountered in more traditional forms of employment, such as gender inequality (Howcroft, Mumford & Bergvall-Kåreborn, *this volume*) and precarity (Woodcock, *this volume*), seem to be repeated in the gig economy. This also means that we need to pay greater attention to the politics of work and their implications for community (de Vaujany & Leclercq-Vandelannoitte, *this volume*). Importantly, reflecting more holistically over new work practices entails rethinking the boundaries between what constitutes work and what does not, and also what we see, from our position, as the 'new world of work'. As such, there is much interest in pondering over the meaning of new work practices when such a focus is translated to a setting that would not be seen as part of these transformations, such as the peasantry (Burrell, *this volume*).

Finally, the role played by methodological endeavours in the exploration of new world phenomena should not be overlooked. Despite claims that work is becoming increasingly digitalised and disembodied, it seems more important than ever to remain attuned to the role played by experiences and embodiment processes (Küpers, *this volume*) as we explore work practices. As such, ethnographic endeavours (Peiro, this volume) are particularly relevant if we are to delve into the minutiae of new work arrangements. In addition, there is clear scope for the development of new forms of methodological inquiry, such as approaches engaging with co-inquiry (Woodcock, *this volume*).

Overall, this volume has sought to highlight the importance of capturing the macro-social conditions in which micro-level experiences of work unfold and are experienced. We argue that ignoring one of the two would lead to partial accounts of the new world of work. Second, we believe that it is key to be receptive of the historical context from which these changes have emerged, so as to critically unpack the narrative and rhetoric surrounding new ways of working. This plays an important role in de-romanticising contemporary discussions connected to the emancipatory and revolutionary aspects of the new world of work. Finally, we argue that as researchers, we need to carefully consider research practices and philosophical concepts that would speak directly to the phenomena explored, either through methodological innovation (rethinking methods in the light of changing phenomena) or through politico-ethical engagements with the new world of work and serious explorations of experiential, sensible, embodied or affective perspectives of the lived experience of work.

References

Anderson, C. 2012. *Makers: The New Industrial Revolution*. New York: Crown Business.

Aroles, J., Mitev, N. & de Vaujany, F. X. 2019. Mapping themes in the study of new work practices. *New Technology, Work and Employment*, 34 (3): 285–299.

Becker, G. S. 1964. *Human Capital: A Theoretical and Empirical Analysis, with Special Reference to Education.* Chicago: University of Chicago Press.

Bell, E., Mangia, G., Taylor, S. & Toraldo, M. L. 2018. *The Organization of Craft Work: Identities, Meanings, and Materiality.* London: Routledge.

Farrugia, D. 2018. Youthfulness and immaterial labour in the new economy. *The Sociological Review*, 66(3): 511–526.

Felstead, A., Jewson, N. & Walters, S. 2005. *Changing Places of Work.* Basingstoke: Palgrave Macmillan.

Felstead, A., Gallie, D., Green, F. & Inanc, H. 2013. Work Intensification in Britain. *First Findings from the Skills and Employment Survey 2012.*

Fleming, P. 2015. *The Mythology of Work.* Chicago: University of Chicago Press Economics Books.

——— 2017. The human capital hoax: Work, debt and insecurity in the era of Uberization. *Organization Studies*, 38(5): 691–709.

Foucault, M. 2008. *The Birth of Biopolitics: Lectures at the Collège de France 1978–1979*, edited by M. Senellert and translated by G. Burchell. Basingstoke: Palgrave Macmillan

Hardt, M. & Negri, A. 2000. *Empire.* Harvard. MA: Harvard University Press.

Huws, U., Spencer, N., Syrdal, D. S. & Holts, K. 2017. *Work in the European Gig Economy: Research Results from the UK, Sweden, Germany, Austria, the Netherlands, Switzerland and Italy.* FEPS, UNI Europa, University of Hertfordshire.

Kaufman, J. C. & Sternberg, R. J. 2010. *The Cambridge Handbook of Creativity.* Cambridge: Cambridge University Press.

Lallement, M. 2018. *L'âge du faire – Hacking, travail, anarchie.* Paris: Points Essais.

Lazzarato, M. 2014. Immaterial Labor. In A. Pendakis, J. Diamanti, N. Brown, J. Robinson & I. Szeman (eds.) *Contemporary Marxist Theory.* New York and London: Bloomsbury Academic, pp. 77–92.

Luckman, S. 2014. Precarious Labour Then and Now: The British Arts and Crafts Movement and Cultural Work Revisited. In M. Banks, R. Gill & S. Taylor (Eds.) *Theorizing Cultural Work.* Routledge, pp. 33–43.

Morgan, G. & Nelligan, P. 2018. *The Creativity Hoax: Precarious Work and the Gig Economy.* London: Anthem Press.

Sewell, G. & Taskin, L. 2015. Out of sight, out of mind in a new world of work? Autonomy, control, and spatiotemporal scaling in telework. *Organization Studies*, 36(11): 1507–1529

Schultz, T. W. 1961. Investment in Human Capital. *American Economic Review*, 51(1): 1–17.

Sharma, S. 2014. *In the Meantime: Temporality and Cultural Politics.* Durham, NC: Duke University Press.

Tassinari, A. & Maccarrone, V. 2017. The mobilisation of gig economy couriers in Italy: Some lessons for the trade union movement. *Transfer: European Review of Labour and Research*, 23(3): 353–357.

Townley, B., Roscoe, P. & Searle, N. 2019. *Creating Economy: Enterprise, Intellectual Property, and the Valuation of Goods.* Oxford: Oxford University Press.

Veen, A., Barratt, T. & Goods, C. 2019. Platform-capital's 'App-etite' for control: A labour process analysis of food-delivery work in Australia. *Work, Employment and Society.* Doi: 0950017019836911.

Wood, A. J., Graham, M., Lehdonvirta, V. & Hjorth, I. 2019. Good gig, bad gig: Autonomy and algorithmic control in the global gig economy. *Work, Employment and Society*, 33(1): 56–75.

Wood, A. J., Lehdonvirta, V. & Graham, M. 2018. Workers of the Internet unite? Online freelancer organisation among remote gig economy workers in six Asian and African countries. *New Technology, Work and Employment*, 33(2): 95–112.

Afterword

STEWART CLEGG

The future is uncertain and the past, even yesterday, so far away. We live in a world of unparalleled immediacy in which 'now' is the dominant mode of being, living and working in the moment, less aware of how, historically, we might have arrived at the now we are in because of its immediacy and insecure about how being here-and-now might translate into futures imagined. Consequently, the newness of now is capable of being experienced in a multitude of ways, unrooted in history and unlimited by imaginary futures. For some, as the book sketches in its early chapters, now is the age of collaboration, often digitally mediated in such a way that one is rarely in the presence of the other or others with whom one is collaborating, often disembodied as a virtual co-creator. The non-newness of the potential of this now of makerspaces, their potential links to historical practices of cooperation, industrial democracy and worker participation, have become less than visible in a world made fit for the digital age. In the immediacy of now, solidarity finds new forms in activist communities of practice, such as hackers, who strive to disturb and disorder the architectonics of authority that corporate and political empires have fabricated. Ethically, those claiming this identity do what they are able to do, sometimes for ulterior motives of a common good; at other times, for reasons of less noble ideological persuasion. Seen in one ideological light, the hacker is engaged in a noble pursuit; from another perspective, they are wreckers of the social and moral order, irrespective of the substantive nature of that which is hacked.

In understanding the newness of any now that we inhabit, social scientists have some well-tested concepts for making sense. Technologies always pose a duality: they can serve to deskill or to augment skill, depending on the political economy of their introduction.

Digitalisation has led to an augmentation of inequalities and power relations as platforms have transformed the nature of craft as an individual preserve into a standardised set of practices from which the craft has been removed. Workers in the gig economy that platforms enable have stories to tell of the freedoms that this kind of economy can enable them to practise. Freest of all, perhaps, at least until families and children beckon, are the digital nomads in the gig economy, working much as itinerant musicians and troubadours of old, putting a spatial map of gigs and opportunities together, perhaps less a contemporary leisure class and more their digital hands for hire, freely ranging.

Marx probably did not have copper wire in mind when writing that everything solid melts into air; nonetheless, the development of digital telephony is the material realisation of the dematerialised future he envisaged as everlasting uncertainty. Traditional agrarian practices, even in the most traditional of rural lives, are being made anew in the immediacy of now. However they are remade, the labour of cultivation and pastoralism is never likely to be one of post-work; rural utopias exist only in the imaginings of those who can afford to neither reap nor sow, to harvest nor husband.

Managers are potentially powerful political agents, the more so they effect mastery of the new technologies characterising the contemporary and future world of work. In their futures is inscribed the imaginaries, dualities and dynamics of how we humans and other actants might relate to each other and the effects that might be engendered on both global and local scales. The future is never a one-way street; tendencies can be reversed; de-civilisation, de-globalisation and destruction are as likely as any utopia of peace, love and understanding. Managers, linguistically descended from horse trainers, need to be taught well that in their hands, wrangling is not merely a technical skill, but a world-making capability. Framing the future well is a heavy responsibility that the present generation owes to those who come after; the now lived thoughtlessly threatens all those futures to come. It is not now or never, as the old refrain has it, so much as never now, because now is always subsumed as a moment in process as soon it elapses. Nonetheless, what is done now is sedimented into structures constraining and enabling all those futures to come. Looked at like this, we may well think the future is, for all intents and purposes, so open temporally as to be infinite, but infinity is not eternity. What is practised today, even at the cutting edge of now, has that potential to enable or constrain futures that may or may not unfold. This book has glimpsed some of the parameters that frame that unfolding now in the design and construction of the worlds of work.

Index

Printed in the United States
By Bookmasters